LOVE AFFAIRS & MARRIAGE

MY LIFE IN FOOTBALL

HOWARD KENDALL

LOVE AFFAIRS & MARRIAGE

MY LIFE IN FOOTBALL

In memory of my late father, Jack Kendall.

'When you talk about Everton you are talking about a marriage.'
6 November 1990

Published by deCoubertin Books Ltd in 2013.
deCoubertin Books, 145-157 St John Street, London, EC1V 4PY
www.decoubertin.co.uk
First hardback edition.
978-1-909245-06-8 – Standard Edition
978-1-909245-09-9 - Holy Trinity Special Limited Edition
978-1-909245-10-5 - 1970 League Champion Special Limited Edition
978-1-909245-11-2 - 1984 FA Cup Winner Special Limited Edition
978-1-909245-12-9 - 1985 European Cup Winners Cup Winner Special Limited Edition
978-1-909245-13-6 - 1987 League Champion Special Limited Edition

A CIP catalogue record for this book is available from the British Library.
Cover design and typeset by Allen Mohr.
Limited Edition covers by Milkyone Creative.

The publisher would like to thank: Les Read, Carena Duffy, Sabahat Muhammad,
Kate Highfield, Daniel Lewis, Allen Mohr, Thomas Regan.

Printed and bound by CPI Group (UK) Ltd, Croydon, CR0 4YY.

CONTENTS

F O R E W O R D

Howard had been a very successful player for Everton Football Club, being a member of the 1970 Championship side. He moved on to Birmingham City in 1974, then to Stoke City where he became player coach, preparing to stay in football when his playing career had ended.

The next move was to Blackburn Rovers as player manager bringing success in his two seasons with them. Towards the end of his second season there, at Everton results were very poor and the board of directors decided to change the manager, who was Gordon Lee. I made contact with the chairman of Blackburn to approach Howard. As a board we were unanimous to want Howard as our next manager. He had a compensation clause in his contract, which we agreed and Howard became our next manager. He made a number of changes at the start of his first season. We finished seventh compared to nineteenth the season before.

It was in his third season at the start when a run of poor results and low attendances put pressure on Howard's position. I came out publicly to give Howard a vote of confidence; I really meant what I said. At the turn of the year things started to improve. As well as finishing strongly in the league, we reached the Milk Cup final against Liverpool, losing in a replay, then going on to win the FA Cup.

My vote of confidence had paid dividends. The rest is history. Great times for our great club.

It was nice to play a part in Howard's success at Everton, our most successful manager of all time. Good luck with the book.

Sir Philip Carter
Spring 2013

INTRODUCTION

AT THE CHECK IN DESK OF A MADRID HOTEL, the receptionist was looking at me with confused eyes.

'The name's Kendall,' I repeated, 'Howard Kendall.'

She shuffled through her papers once more, but couldn't find the reservation details that I had been assured would be awaiting me.

'Sorry, sir, we have nothing for you under that name.'

It was May 1987, and I was one of the most famous managers in English football. The Everton team that I managed had just lifted their ninth league title, their second in three seasons. Two years previously I had led the club to their first European trophy, and a year before that their fourth FA Cup.

Before moving into management I'd had a successful playing career with five different clubs, winning the League Championship with Everton in 1970. For many years I was the youngest player to take part in an FA Cup final and some said I was the finest footballer never to play for England.

But here in the Spanish capital I was an unknown figure. No one knew me. My anonymity suited me, for I was here on a secret mission. Representatives of the Basque club Athletic Bilbao had arranged to meet me in the city to discuss my becoming their manager next season.

'How about Holmes?' I asked. Jonathan Holmes was the agent I shared with Gary Lineker and he was travelling with me to help in the negotiations. The receptionist shook her head.

'Fernando Ochoa?' I asked hopefully. Fernando was the general manager of Bilbao and leading the Spanish club in the negotiations. Again she shook her head.

I was perplexed, but then I was struck with a brainwave. I said the name of an executive at Liverpool Football Club, and the receptionist smiled.

'Here is your room key,' she said. 'Please enjoy your stay.'

MORE THAN A QUARTER OF A CENTURY LATER I am convinced that the seeds of my move from Everton to Athletic Bilbao were sown – unbeknown to me – in autumn 1983. It was a very difficult period for me as Everton manager. Results weren't going our way, crowds were down, and some supporters were even calling for my dismissal. The Everton board remained fiercely loyal towards me, but at times it was unclear whether I would still be in a job at the end of the year.

Across Stanley Park, where our neighbours and great rivals Liverpool played at Anfield, things were going rather better. The club were riding high in the league and progressing well in the European Cup, which they would win the following May in Rome. In the second round of that competition they met the Spanish champions Athletic Bilbao and narrowly beat them over two legs in an engrossing tie. Sammy Lee, the Liverpool midfielder, later told me that the atmosphere at Bilbao's San Mamés Stadium, known as The Cathedral, was the best he'd ever encountered.

During the course of that tie, contacts were made and friendships formed between members of Liverpool's management and those at Bilbao. It was unsurprising, because both clubs had good, decent people working for them; football people. They shared a passion for the game and a vision as to how it should be played.

Step forward three years and while Liverpool were still Liverpool, things had changed at Goodison and San Mamés. Everton, under my management, had embarked upon the most successful period in its history. Bilbao, by contrast, had declined and were battling relegation for the first time. Now they were looking for a new manager, and I was top of their list.

How had all this happened? Historically, although they utilised only Basque players, Bilbao tended to turn to overseas managers during their fallow periods. William Garbutt, Fred Pentland and Ronnie Allen had all managed at San Mamés during lean spells and more recently Jupp Heynkes and Marcelo Bielsa have managed the club as they sought success. Having won back-to-back titles earlier in the 1980s, the team had gone into decline. A foreigner, or a 'Mister', was what they now wanted again.

Kenny Dalglish, the Liverpool player-manager, had been the top target of the Bilbao board. Kenny had won the League Championship and FA Cup double during the 1985/86 season, his first year in charge at Anfield. Everton, under my watch, came very close – leading the FA Cup final with 33 minutes to go and finishing just two points behind Liverpool – but it was a staggering achievement by Kenny.

Yet when Fernando Ochoa contacted his friends at Liverpool to approach them over Kenny, he was given short shrift. Kenny would not be leaving Anfield under any circumstances, he was told. They did have, however, someone else who they would recommend. That person was me.

A year earlier I had nearly gone to Spain as Barcelona manager. It was expected that Terry Venables would leave the club and I was recommended by him to be his successor. I met a delegation from the Nou Camp in London and we agreed the terms of the move. Everton were kept informed of all the developments and the board agreed that my assistant, Colin Harvey, would succeed me.

The deal never happened. Terry decided to stay in Catalonia and I remained on Merseyside, where I led Everton to the League Championship again. But the interest from Spain created an appetite within me to manage overseas. English clubs were banned from European competition, the result of years of crowd violence that had culminated in the Heysel Stadium disaster in May 1985, where rioting by Liverpool supporters had led to the deaths of 39 Juventus fans. Two weeks earlier Everton had won the European Cup Winners' Cup in Rotterdam, where there had been no such trouble. I loved European football and longed for the chance – that had been stolen from me at Everton – to compete with the best again. Only by managing outside England would that opportunity arise.

The Barcelona affair was an open secret on Merseyside, as was my desire to manage overseas. When I received a phone call from the Liverpool executive (who shall remain nameless) asking if I would like to be introduced to Fernando, my interest was piqued.

'Yes, I would,' I said, and the wheels were set in motion.

I took his gesture to be an act of courtesy, although looking back I'm sure he had his own reasons for wanting the manager of his club's greatest rivals to leave. He had no part in anything that followed, although in that Madrid hotel a few weeks later his name hung over proceedings. To keep the talks under wraps I stayed in a room bearing his name. I had become his alter ego.

Those clandestine negotiations would lead to my departure from Goodison Park. I never regretted my adventure in Spain, but neither Everton nor I would ever quite be the same again.

———⊖———

MANY YEARS HAVE PASSED since I left Everton for Spain and yet it's still the event that people ask me about most. There are some misconceptions and some half-truths that I hope to challenge by – for the first time – telling the full story behind my decision to leave Everton while the club was at the height of its glory days.

Since 1987 I've joined and departed Everton twice more, but the club has honestly never left me. When I returned in 1990 I likened Everton to 'a marriage', while other clubs – Manchester City in that case – were mere 'love affairs'. That still holds true. There have been occasions when I've been hurt by football and times when I've found it difficult to replicate the success I once enjoyed. But nothing can diminish my love for Everton and enthusiasm for football in general.

I have written autobiographies before, once as a player and once as a manager. Lots of things have happened since I last put pen to paper in 1991 and there are many aspects of my life I wasn't able to discuss in that book that I am now. When you're working as a manager you're obliged to keep a lid on many things, even those you might feel compelled to speak out on. Not only are you coach and tactician and guiding force of a football club, but you are politician as well, keeping your constituents in the boardroom, dressing room and on the terraces happy. Sometimes by saying nothing it breeds misconceptions or even in some cases wild conspiracy theories. It can be a tough balance.

I'm long free of those shackles and now able to tell about my life in football as I choose. I've had many years to reflect on not just what I achieved at Goodison Park as a player and manager, but also how I did it, and I hope to explain the reasons behind my success more fully than I've been able to than in the past. Success as a player and manager was down to many factors. There are also some great stories about the many characters I worked with and encountered through my life.

I often feel that my achievements beyond Goodison and as a player tend to be overlooked because of my association with Everton in the 1980s. That's another of the reasons why, after all these years, I have sat down to write this book. As such this is not just a book about Everton, but about all the clubs that I was part of. I'm proud to have played for Preston, to have captained Birmingham and Stoke, to have taken Blackburn to the brink of the top flight in my first managerial job. I'm proud too of taking Bilbao into Europe at the first attempt, of saving Manchester City from relegation, and taking Sheffield United to within a match of the Premier League. There were some not-so-good times in Nottingham, Greece and also back on Merseyside, and I hope to explain why these didn't work out.

I've enjoyed reflecting on my career and hope that those who witnessed my career enjoy my memories of the highs and lows I encountered.

Howard Kendall
June 2013

CHAPTER ONE
RYTON

ALTHOUGH THE MAJORITY OF MY CAREER WAS WEDDED to English football's great northwestern heartland, my origins lie firmly in another of its famous hotbeds. I was born in Mitchell Street, Crawcrook, near Ryton-upon-Tyne, on the semi-rural outskirts of Newcastle in May 1946. Historically, the Northeast may have fallen behind the successes of England's western reaches, but while it lacks trophies it excels in passion for the beautiful game.

My childhood followed the oft-told and predictable pattern of many boys born in the immediate post-war period: a sports-mad kid, who spent his winters with a leather ball attached to his feet and summers with a cricket bat in his hands. Like most of my peers I was infused with the Northeast's passion for sport. There wasn't, frankly, much else to do around there in those days, but that was more than okay by me. All I needed was a ball and I was the happiest and most fulfilled boy you could imagine. While my childhood was typical for my surroundings, what saw me rise to become a famous footballer and the most successful English manager of my generation was the extraordinary and selfless influence of an otherwise ordinary man: my dad.

My father, Jack Kendall, was my hero, my coach and guiding influence. Nothing that I have achieved would have been possible without his encouragement and generosity of spirit. Without a shadow of a doubt I wouldn't have had a career as a footballer without my dad. I owe him everything. Every minute, every spare second, he was out there with me on the field adjacent to our house, in the winter with a football, in the summer with the cricket ball. He had been a good amateur footballer himself and wanted me to be successful.

His enthusiasm knew no bounds. He used to leave me when he was working in the summer and I was on school holidays. He would get a tennis ball and punch a hole through it, put it on the washing line in the back yard and let it hang down so I could practise cricket shots all afternoon on my own. Even in the middle of winter when you couldn't get out on the fields, he used to blow a balloon up and we'd get two doors opposite each other which served as the goals. The two of us would be jumping and heading and volleying the balloon. It's crazy thinking back that he could work as hard as he did each day and come home and play with me for hours and hours to try and make me a success. (Years later I always took great pride in the Everton trainer, Wilf Dixon, telling me I was the best volleyer he'd ever seen; clearly my father's balloon trick reaped dividends).

I was an only child and thus the beneficiary of my parents' undivided attention. My mother used to joke about what a heavy baby I was – 11 pounds, she reckoned – and it put her off ever having any more. Although

I never knew what it was to have a brother or a sister, it made me the entire focus of my parents' existence. I suppose, looking back, this was the making of me.

Like many of the men in our village, my dad was a coalminer. It was a hard, back-breaking, dangerous and dirty existence. I remember him coming back home from work and my mother preparing the bath in front of the fire. As a child you're oblivious to the hazards of the pit, the dangers that men at the coalface were exposed to every minute of their working day. The work that he'd done down the mines would eventually claim the life of my father, but it was long after he had last made the long trip underground. When I was eight or nine he developed pneumoconiosis, an illness caused by dust on the chest, and he was advised to leave the mines and go and work in the country, which is what we did. It was not until many years later that I learned the real reason behind our departure and another 25 years before the dust on his lungs took him away from us, aged just 65. I have no doubt that the work took it out of him.

After he left the pit we moved to Corbridge, near Hexham, and he was caretaker at Mowden Hall public school. We would move a few more times after that, but wherever we went my dad always made sure there was a field to play football on next door. The two of us would be out there every second that we could, practising, practising, practising.

His routines were simple, but I suppose he was ahead of his time. Dad used to go out there with me and put a stick on the ground; he'd stand about 15 yards away from it, and I'd be 15 yards the other side of it, and I had to pass it with either foot and hit the stick. If I didn't concentrate or look interested he'd pick the stick up and in we'd go. I didn't do any fitness work; I didn't need to. It wasn't like the present day or how I saw things in Bilbao (which are increasingly the norm in England now) where they start so early on fitness and exercising. I was naturally fit because I was always moving.

My father encouraged me, but he never praised me. He would come along and watch me in schoolboy games and assess my performance, but there was no acclaim. He'd pick out one instance in which I hadn't done something right, and would tell me about it. There was no danger I would become big-headed or anything like that. He kept my feet on the ground. Much later on, when I was at Preston, we went to watch Blackpool one night. I'd organised some tickets and got to the ground late; we'd struggled finding a parking space and a couple of kids came up with autograph books.

'Howard, would you sign this please,' said one of them.

'We're late,' I replied. 'Now piss off.'

Well, I got such a telling-off from my dad; it was absolutely unbelievable. 'Who do you think you are?' he asked, and he was right. I never did it again. But that was just my dad; always seeking to improve me as a player and as a person.

Invariably all my toys were related to sport. We had one of those magnetic football tables, a precursor of Subbuteo, where you put the magnet underneath the table and could move the players. We played it that often that it would feel like my wrists were hanging off at the end of the day; and my dad's would be as well.

I think one of the things that worked to the advantage of all my generation was the surfeit of other things to do. Like many homes in the 1950s we had no television and although there was a wireless set, it was only during the summer holidays when the Test matches were being played that I tuned in.

Cricket was my second love; I really enjoyed the sport both as a participant and fan. During those endless summer holidays I'd be sat in front of the family wireless set with a scorecard and never missed a ball; I'd meticulously write all this information down. It sounds strange, but that's just what I liked doing. It was all part of my magnificent inheritance from my dad; he was sports mad and he passed it down to me.

My mother was also a major influence, but in a more circumspect way. My parents were ambitious for me and, I suppose, quiet aspirational. They saved up to buy me boots, whereas all my friends went to the sweet shop. I remember telling them, 'My friends are getting sixpence pocket money, but you're only giving me threepence.' They replied, 'Yes, but we're saving up to buy you some football boots.' That really brought me down to earth. Football gear was nevertheless quite rudimentary at the time. My dad bought me some Timpson's boots at one time, with steel toecaps so I didn't get hurt in a tackle and to 'protect' me. It seemed like a great idea; the boots were harder so I'd hit the ball harder, right? Wrong. In practise it was a terrible idea; they were awful – very heavy, like workmen's boots – and I soon got rid of them.

As well as sport my parents also encouraged me in my studies. I was lucky in primary school because there were schoolteachers every bit as committed in seeing their pupils realise their sporting potential as my dad was with me. Two of my teachers, Mr Elliott and Mr Storer, put in endless hours of their spare time coaching and organising games. They didn't have to do it, but they loved putting that extra bit in. It was not just football but cricket as well.

With their encouragement and my parents', I progressed well at primary school and passed my eleven-plus examination. When I started Washington Grammar School I was part of the same intake as Bryan Ferry. I don't remember much about him other than that he played on the right wing for the school team. Years later, one of my classmates, Alan Slowther, who worked with me as a scout, called me up and asked if I'd seen this band named Roxy Music. 'Check out who the lead singer is!' It was, of course, Bryan.

With my mother in the late-1990s.
She and my father did everything they could to
help make me a success. (Author's Collection)

Mum worked at the local cinema selling tickets.

I always remember walking down to go in and watch a film one night when I was 11, and people were running out.

'What are they running out for?' I asked her.

'There's been a plane crash, Howard,' she said. 'The Manchester United team were on board.'

It was the Munich air disaster and news had just come through. I turned back and went home; like everyone else, I didn't want to be out any more.

I always considered myself unquestioningly a Geordie until I joined Everton, where I met Jimmy Husband, who was from Newcastle itself.

'What are you?' he asked.

'I'm a Geordie,' I said.

'No,' he replied. '*I'm* a Geordie. Could you hear the hooting and the tooting of the Tyne from where you're from?'

'No,' I answered.

'Well then,' he laughed, 'you're not a Geordie!'

I did, however, class myself as one and was a Newcastle United fan. My childhood and my growing love affair with football was set against the context of Newcastle United's greatest era. During the 1950s Newcastle lifted the FA Cup on three occasions within a five-year period. In 1951, when I was five, they defeated Blackpool 2-0, a year later Arsenal were beaten 1-0 and in 1955 Newcastle beat Manchester City 3-1.

My hero was the inside forward George Eastham, who, as a manager, would one day sign me for Stoke City. I thought he was absolutely fantastic. There was Len White and Ivor Allchurch, a spectacular goalscorer from midfield; Bobby Mitchell on the left-hand side; Jimmy Scoular in the middle of the park; Ronnie Simpson, the goalkeeper who went to be part of Celtic's Lisbon Lions team. It was a great side. I would go in the boys' entrance and be tossed to the front, where we'd sit on the cinder track that went around the side of the pitch. We were literally part of the action; it was wonderful. Afterwards I'd meet my dad outside and we'd talk all about the game on our way home. Because we were living in Washington, which was situated between Newcastle and Sunderland, we also used to go to Roker Park on the Saturdays when Newcastle were playing away. Len Shackleton and Charlie Hurley were my heroes in the red and white of our rivals; I thought Hurley was an unbelievable player.

Although I had my favourites and my heroes, I never studied players as such. However, I always remember seeing Danny Blanchflower do something at St James' Park that absolutely amazed me at the time. It was a back-flick or something that would be considered normal now, but back then I was in awe. So much so that I wrote to him asking how he'd done it. I still don't know how he did it – he didn't reply to my letter!

My extended family was small and very close knit. I have only vague recollections of my grandparents, who all died when I was still a young boy, and my mum only had a couple of sisters. One of their husbands, my Uncle Billy, was blinded in a mining accident and my father used to go and commentate on games for him at St James' Park. This assumed added importance when his son – my cousin – Harry Taylor pulled on the famous striped shirt and stepped out onto the hallowed turf as Newcastle's outside right. He didn't play many first-team games for Newcastle, then moved on to Fulham when he was doing his National Service.

Although my cousin Harry was only really ever on the fringes of the Newcastle team it was a big thing to have a relative on the books of a First Division club. I vividly remember my dad bringing him along to see me play in a match when I was aged 13 or 14. What I think he was doing was asking Harry if I'd measure up to the standard demanded of young players by Newcastle at that time.

Harry gave the thumbs-up, but his advice was surprising: don't sign for Newcastle. At the time Newcastle had a near monopoly on the most promising local youngsters, but the pull of being the local giants was not matched by resources in developing that pool of talent. Newcastle encouraged youngsters to stay on at school and pass their GCEs, which was fine, but games were played only once every three or four weeks, with training in the St James' back car park twice a week. Harry was quite unequivocal: 'I'm not recommending that you come to Newcastle.'

I was never really marked out as a special teenager or someone who was endlessly told I was destined for greatness. My dad made sure my feet were firmly bedded on the ground. Attention in me was nevertheless increasing. When I was 14 Chester-le-Street Schoolboys had a tremendous run in the English Schools' Shield and we eventually made it to the quarter final. For a small district of seven or eight schools it was a tremendous achievement given that there were dozens drawn from the big cities. We eventually fell to Manchester Boys, who had it wrapped up most years, but it was a hell of a run to get so far.

It was around this time that I started to be noticed beyond my area and I was called for trials for England Schoolboys. This was selected according to a series of regional trials; I was called to the last one at Bourneville in Birmingham and made it through to be selected to play against Wales. My fellow players included several who I would come up against in the First Division a few years later. These included Alan Ogley (Manchester City), Glyn Pardoe (Manchester City), John Sissons (West Ham) and Peter Storey (Arsenal).

With the England Schoolboy team. (Author's Collection)

We won 7-3, but I was not happy with my performance. It was my own fault because I was so desperate to do better that I ended up doing a silly thing in the build-up to the game. The television cameras came to the school and set up on the asphalt. We were given instructions to do a routine for the cameras; just passing around, running, and to make it look as if we were tackling. I was desperate to impress for the television cameras and went in a little too eagerly to my tackle and ended up scraping all the side of my leg. It was such a mess, but I didn't tell anyone because I didn't want to miss the game. John Sissons scored four on the night, but I had a quiet game, and I knew why. It was the only time I played for England Schoolboys. My naivety may have cost me more caps, but I was delighted to get that precious one.

Playing for England Schoolboys immediately thrust me under the noses of a whole host of professional clubs. As well as Newcastle and Sunderland, Arsenal were also interested in signing me, but it was a less fashionable club that made the most persuasive case.

Preston North End were in the process of being relegated from the First Division in 1961, but its Northeast scout Reg Keating was a persistent and persuasive advocate of the club. In the end he became a good family friend and would share Sunday lunch with us. There's an art in that, I suppose; but I think it was genuine with Reg. He was the first scout to make himself known when I was playing schoolboy football and I and my parents liked and trusted him. What he got from my parents was the promise that we'd go down to look at Preston before anybody else and see what they had to say.

My parents promised him that we'd certainly go there and have a look at the facilities and where I might stay, and where I might carry on my education. You could still leave school at 15 in those days, but my mother was keen for me to continue my education.

When we visited Preston we couldn't find a fault. It was a small club underpinned by a strong family ethos. My father, however, was already looking beyond Deepdale. He wasn't pushy about it, merely wise. He told me: 'If you make it there, the big clubs will come for you.' He could see that there were chances beckoning. The club was in transition: it had just been relegated and Tom Finney had retired. I'm sure it was a very unsettling time for the more established players, but for an ambitious teenager my dad could see that the situation was ripe with opportunities. And he was completely right in everything he saw.

In May 1961 I turned 15. A few weeks later I left the family home and signed on to become an apprentice footballer at Preston North End.

CHAPTER TWO
PRESTON

PRESTON NORTH END had been English football's first great club, winning the two inaugural Football League titles and going an entire season unbeaten – a feat that went unmatched until Arsenal went a season undefeated in the early years of the 21st century. The club's halcyon era had been in the Victorian age and although they won the FA Cup in 1938, it wasn't until the 1950s that, inspired by Tom Finney, they threatened a renaissance. Twice – in 1952/53 and 1957/58 – they finished league runners-up (in 1953 by 0.1 of a goal, using the old system of goal average) and were runners-up in the 1954 FA Cup final, a match they had led.

By the time of my arrival in August 1961 they were, however, a club in a state of flux. Relegation, invariably, had not gone down well with the supporters, and the sense of loss was deepened by the retirement of the club's talisman, Finney. I wouldn't say there was a sense of depression in the dressing room, but there was a degree of anxiety. Everyone knew we had to get straight back up. Expectations were high in the town.

As a young apprentice I was far away from first-team affairs at that stage. Because this was still an era before substitutes, people tend to think of playing squads as quite small, but that wasn't the case. Even at a club like Preston there were a succession of teams – first team, reserve team, A team and B team – and my starting point was with the B team, or Preston's fourth team.

For most of my first year at Deepdale, I played for Preston's B Team in the Lancashire League. It wasn't glamorous, but we weren't ignored. The town had a great appetite for football, and in the FA Youth Cup we would play in front of crowds of two or three thousand people – attendances that many clubs at the lower end of the league spectrum would find acceptable. Newspapers reported on our matches. There was a level of recognition. According to one report I played 'the Blanchflower type of attacking game', which was nice, and came despite the great man previously shunning my attempts to find out his footballing secrets.

With Jimmy Milne and Danny Blanchflower, with whom some newspapers were kind enough to evoke comparisons. (Author's Collection)

I was put up in digs, just around the corner from the ground. I was looked after by an elderly couple called Emma and Tom Rawlinson, who were great to me. Other lads, I felt, weren't so lucky. There was one house in Preston with six or seven apprentices and young professionals, like Peter Thompson, living in it. It was quite a tame way of living – I remember them saying they used to put two shillings together and buy a Fats Domino record once a week – but it wouldn't have been my thing. I think being on your own, with a couple of parental substitutes, was a better move.

Coming from the Northeast when I was still only really a child might have been harder for me to take were it not for the kindness of Emma and Tom. I think anybody leaving home at 15 would find it strange living with another family, but they helped me settle and by taking me into their home it eased whatever anxieties I might have had. At first I used to go back home once every couple of weeks and then it would be once every four weeks. I suppose I was quite quick to bed in, looking back. I was very friendly with a lad round the corner called Willie Watt who came from Scotland and that certainly helped. But there were only three or four of us there doing the apprenticeships and it was close knit.

My parents had been insistent on one thing when I moved to the Northwest: that I continued my education in case professional football didn't work out. It was a wise outlook, as the professional footballer's life was even more perilous then than it is today. There was huge competition, of course, simply to make it, but even if you did this was an era where the maximum wage of £21 per week had only recently ended. It was not a lucrative profession and having other options was sensible. As such, three nights a week I and a couple of the other apprentices went to night school to study English, maths and geography. There was no interest from us; it was really just a case of doing what your parents had asked the clubs to do to make sure you furthered your education. There was only one thing on our minds, and that was playing football. In the classroom we were simply going through the motions.

Night school was quite conventional compared to another of the side-lines I briefly pursued. I was very friendly with one of the directors' sons and we were chatting one afternoon and the issue of alternative careers came up.

'You know if you have a serious injury and you have to finish playing, what are you going to do?' he asked.

'I don't know,' I replied.

'Why don't you think about it, instead of going to the cinema nearly every afternoon,' he suggested. At the time we had free cinema passes and this was how we filled our days when we weren't training. I think I saw The Guns of Navarone 12 times. 'Why don't you think about another profession, learning something else?'

'Yeah, that's a good idea,' I said, although maybe I wouldn't have been so enthusiastic had I known what he had in mind.

'What about ladies' hairdressing?'

'Oh no!'

But he told me to give it a go and I used to visit a salon a couple of days a week and actually quite enjoyed it. I even used to practise on my mother. They wouldn't let me cut the hair, mind you, but I put the rollers in and did everything else! It's not something I continued, although I've still got the certificate somewhere at home.

Becoming a footballer, as I've said, wasn't the route to riches that it has since become. There was no great incentive to join as an apprentice. I had received a signing-on fee of £5 but also had to pay £5 to get myself out of grammar school. Preston, in fairness, paid that as well, so I had my £5, but it wasn't much. My weekly wage as an apprentice was £7, half of which went for board and lodgings.

We had our duties as players, but we also had work to carry out in and around the ground. On Fridays we'd clean the bathrooms, the tunnel area and the stands. There were big crowds at Deepdale back then, and although they had dropped down a division they still had a good side. In the summer we didn't get the whole time off, we'd be in painting the crush barriers and helping in the stadium's annual maintenance regime. It was a fine up-bringing and I think it did us good long-term, a view I held even at the time.

Twenty years later, when I became a manager, working around the stadiums and backrooms was something that the apprentices were still involved in, but it died over the duration of my managerial career. Cleaning boots and kit became something young players didn't want to do and with the advent of academies and expanded youth set-ups it became too big a job to hand to the kids anyway. At Everton I ended up appointing Jimmy Martin as our kit manager. He's still at the club and has now got half a dozen people working under him, which I think tells you something about the way modern football has evolved.

Although I missed home and missed my parents, I was very happy with the routine of the young footballer. There was a simplicity to my life: training, helping out around Deepdale, a chat with my team-mates, the cinema, home. I had money in my pocket but nothing to spend it on. In my first year I managed to save £100, which given that I only had £3.50 a week spending money wasn't bad! We didn't need to spend any money; the only thing we were concentrating on was becoming professional footballers.

There would be a match between the reserves and the first team on Friday mornings, which would last until the first team won. The apprentices and reserves would play again on Saturday morning. I was progressing well and, towards the end of that first year as an apprentice, progressed from the B team to the A team. By April 1962 I was playing for the reserves in the Central League. Again, it was a step up in standard, but not only that, it meant I was playing in some of the biggest and most famous stadiums in the country. This included the vast empty expanses of Goodison Park. Even then, long before my life would become entwined with that of Everton Football Club, there was something magical about the wonderful pitch and those huge stands, with their Archibald Leitch ironwork criss-crossing their fronts.

Summer came and I returned to the Northeast. I was happy with my progress in that first year at Preston, but glad of the chance to indulge my other great love. As well as football I was a decent cricketer; another result of my dad's endless playing with me as a child. I enjoyed the way that the year was split into two discernible halves, the cricket season and the football season; there seemed a natural symmetry to it. Back then the football season was finished fairly early and you had a decent summer, a couple of months at least to play your cricket. It kept you fit as well, especially if you knocked a few runs off.

During the summer between the ages of about 15 and 19 I played for Philadelphia in the Durham Senior League, which was a very high standard. It had professionals and it had foreign players, usually internationals, who had to serve 12 months at club level before they could go and play for a county. Although I didn't play for the first XI that often, I did have the honour of playing against Lance Gibbs, the famous West Indian bowler, who played for a club called Whitburn, near Sunderland.

When I was older I was offered trials with Leicestershire and Warwickshire (my native Durham were a minor county until the 1990s) and could probably have combined county cricket with professional football, as some of my contemporaries – such as Chris Balderstone, who played for Carlisle United and Leicestershire CCC, and subsequently played against me at Goodison – did. But no matter how appealing the idea of filling my summer months with more professional sport was, I felt the idea of coming in and taking up a regular player's place for a couple of months was wrong.

My second year as an apprentice at Preston was dominated by the so-called Big Freeze. Britain encountered its coldest winter of the century and for almost three months the country suffered conditions more familiar with Siberia. The Deepdale pitch was covered in snow and ice and between Boxing Day and 9 March the first team played just a single league match. By creating a huge backlog of fixtures, the weather would play into my hands. In the last two months of the season, the first team had to play no fewer than 17 league games. Inevitably there were injuries and fatigue.

On several occasions the Preston manager Jimmy Milne had me travel with the first-team squad. It was exciting travelling with the senior players, but I took it in my stride. I suppose, looking back, I was quite unfazed by most things. I was confident, never arrogant, but knew what I was capable of. All the careful supervision of my father had taught me so much about the game that when it came to stepping up at the highest level I knew I'd be ready.

Three games out from the end of the season came a trip to Newcastle on Saturday 11 May. There wasn't much to play for. Promotion was just about beyond Newcastle's reach, while we were miles off, stuck in mid-table. I didn't really give the game against my boyhood club much thought, until shortly before the game Jimmy announced his starting line-up. To my astonishment, I was in it.

I was ecstatic, not just that I'd be making the step up, but doing so in front of my own people. It was the biggest thing that had happened in my life at that point. I was just shy of my 17th birthday and the manager had probably seen me in reserve-team games and maybe it was a little gesture to say, 'Here's your reward for the season.' But what a reward it was too – it was absolutely fantastic. To think that a few years earlier I had been standing on those same terraces cheering Newcastle on and now I was on the same field as my heroes, playing against them.

We drew 2-2, which a was a fair result, and I don't think I let anyone down, which in these situations is your first priority. Jimmy included me to play

The programme from my debut match against Newcastle United.

NEWCASTLE UNITED FOOTBALL CLUB
ST. JAMES' PARK · NEWCASTLE
GROUND CAPACITY — 70,000
RECORD ATTENDANCE — 68,386

WE WELCOME TODAY–
PRESTON NORTH END
Saturday, 11th May, 1963. Kick-off 3-0 p.m.
OFFICIAL PROGRAMME
3d

against Middlesbrough at Ayresome Park the following Wednesday, but I was swiftly brought down to earth. Cyril Knowles, the Middlesbrough full back, *did* me. It was a late and brutal hack that saw me carried off with a knee ligament injury. My mother was so upset that she vowed she'd never go and watch me again (a promise she maintained until I appeared in the FA Cup final a year later).

I don't think that this was a lesson to the young prodigy, or at least I didn't believe at that particular time it had been deliberate. But you soon learned as a professional footballer that certain players had this in them; they didn't care what was going to happen to you, they were going to do you, and this was one of those occasions. Certainly it wrecked my summer plans. It meant I couldn't play cricket, which is how bad the injury to my knee was. It was a naughty one.

○

MY ASCENT FROM HOPEFUL APPRENTICE to fully fledged professional was completed a few weeks later when I turned seventeen and signed professional terms with Preston. My wages went up from £7 (the maximum available to an apprentice) to £15 per week. My parents left the Northeast, our home and their jobs in order to support me in fulfilling my dreams. It was a typically selfless gesture. It must have been a wrench for them to leave and I was grateful for yet another sacrifice, as I was for everything they did through my career.

We moved into a house rented from the club. My dad got a job at English Electric in Preston and Mum stayed at home. Dad had also done a little bit of scouting for the club in the Northeast as well, and was responsible for sending down Frank Clark, who was playing as an amateur for Crook Town. Frank played for Preston in the FA Youth Cup but was well wanted and went back to the Northeast, spending 13 years at Newcastle before moving to Nottingham Forest, where he won the European Cup.

Becoming a professional didn't change me off the pitch. People I'd grown up with in the Northeast were pleased for me and I was grateful for their support. Mr Storer and Mr Elliott, the two primary school teachers who had been so patient coaching me when I was a kid, even came down to Preston to see me, which was a tremendous gesture that I appreciated enormously. In essence I was still just a teenager, living with my parents; I certainly wasn't some 'big-time Charlie', living the high life. The social scene, such as it was, was pretty tame. Naturally you met up with friends and went to parties. Back then it was parties at people's homes more than going to pubs or nightclubs, but it was very tame. I didn't start going to the pub until I was 18.

In fact my Friday night entertainment was unbelievable given the preconceptions people have about footballers now. I'd head out to the local Methodist church to practise on the organ ahead of Sunday Service. It just took my mind off the game the next day. I'd had piano lessons in Ryton and one of our neighbours when we got to Preston suggested I try the organ. I learned one hymn – 'Tell Me the Old, Old Story' – and that was the only one I could do because I couldn't use the pedals. A footballer who couldn't use his feet on the pedals! It was funny because on the Sunday you could see the children's faces drop when they saw me because they knew it was going to be 'Tell Me the Old, Old Story' again.

As a professional at Deepdale I was absolved from the domestic chores of the apprentice pool, but life didn't change too much. Training was fairly mundane, consisting of a lot of running. Pre-season at the time consisted of eight to ten weeks and it was a heavy schedule going back. There was lots of road running, but it wasn't really very professional. The trainer, Walter Crook, was also the physio. He would ride his bike at the front of the squad, when all of a sudden a bus would go past and a couple of players would be waving out of the back window. That's what happened in those days. Alec Dawson, our Scottish forward, used to put so much weight on in the summer that he'd have a bin bag underneath his tracksuit, so that he could try and sweat the weight off. Afterwards there'd be a huge puddle in the dressing room.

Jimmy Milne wasn't a tracksuit manager, but managers generally weren't in those days. I think the first that I experienced was Billy Bingham. Harry Catterick certainly never was unless there was a TV crew at Bellefield or the chairman was coming down. You didn't really have coaches, either. We had Walter, who was trainer, physio, and also organised the apprentices. As a concept coaching didn't really exist. You went out and ran to get fit. You played five-a-side, or played a practice match, and the team gelled into its way of playing that way. Tactics was largely a foreign word.

We used to have team meetings every Friday, when we'd go to an up-stairs room in Deepdale to talk about the match. This was as far as a tactical talk went. Jimmy Milne was quite a nervous character. I never felt he was fully comfortable addressing the men in his charge. At pre-match meetings he had counters and a table laid out like a football pitch, but his hand would be shaking as he laid them out. His pep talks didn't always work, either. I'll always remember one meeting when he focused on our left back, Jim Smith, who hadn't had the best of times.

'Jim, I don't know what's wrong with you,' he pronounced. 'You're looking sluggish, you're not winning the ball in the air, you're giving the ball away too often. In fact, it looks as if your confidence is gone, lad.'

'Boss,' Jim responded drolly, 'you've given me all the confidence I need for tomorrow.'

As a young player you picked up things and absorbed advice that was given to you. Tom Finney had finished a year before my arrival at Deepdale, but he was still a big presence in and around the club. 'Legend' is a term that is bandied around too freely in football, but in Tom's case it was true and as a young player I was in awe of him. I needn't have been because he was a great man, decent and humble, and he gave me some lovely advice. Even though he had played until he was in his late thirties, he felt he'd had to finish his career earlier than he should have done (he didn't play as a professional until he was 24 due to the Second World War) because of playing through injuries.

'I've seen you play when you shouldn't have played and that's silly,' he told me. 'It's not how many games a season you play, it's how many seasons.'

What he was saying was, don't play if you have any injury concerns. Those words always stuck with me; indeed it was some of the finest advice I ever received and helped my career endure.

Preston might have been stuck in the Second Division, but we possessed First Division quality throughout our ranks. It was a really good team and there was a tremendous atmosphere. As the rookie, I just swallowed it all up.

In goal we had a fantastic keeper in Alan Kelly. Years later I had Alan as my goalkeeping coach at Everton. One of the biggest compliments you can pay him is that the eternally demanding Neville Southall actually loved working with him. Neville was very fussy and if he didn't like his coach he'd tell you. But he loved working with Alan.

The full backs, George Ross and Jim Smith, were tremendous players but brought much more to the dressing room with their humour and leadership. Jim was a big, tall lad, a very solid defender and good in the air too. His humour, as I've recounted, was dry as a bone. George was solid and hard, a tireless worker. Indeed, 50 years later George is still working hard with the club in their commercial department. It's amazing how many Scottish players come down to England and settle here.

The deal Jimmy Milne conducted with Manchester United in 1963 to bring Nobby Lawton and Alec Dawson to Deepdale was a masterstroke. Maybe they were just a bit below the level demanded by United but, I tell you what, they weren't far off. They were excellent for Preston. Nobby, like me, was a wing half. He was a terrific player, but he was also a leader. He took responsibility on the field, as a good captain should do. Alec was our main goalscorer. He'd bring us very close to glory.

Supplying Alec on the wing was Davey Wilson. Davey was a highly talented but precocious flanker, who made us all laugh with his unstinting admiration for Stanley Matthews. I'll always remember sitting in the dressing room and hearing some heavy footsteps – a clonk, clonk, clonk – coming down the corridor towards us one morning. The changing room door opened and there was Davey.

'What have you got on your feet there?' one of the lads asked.

'I've just been reading about Stanley Matthews,' Davey replied. 'He wears heavy boots and shoes during the week and when he goes out on match days he puts his ordinary football boots on and they're as light as a feather!'

We didn't let him forget that in a hurry. Basically, anything Stanley Matthews did, Davey did too. But he got his move to Liverpool and rightly so; he could glide past players, he was that quick.

On the other wing was the veteran Dougie Holden. In 1958, when I was aged 11, my father took me to the Bolton v. Manchester United FA Cup final and Dougie was playing for Bolton. Little could I have imagined that just a few years later I'd be playing with Dougie – in fact playing alongside him in an FA Cup final. He was one of those wingers that picked the ball up outside his own penalty area, and would end up in the opponent's penalty area without being tackled. He just would dummy, as if to say, 'I'm going past you,' but then wouldn't go past his opponent; he'd drop the shoulder again, forcing the defender into a retreat, and he would somehow end up at the other end of the park. He used to have a little go at me because when balls came to my right-hand side I swept them out to him, to the left wing, and of course there was spin on them and if he miscontrolled it and it went out of play, he'd point the finger at me. Of course, it wasn't my fault if he couldn't control the spin of the ball. But he was the veteran and I was the kid. It wasn't my place to challenge.

I wasn't a regular and I wasn't first choice. The team was good enough to be able to pick itself. I got opportunities through players being injured; other-wise I was playing in the Central League or for the youth team – this being the era before substitutes were allowed, it was just an eleven-man game.

One of those chances came in the third round of the FA Cup. We had been drawn against First Division Nottingham Forest at the City Ground and no one had given us much of a chance. But a display of dogged defending kept the scores goalless and earned us a replay at Deepdale. That's when my opportunity came. Jim Smith was struggling with an injury and the call came to abandon my youth team-mates, with whom I was preparing for a match with Manchester City, and join up with the seniors.

Deepdale was engulfed in a blizzard, but it didn't affect our brilliant and loyal fans. More than 30,000 turned out on a bitterly cold night. They watched an engrossing and evenly matched tie, which was lacking everything but goals. The game went to extra time. Often games stretch in these instances and I suppose that's what happened this time around. I found myself pushing forward and on one of these attacks, around 20 yards out, found the ball at my feet with a bit of space. I always had a good shot, another of the fruits of my father's labour. There was no art to what I did; it was just hours of practice off the pitch, and smashing the ball when I had the chance. And that's what I did. I just hit it, and it almost tore the back of the net. It was enough to send us through.

The FA Cup was big news in those days, and so – all of a sudden – was I. I woke to find myself on the back page of every newspaper. 'The KO Kid', they dubbed me. I was ecstatic.

I also kept my place for the fourth-round game with another First Division team, Bolton. This was another away tie and another draw, 2-2. We took the replay 2-1 and beat Carlisle United 1-0 in the next round.

Sometimes in cup football fortune favours you. That year Preston might have faced Liverpool or Manchester United in the quarter-finals of the FA Cup. Instead we got Fourth Division Oxford, and we beat them 2-1. Then in the semi-finals we avoided top-flight opposition again, drawing Swansea Town (soon to be Swansea City), who were struggling against relegation to the Third Division.

It heightened my belief that this might be Preston's year. But by then, as is often the fate of a young footballer, I'd dropped from the side. I was absent from the victory over Oxford, and watching from the Villa Park stands when we faced Swansea. The sense that our name 'might be on the cup' increased when we turned around a 1-0 half-time deficit to win 2-1, after goals by Alec Dawson and Tony Singleton. Preston were Wembley bound and I had played a small part in that run. That, as far as I was concerned, was my contribution done.

In any case, I had more pressing matters to think about. I had been selected to captain England during the so-called 'Little World Cup', a 24-nation European youth tournament hosted by the Netherlands. England were defending champions, having beaten Northern Ireland 4-0 in the previous year's final in London. There was a lot of prestige attached to the competition and it was an enormous honour to lead out my country. My team-mates included Don Rogers, John Hollins, John Sissons and, of course, Harry Redknapp.

Don was the outstanding player in that team, and was absolutely superb for us, winning player of the tournament. At club level he could have been one of the best players of our generation, but he wouldn't leave his beloved Swindon Town, to all our amazement. I think if it was today there's no doubt he would have made the move to a bigger club, but back then the incentives were not so great. He was a country lad and happy where he was, so why move to the city for the sake of a few extra quid a week?

I always knew Harry would never become England manager as the FA had his card marked from an early age. He wasn't a hell-raiser or anything like that, just constantly taking the mickey, which the strait-laced committee-men liked not one little bit. He was fun to be with, but it was clear that they considered him a 'disruptive influence'. Even though he was eligible for selection the next year, they didn't pick him – probably for that very reason.

England were untouchable in that short tournament. We topped a three-country group with Poland and Ireland, beat Austria 2-1 in the quarter-finals and Portugal 4-0 in the semis. It set up a final with Spain at Amsterdam's Olympisch Stadion. They were a formidable team, and included among their number the goalkeeper Miguel Reina, who would be capped by Spain, win six major trophies in a glittering career with Barcelona, and whose son, Pepe, would keep goal for Liverpool for many years. I led out my country in front of a crowd of 12,451 and we were just too good for them. Don Rogers scored a brace, and John Sissons and Peter Knowles got a goal apiece as we ran out 4-0 winners.

The Little World Cup took place during the seven-week interlude between the FA Cup semi-final and the final against West Ham. When I returned to England Preston was consumed with growing cup fever. Our league form since the start of the year had been really good, but we didn't have quite enough to catch up with either Sunderland or Don Revie's Leeds – who would follow up their Second Division title that season by finishing runners-up to Manchester United in the League Championship a year later, only missing out on goal difference. I think that said a lot about the quality of our division.

There was no sign that I would be anything other than a spectator at Wembley. A week before the final I was selected in place of Ian Davidson in the team to play Northampton Town. Ian, we were told, had to attend a funeral in Edinburgh and his return to the team was considered a formality. But three days before the final Ian's world collapsed and I was catapulted centre stage.

'Davidson was chosen to play in the home game with Northampton last Saturday but was given leave of absence after informing the manager of a bereavement and asking to be allowed to attend the funeral in Edinburgh,' explained a statement by the Preston chairman, Alan Harrison. 'The reasons Davidson had given were found to be untrue. The manager reported the facts to the board and he agreed that they had no option but to suspend the player.'

What this meant was that I would be taking Ian's place in the FA Cup final. My friend and England youth team-mate, West Ham's John Sissons, had been set to be the youngest ever participant in such a match at Wembley, but at the age of 17 years and 345 days, I would beat him by a good 250 days.

Fifty years later I am none the wiser as to what went on that week. I don't know whether or why Ian lied about having to attend a funeral. I don't really understand why it wasn't hushed up. We never talked about it, and if it was discussed by the other players in the dressing room I was out of earshot.

But I felt – and still feel – very sorry for Ian. I thought it was very tough what Jimmy Milne did to him. When you're a regular and your team gets to the cup final and you're suddenly suspended – I thought that was harsh. I think at the back of it all, though, was that Jimmy wanted to play me. I'd played in three of the cup ties, scored the winner against Forest and got the headlines. I'd had a good match a couple of weeks before the final and Milne wanted to play me. It was unforgiving, because Ian was a regular, but there are certainly parallels with the 1966 FA Cup final when Harry Catterick left Fred Pickering out of the Everton team, citing injury, picking Mike Trebilcock instead. It was a case, I believe, of the manager favouring the form player.

I had tremendous help from the players in the build-up to the final. It was different then; you used to go down on a Tuesday and spend time in a hotel preparing. Nowadays you go down the day before. We'd be shut away somewhere and I was guarded from the media, which I think was very shrewd. It was a different media culture, but I was still the big story. It took a little bit of pressure off the senior players; but they were more concerned about me and about what I'd be doing on the day.

West Ham were clear favourites for the final. They had the top-flight pedigree and great players like Bobby Moore and Geoff Hurst, who would win the World Cup for England two years later, and other internationals like Peter Brabrook and John 'Budgie' Byrne.

Nothing fazed us, however, and I don't think I was overawed by the occasion. As with everything, I just took it in my stride. I slept well before the match, and although there was the tingle of excitement as the coach inched through the masses towards the famous old stadium there were no nerves. Awaiting me in the Wembley dressing room was a telegram from the former Arsenal winger Cliff Bastin, congratulating me on beating his record – set in 1930 – as the youngest player to appear in a Wembley FA Cup final.

We played well that afternoon against a side that bristled with quality. Twice, through Dougie Holden and Alec Dawson, we took the lead, but held it for just a few minutes each time, John Sissons and Geoff Hurst restoring equilibrium. The game seemed to be drifting towards extra time, both sides possessing tired legs when, in the final seconds, Brabrook teased some space and Ronnie Boyce knocked home his cross to win the cup for West Ham.

Inevitably there was disappointment at the end of the game, but pride too. I remember our inside left Alan Spavin saying in the dressing room, 'You know what, lads? We've done ourselves proud today.' It gave everybody a lift for we knew that they weren't just empty words.

The next day I picked up the Sunday papers and although we had lost there was some personal consolation. Many journalists named me as Preston's man of the match. My view was the same as it had been a year earlier when I'd made my debut up at St James' Park: relief that I hadn't let anybody down.

Going back to Preston on the train I simply couldn't believe the reception as we approached the town. There were crowds of people and banners laid out for us, and the sight that greeted our arrival was absolutely amazing. For a while I was amazed: we'd lost. Yes, we were a Second Division side and they were a First Division side, we realised that. But we'd lost. What were they doing out there?

They were applauding the effort, I suppose, but it was a small consolation.

THE YEAR WE REACHED WEMBLEY, Preston finished third in the Second Division. We were very close to regaining our top-flight status, but things started to fall away after that for the team. We finished the 1964/65 season 12th and the following season 17th. We reached the quarter-finals of the 1966 FA Cup, beating Tottenham on the way, but that was as close as we got to glory.

As the club's fortunes dipped, however, so mine rose. Not only did I establish myself in the Preston team, but I became one of its star players and the subject of endless transfer speculation. Liverpool, in particular, were closely linked with a move for me. The rumours were to some extent inevitable. Peter Thompson had gone there; Davey Wilson had gone there; Gordon Milne, the manager's son, had also gone there. The club was managed by Bill Shankly, a former Preston player. But the supporters were not happy: they didn't want Preston to become a nursery club for Liverpool.

I wasn't too sure that the board shared those sentiments. If the money's right, directors don't care where you go. Football, of course, was far less commercially driven than it is now, but after the end of the maximum wage in 1961 agents started to appear on the scene. I had one of the first agents, Paul Docherty, who used to work for ITV. He was aware that I was seeking fresh challenges and asked me if he could handle things on my behalf. His advice was to put in a written transfer request. I wasn't sure, but put one in and it was ignored by the board. He told me to put another one in. Then another one if that failed.

I just wanted to play at the top level. I was very honoured to be linked with Liverpool and there seemed some inevitability about the transfer. I'd even been over to stay with Peter Thompson at his digs for a weekend. It was a matter of if I was moving I was going there.

It was March 1967 and the transfer deadline was approaching. The transfer talk hadn't quietened. Liverpool had signed Emlyn Hughes a month earlier and Shankly had publicly stated the club 'wouldn't concede another goal all season' if they signed me as well. The Preston chairman had been upset by some off-the-record comments I'd made about my failure to secure a transfer that had been made public in a national newspaper. I hadn't fallen out with the club, but the situation wasn't great. That evening there was a knock on the door. It was Jimmy Milne. Despite me now being almost 21, it was my dad he did all the talking to.

'I've got a club for your lad; we're going to let him go,' he said.

'Is it Liverpool?' my dad asked.

'No; across the road.'

There had been no hint whatsoever that Everton were interested in buying me. Not a whisper. It emerged later that Bill Shankly was so infuriated by this transfer coup and Liverpool's inability to sign me that he resigned his post as Liverpool manager, a demand that was rejected by the club. (The resignation letter remained unopened in the desk drawer of the Liverpool chief executive, Peter Robinson, until the day he died.) But Everton manager Harry Catterick and Harry Cooke, their chief scout, were waiting for me to go to Deepdale and have talks with them. The following day we went to Goodison to finalise the move. I returned to Preston that night with what I thought was a straight choice: sign for Everton in the morning, or travel down to Plymouth with Preston.

But when we got back home there was another knock at the door. This time it was the Stoke City assistant manager, Alan Ball senior.

'We'd like a word with you,' said Ball. We went with them to an acquaintance's house, where I spoke to the Stoke manager Tony Waddington over the phone. Ball then tried to use his charm to persuade us that The Potteries was the right move. He produced a bottle of Scotch and put it on the table.

'You can get rid of that for starters,' said my dad.

Stoke at the time had a reputation for being slow in settling transfer fees, but for players they were an attractive proposition because they paid well. I suppose that's where the money was going.

Ball started unveiling promise after promise. A house for me. A house for my parents somewhere between Preston and Stoke. More money. A car. And on and on it went.

My dad, however, was wise to all this. He took it all in and didn't say a word until Ball had stopped his spiel.

'Why should my son not sign for Everton?' he asked. 'Your son is there.'

Alan Ball senior didn't know what to say.

'Yes, well, my son will be playing for Stoke City in twelve months' time,' he vowed, rather unconvincingly. I knew then that I was Goodison bound.

CHAPTER THREE
BELLEFIELD

BEFORE I JOINED THE CLUB with which I would be synonymous for more than 30 years, my experience of Everton was limited to a couple of visits. There had been an appearance for Preston reserves when, as a slightly awestruck teenager, I'd marvelled at the vast empty expanses of Goodison Park. Not long after, at the start of the club's 1962/63 League Championship winning season, I'd returned as a spectator. Manchester United were playing and all the talk was of Denis Law's return to English football from Torino. It was an evening game and one of my team-mates who was in digs around the corner suggested we made the journey to Liverpool to see him. We knew that we'd have to leave at half-time in order to get the last train home, but we figured it was still worth it to see the returning idol.

But it wasn't Law I was captivated by. Just under 70,000 crammed into the ground as Everton roared to a 3-1 victory. I think Alex Young scored a header. It was an unbelievable atmosphere and never could I have imagined that a few years later I'd be on the same pitch, lining up alongside Alex in the famous blue shirt.

On that first day at Goodison Harry Catterick came out to greet me. He was unimpressed straight away by my car, a brand-new bright red MGB.

'You'll have to change that,' he said, referring to the colour of the car. 'You've no idea what they're like around here.'

We went inside Goodison, which still had the old Archibald Leitch-designed Main Stand. There were no negotiations as such, no image rights or incremental pay rises like you might get today. I was doubling my money to £60 per week and there was appearance money and win bonuses. Nobody talks about those elements these days because basic salaries are sky-high, but it meant something to us. I think we got £5 for a win and £2 for a draw. In European competition we got paid extra if the attendances were over 20,000, which led to all sorts of conspiracy theories among fans about attendances being under-reported.

The pay structure was still basically the same when I was manager during the 1980s. I remember Sir Philip Carter coming around the dressing room ahead of a European match wishing everyone good luck, and Adrian Heath piping up, 'What's the gate tonight, Mr Chairman? 19,999, again!?'

I went to live in Ainsdale with my parents, which was roughly halfway between Bellefield and Preston, where they still had a lot of friends. I kept living with them until I was married; it was just the way things were done in those days, but I was still very grateful that they'd come down to live with me from the Northeast.

It was when I walked into the Everton dressing room for the first time that I realised the world I'd entered. Football dressing rooms the length and breadth of the world are essentially the same: benches, showers, the smell of liniment and soap. It's the people inside them that make it, and it was clear from the faces in front of me that I'd entered a new and very special world. Gordon West, Tommy Wright, Ray Wilson, Brian Labone, John Hurst, Colin Harvey, Johnny Morrissey, Jimmy Husband, Alan Ball, Alex Young, Fred Pickering and Joe Royle. There were two World Cup winners – Wilson and Ball – among their number and most were internationals or soon would be. The majority of the 1966 FA Cup winning team were still at the club and several had won the league title three years earlier. I had arrived for a big fee, and I realised that expectations would be high from the supporters. But it was these men I would need to win over first. I think your initial task when arriving at a new club is to prove to the other players that you can play; then you have to worry about the fans.

Harry Catterick had a very ruthless way of discarding players. When someone had performed well for him but he felt there was need for a change, very rarely did a player move locally. The risk that Harry saw was that a player would maybe do well for a club in the same area so Evertonians would be reminded of it every other day. He sent Alex Young to Ireland; Jimmy Gabriel, Southampton; Mike Trebilcock to Portsmouth. They were going all over the place, as long as they weren't in the Northwest. You tend to accept the hand that is dealt to you in football, but it showed quite unequivocally where the power rested within a club in those days: the manager.

At Preston I'd been considered a wing half, but at Everton I was classed as a midfielder. The change in classification reflected the evolution of football tactics at the time, but it was basically the same position. What I don't like these days is the term 'attacking midfielder' or 'defensive midfielder'. I don't think there should be a place in football for those words. If you're a midfield player you should combine the two, without a doubt. That said, I played within different systems at Deepdale and Goodison. At Preston it was a more defensive system; I was virtually playing as a central defender sometimes. But I hated the idea that I'd just defend and I would set myself a target of between six and eight goals a season.

I'd come in to replace Jimmy Gabriel, who was popular among the players and supporters and had been crucial to the league and FA Cup successes. I'd seen him play and he was an absolutely tremendous wing half. He could tackle, get forward; he was the perfect wing half, a superb player. It can be difficult, sometimes, coming to take over from someone who has such a bond in the dressing room and on the terraces, but he was fantastic with me. On the day of my debut there was a telegram waiting for me; it was from Jimmy wishing me luck. I think that was the measure of the man.

So I arrived at Goodison with Jimmy's blessing, but others could be more testing. The captain, Brian Labone, for all his geniality, was somewhat petulant, at first at least.

'Who are you?' he'd sneer. 'You've only played in the cup final.'

On other occasions he'd give me a flick with his hand on my temple and bang my head against the wall, muttering, 'Good morning'.

Don't do that,' I'd say, but he was deaf to me and did it the next day, and then the next day.

The day after that I'd had enough of him, so I picked up his underpants and socks and chucked them into a bathtub.

Brian was furious. 'Don't you ever do that again,' he shouted.

'Well, don't you bang my head against the wall,' I said. And that was it; finished. I was accepted, one of the boys, an Evertonian – just over something silly like that. It was a test of character I realise now.

Brian's great mate Gordon West was testing too, but in a very different way. He would make all newcomers stand on a table in the dressing room and ask them to sing a song. If you didn't you were in trouble, but that was your welcome. Something like that would happen in most clubs, but not a physical thing like Brian was doing; I had to stop him.

The start to my Everton career was a slow one for me. The £80,000 deal to sign me had beaten the transfer deadline, but I was quickly forgotten about as all attention focused on the weekend's FA Cup fifth round tie with Liverpool at home. I was cup-tied and could only watch as an envious onlooker – one of 100,000 who crammed Goodison and Anfield, where the game was being relayed on a giant TV screen – as Alan Ball scored the only goal of the game.

My debut, at home to Southampton on 18 March, was a nightmare. It was the sort of fixture Evertonians expected – demanded – to win. But I just froze. I missed an open goal, was sloppy in my play and just didn't seem to be able to do anything right. Everton lost 1-0.

Despite the high expectations, the Everton supporters were fantastic about it all. After the match I was with my dad as we filled up with petrol at a garage near to Goodison, on the way back to Preston. It was pouring down with rain and I was recognised by a couple of the supporters. I'd just had a nightmare and we'd lost at home, but they didn't care. They were kneeling in puddles bowing to me. It reaffirmed the realisation that I was at a special club.

I only played three more games during the final two months of the 1966/67 season. I think Catterick was reluctant to use me and disrupt the team while Everton were in the FA Cup (they fell at the quarter-final stage to Nottingham Forest) and after that an injury flared up.

Expectations nevertheless remained high, as well they might, for I had cost a lot of money. I recall meeting John Moores, the Littlewoods magnate who owned the club, in a lift after a game I hadn't played in. Moores was a great patrician: always looking after his own, whether they be the people of Liverpool, his workforce or Everton Football Club. But as a player and later manager we had very few dealings with him. He had an annual event where he'd oversee disabled children being taken for a day out at the fairground in Southport and we'd take them on the rides, but that was it. He was a good man, but never beat about the bush.

'You're Kendall, aren't you?' he said in his typically direct manner.

'Yes,' I said.

'Well, when are you going to start playing for us, because you've cost us a lot of money?'

And with that he was off, point made, me not really knowing what to say.

The Everton dressing room, I soon learned, was full of characters. Sandy Brown was the butt of a lot of Labone and Westy's fun. It was a shame that everyone remembers him now for his derby day own goal, because he was a very good player. He was as fit and hard as any player I ever knew. His stomach was like a washboard; it was all muscle. He used to say in his thick Scottish accent, 'Punch for punch', challenging you to hit him so he could wallop you back. 'You can have a free one, if yer like,' he'd add; meaning he didn't do it back to you first time around. Not many people took him up on it.

It was Alan Ball who was the greatest help to me in those early days. He was confident, he was cocky; infectious as a player on the field but bubbly off it as well. I remember one occasion in those first days at Everton when he came into the dressing room and announced: 'One day, when I finish playing, I'm going to own my own house.' We all thought, 'You cocky little bugger!' A Premier League player could buy one a week these days!

He had arrived the previous summer and I signed on the deadline day, and the norm was that the players went for a night out when a new player arrived. We went into Liverpool, and Bally gave me some of the best advice anyone could give. 'Don't take the ball off Johnny Morrissey in training.' Johnny was a fearsome character and you wouldn't want to get on the wrong side of him. He did not suffer fools gladly. I've seen Johnny chase people around Bellefield simply for tackling him; Terry Darracott was one who was naive enough to try it. We were his team-mates too; among opponents he was hated and feared. He was number one in Jackie Charlton's 'black book' and completely ruthless. Luckily I was warned before it was too late.

I think Bally was deeply affected by being rejected as a teenage foot-baller. Whereas I'd had a line of clubs, both local and from far afield, vying for my signature, his local club, Bolton, had turned him down on account of his size. It had instilled a 'I'll show 'em attitude' that drove his relentlessly high standards. After finding a role with Blackpool, he'd vowed to his father – who he idolised – that he would play for England before his 21st birthday, a promise he'd kept. I think possibly Alan took more pleasure about being successful than I ever did. I was lucky never to have been turned down and didn't have that attitude. But we were united in an appreciation of our fathers: mine had made me the footballer I was; his had refused to give in and was determined to see his son play professional football.

Because he was so highly strung, Bally – like Sandy Brown – was always the subject of mickey-taking too, but he could take it. He and Alex Young owned a horse together, called Daxelle, which was the butt of many jokes. When it raced, Gordon West would get a cutout of a donkey and affix the name 'Daxelle' underneath it. I don't think it won a thing.

Alex was the Goodison idol, and it was easy to see why. I didn't play with him for very long, but his technical ability was absolutely fantastic. He was so silky; his movement brilliant. You could understand why he was called the 'Golden Vision'. He combined the skill with magnificent aerial ability; he had great spring for his size. It was an unusual combination, this grace and power, but the fans loved him for it. Even now, every time he goes down to Liverpool from his home near Edinburgh, he's absolutely mobbed. When you talk about Everton you talk about skill and you talk about quality; Alex certainly had those in abundance.

At the same time I think there was a physical side he didn't want to get involved with too much. Away from home he could go missing and Harry was never one to shirk in criticising a player. Harry Catterick used to have team meetings every Monday lunchtime after a game. Alex, however, had trouble with his hearing and if he had played at home and scored a couple then his hearing aid would be in.

'Alex, you were superb, well done; great goals,' Catterick would say.

But after playing away from home, knee deep in mud, Alex would be the first one he'd point the finger at.

'You didn't try a leg, you didn't run up and down, you weren't interested.'

On a day like this Alex would have the hearing aid out. Catterick would finish his speech and whoever was sat next to Alex would nudge him. 'He's talking about you, you know.'

'Oh, was he?!' he'd say obliviously.

Catterick was enigmatic. We feared and respected him. He never ranted or raved and was always straight to the point. There was never any arguing with him and you had to be respectful because of his record. But we didn't know him at all. He was distant and we'd rarely see him on the training ground. But we knew he was there. You'd see the blinds twitching in his office at Bellefield and step up the pace because you knew he was watching. He wasn't someone you'd warm to. Even his own staff didn't like him. But he knew what he was doing: you don't win two League Championships if you don't know what you're doing.

I remember one match when we were playing Tottenham and we stopped off overnight in Buxton. Catterick put a curfew on, as was normal. I'd not long been at Everton and although I joined the other players when we went out, I was anxious as curfew time approached.

'Right, I'm going now,' I announced as the other players started on another pint.

'You're not,' said Brian Labone, 'You're staying.'

'Time's nearly up,' I said. 'I'll just head back, you can follow me on.'

'You're STAYING,' ordered Brian.

And so, trapped between the will of the Everton manager and the Everton captain, I stayed. But when we got back to the hotel, there was a problem. Harry had taken all the room keys into his own room. To get to bed you had to knock on the boss's door and ask for your key back. He knew exactly who'd broken his trust.

The next morning he held a team meeting. The trip to the pub was top of the agenda. Harry handed out fines to everyone who'd broken the curfew. Everyone, that is, except me.

'Boss,' said Labby, 'don't fine Howard. It was my fault that he stayed.'

It was something I'll never forget about Brian. It was bold and brave, but as a player it also won me over to the captain.

I don't think anyone else would have stood up to Harry, though. I'll always remember Tommy Wright – an England international – complaining about his contract when we were having lunch. So Gordon West picked him up – physically lifted him up onto his shoulder – from the dining room, took him down the corridor, knocked on Harry Catterick's door, and left him there.

Catterick announced, 'Come in', but Gordon was away.

Poor Tommy was left stranded there, not sure what to say.

'What do you want?' barked Catterick when Tommy entered the office.

'I've … I've … come in to apologise for disturbing you, boss.'

Most of Harry's time was spent in his office silently observing. Only if the TV cameras or John Moores were around would the tracksuit come out. Strangely, he would be there for pre-season training on the sand dunes at Ainsdale. Maybe it was the sadist within him, as to a man we all detested it. We always lost about three or four players running up and down those dunes With Alex Young it would be blisters; others pulled hamstrings. It was carnage. Harry would sit in his Rover at the bottom, looking up at us, just to keep a check on it. Of course, like fools, we tried to go faster when he was there.

As a man-manager he was lacking. The only thing Harry ever coached me was this: I was always getting hurt on the front of my leg; I always used to go into a tackle front-on and my opponent would come in like that too. I used to get caught there and have to wear pads. He taught me how to adapt my stance in order to tackle more safely. 'Go in from the side,' he'd say. It was simple advice, but blimey, he was right. In six and a half years playing under him that was the only information he passed on to me that helped my career.

What did Catterick do, then? He bought good players. That was it:

simple. He didn't give good team talks; his coaches did that. We seldom saw him on the training ground. We had a meeting on a Monday in which he'd dissect our performance and praise and criticise accordingly. None of us liked him. His own staff loathed him, or at best disliked him. In the dressing room we all feared him.

MY FIRST FULL SEASON AT EVERTON – 1967/68 – was one of steady consolidation for me and the club. After my slow start the previous season I knew that I had to gain the trust of my team-mates and the supporters. Sureness in my own ability was never an issue, but you have to earn the confidence of others. In my experience the best approach in these situations is to keep your head down, work at what you know and are good at, and you will slowly enjoy the fruits of recognition.

Lining up with my Everton teammates ahead of the 1967/68 season. (Author's Collection)

Everton were also in a state of transition. Catterick was ruthlessly dismantling the FA Cup winning team, and I was part of this new guard.

Jimmy Gabriel was moved on that summer and other old favourites were also ushered out of the door. Alex Young, Fred Pickering, Derek Temple and Alex Scott would all follow him out of Goodison's revolving door in the year or so after my arrival.

The club had a reputation as the 'Mersey Millionaires' after going on a spending spree, partly underwritten by John Moores. But I was one of the last big buys. Harry brought in Ernie Hunt from Wolves in September 1967, a move that never worked out (he was sold to Coventry after just 14 games), but that was it for nearly three years. Instead he promoted from within, reaping the rich yield bestowed upon him by Everton's bountiful youth development scheme.

Colin Harvey had already stepped through those ranks. I played against Colin when I was at Preston in the A team, when we were both young, and his quality was immediately obvious. I think Colin was technically better than me; possibly my ball-winning attributes were better than his. With Bally the three of us would soon earn the admiration of English football. We just gelled and it was one of Harry Catterick's great gifts to the history of Everton Football Club bringing us all together.

John Hurst had followed Colin into the Everton first team in 1966/67 and never once looked out of place in the defence. We used to call John 'The Magnet'. It may have been the time he spent as an England schoolboy international centre forward, but he had this knack of going up at set pieces and scoring for fun. He didn't say much on the field, but he knew the game. His was a great defensive partnership with Brian Labone and they read the situations superbly well.

The 1967/68 campaign would be the breakthrough season for Jimmy Husband and Joe Royle. Joe had had an early start. People looked at his age – he was just 18 when he started playing regularly for the first team – but physically he was capable of succeeding at the top level even then. He was, in many respects, a man as a boy. When you're looking at centre forwards, Joe's got to have been one of the best in the club's history. Everton are renowned for number nines and he's well up there with them. He could hold the ball up, he was great in the air and had a terrific shot on him. And as a target man, Joe technically was very good as well.

Jimmy was as quick as lightning. I think credit is due to Catterick, who moved him from a wider position to start with and allowed him a free role just behind Joe. He wasn't the most clinical of finishers but nevertheless got his fair share of goals. For the next two or three years he was brilliant for Everton, but then he was on the receiving end of a hell of a bad tackle by Dave Mackay that put his career in jeopardy. Although he recovered, he was never quite as quick again, but in the late 1960s his pace was a crucial outlet for Everton.

When the 1967/68 season kicked off I was still just 21, Colin, Bally and Tommy Wright were 22; even Westy was still only 24. Joe was 18, Jimmy was 19. The average age was just 22. We were exciting and effervescent, if lacking a little experience.

We began the season brilliantly: 61,452 crammed into Goodison to see us face the reigning champions, Manchester United, and none were left disappointed. A brace by Bally and a goal by Alex Young saw us 3-1 winners. We played good football, but our lack of experience let us down on occasions. In our first ten league games we won four, but lost five.

Slowly we built momentum as the footballing relationship between me, Bally and Colin began to flourish. Our brand of football was about retaining possession, passing quickly and incisively, and moving into space. It was largely intuitive, perfected over endless, joyous games of five-a-side in the Bellefield gym. 'Sometimes I wished I could have got the games televised,' Catterick would recall years later. 'It was absolute magic.' It came easily to us, naturally. There were no get-togethers where we thrashed out what we were going to do on a Saturday. We knew instinctively what we'd be doing. It just happened.

Alan played in such an advanced position that he was like another striker. Certainly he was as prolific as one, finishing the season with 20 league goals from just 34 appearances, including four in a 6-2 hammering of West Bromwich Albion at the Hawthorns.

As spring came we hit a rich vein of form. We won 12 of 13 games, including nine on the spin. The run carried us through to the semi-finals of the FA Cup after we dispatched Southport, Carlisle United, Tranmere Rovers and Leicester City.

It set up a semi-final at Old Trafford with Leeds United, a side Catterick's Everton teams had struggled against since their promotion in 1964. They were hard, ruthless and dirty; and antipathy seeped between the football purists of Goodison and the brutal but brilliant Yorkshiremen. When Everton had faced Leeds at Goodison in November 1964 the referee took both sides off for a 'cooling-off period' after a waist-high tackle by Willie Bell had left some fearing for Derek Temple's life and nearly caused a riot in the stands and on the pitch.

We would be missing the suspended Bally for the semi and John Hurst was absent with jaundice. While everything had seemed to favour Preston four years earlier, now nothing seemed to go the way of Everton. We knew this was the final by proxy; that if we got through we would face at Wembley either Second Division Birmingham or a West Brom side we'd torn to shreds in March.

We discussed tactical ploys to overcome Leeds beforehand, and Harry Catterick was fixated with Gary Sprake's kicking. He felt that the left-footed kicking of the Leeds goalkeeper wasn't up to much and that we could gain an advantage by stopping him from using his right foot. Joe Royle and Jimmy Husband were thus instructed to stand directly in front of him whenever he had the ball, simply to stop him from clearing.

Harry's input in these matters was usually minimal, but this time it was a masterstroke. We followed his instructions and just before half-time they paid off. Joe stood in front of Sprake who, in his rush to clear, sent a weak and misdirected clearance into the path of Jimmy Husband. His goal-bound shot was blocked on the line by Jack Charlton with his hand,

and who else – in Bally's absence – was to take the resultant penalty than Charlton's nemesis, Johnny Morrissey? Johnny made no mistake in scoring the only goal of the game.

Being presented to Princess Margaret ahead of the 1968 FA Cup final. (Author's Collection)

It meant that at the age of 21 I would be lining up for my second FA Cup final. At Wembley we would be facing West Bromwich Albion, a team we'd already beaten easily at their own ground, and also at Goodison the previous November. We had done the hard job, beating Revie's fiercely competitive Leeds team, and we were overwhelming favourites. For me it was quite a different scenario to 1964, when I was thrust into the limelight and yet nothing was expected of me. I won't say I felt the pressure, but certainly all the Everton players were deeply aware of the expectation.

Although we might not have really been aware of it at the time, I think this preyed on one or two minds. On the bus on the way to Wembley I fell out with Ray Wilson. It was totally ridiculous looking back; just nerves, really. I was sitting next to him, listening to Gene Pitney's '24 Hours from Tulsa' on the bus's radio.

'Get that off,' he snapped.

'No, I like that, Ray.'

'What? Listen to that voice; and he comes over here and earns his money over here.'

I can't even remember what I said after that. The very idea that we had a bust-up on Wembley Way about Gene Pitney was absolutely ridiculous! I thought Gene Pitney was great, Ray didn't. That that difference would come out at that point in time said something about the tension lying beneath the surface.

I don't know if this undermined our performance that May afternoon, but we struggled against an organised and defensive Albion side. The space that normally opened up before our midfield play was lacking. Whatever we tried, we just couldn't break them down. Even the crowd started chanting 'We want football.'

Four minutes from the end I burst forward and sent a diagonal ball across the Albion penalty area. There was no one to meet it, but Johnny Morrissey retrieved it on the left and sent another cross into the six-yard area where Bally and Jimmy Husband were both unmarked. Jimmy, with time and space, got to it, but he was underneath the ball when he headed it, and while he should have buried it in the back of the net, it floated harmlessly over. He said later that he could have 'swallowed it' and that Bally put him off by yelling for it – both of which were probably true. If only he had left it, though, you would have put your house on Bally finishing it.

I don't think you can point the finger at Jimmy though. It was one moment in one game; had it been at any other moment in his career it would have been forgotten about.

Jimmy was sharp as a razor, a great worker and member of the team, but he was never a clinical finisher. I'd liken him a little to Adrian Heath, who would get into great goalscoring positions, but you weren't always guaranteed a finish. I think sometimes players are defined by one particular incident and this was the one for poor Jimmy. It's unfortunate because it overlooks what he did throughout his career at the club.

Extra time came and both teams tired on a warm afternoon. Four minutes into extra time, Jeff Astle's volley broke our hearts. We just couldn't find a way back.

We were devastated. We hadn't covered ourselves in glory, but we had been the better team. Sometimes you don't mind losing if you've played badly, but defeat is always harder to take when you know you've edged a match. We retreated to the Grosvenor Hotel and drowned our sorrows, taking comfort in the assumption that as young players our chance would come again. I think we would all have been shocked had we known then that of the eleven of us, only Bally would get another stab at Wembley glory while still a player.

The following Tuesday we returned to Goodison to conclude our league campaign. We put in the sort of performance we should have done at Wembley and trounced Fulham 5-1. It ensured we finished fifth, just six points off champions Manchester City. We'd won nothing, but the crowd sang and chanted our names as if we were the champions long after we'd left the pitch. When we reached the dressing room, Catterick ordered us to return to the pitch. There, in a rare display of showmanship, he addressed the crowd himself, promising that the brand of football they had witnessed that night would 'be the pattern of things to come'.

Collectively we had shown our undoubted potential during that first full season. Now we had to fulfil Catterick's promise and, what's more, add a trophy to go with it.

CHAPTER FOUR
HEAVEN

THE MIDFIELD PARTNERSHIP that I struck with Colin Harvey and Alan Ball would define Everton in this era and, in many respects, for all of our careers. We were 'Los Tres Amigos', the Holy Trinity, Goodison Park's 'Three Graces'. We could do anything: control games, break opponents down, win matches.

Looking back, I don't think the partnership needed any time to work itself out. Colin was a very gifted player and knew his position intuitively, as did I. He worked the left, I worked the right and we knew Bally would be up and down through the centre and scoring goals as well. Jimmy Husband would make runs from the right-hand side and I immediately turned round and went into the space that he'd left behind. Or it would come from Johnny into Colin and Colin would switch it over. The opposing full back then would go with the winger, so the space was there. It was something that we, as players, talked about and discussed among ourselves.

When you think of the system that we played, it's very much similar to the one David Moyes deployed in his last three or four years as Everton manager. There was lots of incisive midfield interplay and our opponents just couldn't cope at times. I think it's difficult to compare between eras and you have to judge players over a period of time. But I suppose of today's crop, Darron Gibson is the player I'd look at in terms of my position and liken most to myself. Leon Osman would be of a similar style to Colin. Jimmy Husband, not unlike Kevin Mirallas, had a licence to go off on the right-hand side and join in up the middle.

The difference we had was Bally, who was a once in a lifetime player, someone who was incomparable. The 20 goals a season we would get from him were the difference between us being a very good side that were in the mix (not unlike the Moyes-era Everton) and an outstanding one. If you want a modern comparison, I suppose you would look at the galvanising effect Gareth Bale has had upon a good Tottenham Hotspur team, but I don't think even he is in the same class as Bally.

Alan was definitely the best player I ever played with. He was so consistent. As I've said, the disappointments he had earlier in his career had a profound effect upon him and he never wanted to fail again. Even when he was a World Cup winner, he kept pushing himself and pushing himself.

The other difference with the modern-era Everton was that there was very little coaching or tactics dictated from above. We had trainers rather than coaches; men like Wilf Dixon and Stewart Imlach, who would work on getting us fit. How we played and the pattern of our play was left for us to decide among ourselves.

One time at Bellefield Wilf decided to get involved in our play.

'You give the ball to Colin; Colin, give it to Johnny; Jimmy, you start off your run, put it back to Colin; Howard, I want you to go round there. Colin, try and pick Howard out in that space over there because the full back's gone with it.'

. We just laughed: 'Wilf, we do that.'

That's not meant disrespectfully, but it was something you didn't need to coach. We all knew what we were doing and it was a good balance. I think that's the thing, the balance of it; and by making the signings and promotions from the youth team that he did, that was Harry Catterick's great gift to Everton.

All the talk of the three of us underplayed the contribution made by players like Johnny Morrissey and Jimmy Husband. One Monday morning a newspaper headline read 'Los Tres Magnificos'.

Brian Labone piped up: 'You know what? We're the only three-man team that's ever won the league.'

We didn't think that way, though, because we knew we had tremendous players alongside us. Johnny was a great player. I'd liken him to John Robertson at Nottingham Forest: he could go outside and he could go inside defenders but was rarely touched. I remember we played at Burnley and they moved Colin Bland from centre back to right back, because he was a big solid player, especially to see to Johnny. Colin never got near him all 90 minutes because Johnny was just too clever.

There was, of course, that ruthlessness in Johnny. We knew he was tough and as his team-mates we wouldn't get on the wrong side of him, so who knows how others saw him? He had a streak in him and was involved in a few incidents where the full back was badly hurt, and the finger was pointed at him. So the word got round and he was targeted by opponents. There was often a thirst for a bit of revenge, but nobody got near him.

I wasn't like that at all. That level of confrontation was just something I couldn't comprehend. It was a disappointing aspect of the game for me through the 1960s and 1970s. I've had it done to myself and been kicked out of games. It wasn't something you forgot. When I was at Preston we played

Bolton in the FA Cup and I'd flicked the ball up over the head of Franny
Lee. As I went around him he head-butted me and broke my nose. I couldn't
believe that there was an intentional part of a player's brain that fed down to
say, 'I'm going over the top,' or 'I'll have him, he won't have me,' or 'I'll go
high. If he goes in high, I'll go higher.' I simply couldn't imagine that going
on in a player's brain, but it may have done.*

Although we'd win the league title a year later, 1968/69 in some ways
saw us play better football. Many say that it was the finest footballing side
of Everton's post-war era, maybe because it was new to us and we were
more exuberant. Alan, Colin and I also played more games together that
season than when we won the title. Although Leeds would win the League
Championship, we felt that despite finishing third behind Liverpool we were
the best team. I think you have to have that mentality, that confidence, if
you're going to be successful.

Catterick had let the summer of 1968 pass without making any
signings, despite Alex Young's departure to Glentoran and the serious knee
injury suffered during the pre-season by Ray Wilson. This would restrict Ray
to just four further league appearances, but give the much underrated Sandy
Brown a chance to flourish.

Although we lost the opening fixture 2-1 at Manchester United and won
just two of our next five matches, by the end of September we had risen to
fifth. On the way we exorcised some demons. West Brom came to Goodison
at the end of September and 20 of the 22 players who had turned out at
Wembley were present in a game that Bally ran from start to finish, scoring a
hat-trick. Colin completed the scoring with a spectacular solo effort. That victory sent us on a winning streak that briefly elevated us to the top of the league.

---

* That particular day my Preston team-mates were so preoccupied with avenging my demise
that they lost their heads and we eventually lost the game because of it. I didn't forget the
incident and it always went through my mind whenever I played against Franny. Thirty years
later, when he was the Manchester City chairman, he tried to entice me to Maine Road as
manager. I told him 'no' – there were other factors, but it was partly because the head-butt
still played on my mind.

We'd dominate games. Sometimes it would be like shooting practice. If it came off, then great: we put five past Luton (in the League Cup) and Southampton, seven past Leicester City. 'The sustained play, the intelligent build-up, the remorseless pressure came from an Everton side operating smoothly on all cylinders with the super-charged drive coming from those marvellous men in the middle, Ball, Kendall and Harvey,' wrote Mike Charters in the *Liverpool Echo* when we beat Leicester 7-1 on a mudheap at the end of November. We went off to standing ovations at both half-time and 90 minutes, which wasn't unusual. On other days we'd give away soft goals and draw – or even lose – matches that we should have won easily. Sometimes it left us bewildered. If we had a problem, it was a lack of ruthlessness.

We had another good FA Cup run, albeit one that was fraught with challenges and personal disappointments. Besides a fifth round tie with Bristol Rovers, we faced First Division opposition all the way: Ipswich, Coventry, a quarter-final against Manchester United at Old Trafford, and then a Villa Park semi against the champions Manchester City.

In the run-up to the semi I experienced all the worst of Catterick's scheming. I'd come off injured against Queens Park Rangers on 1 February after taking a whack on the leg. It would heal, but then afterwards in training I'd break down again. It caused me to miss both the Bristol match and the game against Manchester United. Although Tommy Jackson had deputised ably in my absence, I felt the burden of pressure to get fit.

In the end our physio, Norman Borrowdale, agreed to get the doctor to give me an injection to see if they could heal it. Catterick came in to witness the procedure.

'Do you want to play?' he asked as the doctor inserted the needle.

'You don't know me if you don't know I want to play,' I said. I was furious at the implication I'd been dodging training, even more so at his timing.

But the treatment was unsuccessful. The next step was to see a specialist in Manchester. The main difference there was that the needle was longer, and they put cortisone in it.

The specialist this time announced, 'We'll have an X-ray before we do it.'

When the results came back it showed a stress fracture; calluses had already started forming and it had started to heal of its own accord.

Catterick came back to me, this time all apologetic. 'We found it; it's healed, you'll be okay now.'

I was somewhat less than impressed at the level of treatment, but what made it worse was that he'd doubted my injury.

A few weeks passed and my injury improved. The semi-final against City at Villa Park neared, and there was a reserve game on the Tuesday beforehand. I had a good relationship with the local press and one of the journalists called me to ask how the injury was. 'It's going fine,' I replied blandly. 'I'm starting to train again and I'm sure the manager will select me for the reserve team to see how it goes.'

The following Monday I was summoned into Catterick's office, which was never a good sign.

'What's this, Kendall?' he asked. He waved the paper and read it back to me: 'Kendall demands reserve-team spot'.

'Demands?' he asked.

'I didn't say that,' I stammered. 'I just naturally thought you'd play me and see if I'm all right.'

'Well, you're not playing; and I'm fining you.'

I was shocked. I'd never been fined for anything before, not even for being late.

'Pardon?' I asked.

'I'm fining you.'

I went downstairs and all the lads were waiting for me there and they could probably tell by my face that something was up.

'What happened?' they asked.

'He's fined me a week's wages.'

'Get away.'

I missed the reserve game, as he'd warned me. But on Saturday it was my name on the teamsheet to play City at Villa Park, not Tommy Jackson's. I had a painkilling injection before the match and another at half-time, but it was no good, I couldn't stand it and Tommy replaced me. We lost 1-0 to Tommy Booth's last-minute goal. The disappointment was crushing.

That night after the long, disappointing journey back from Villa Park, Harry drove me to the nursing home from Bellefield.

'By the way,' he said. 'I'm not fining you.'

'Great,' I said; but I wasn't really bothered – I was in agony and we'd just missed out on Wembley.

'When I said I was going to fine you, I knew it was because you were going to go downstairs and tell them. There was not a quote in the paper all week, was there?'

Looking back I can laugh at it now. He'd done it to stop Bally talking to the press. But the incident revealed the complex and manipulative way that Harry operated. At the time I was furious.

Because of my injury I made just one more appearance as a substitute that campaign. We ended the 1968/69 season third, ten points behind Leeds United's record haul of 67 points. In most other seasons 57 points would have brought us a lot closer to the League Champions; it may even on some occasions have been good enough to claim the title. We were top scorers with our 77 goals coming from all areas of the pitch. Joe Royle had finished the campaign with 22 goals, Jimmy 19 and Bally 16. I only got one! But things looked good for the following season.

WHAT MAKES A SIDE THAT TOUCHES GLORY go on to actually achieve it? Is there a dividing line between a very good side and a great one? Certainly luck and fate play a role, but I think it can be even less discernible than that: resolve, determination, mentality. I think the main difference between 1968/69 and the following season was simply belief. Just believing that we were the best. If you look at the sides that I managed, you could compare 1968/69 to the 1984/85 season, when we played fantastic football, and 1969/70 to 1986/87, when we utilised a larger squad but dug in for victory.

Certainly we were all aware of our responsibilities to bring the title back to Goodison. We were reminded constantly of people's expectations, sometimes with hilarious consequences. Some of the players had a night out on a Tuesday in Southport; Tuesdays being our day off. We were having a few drinks, but it was tame enough, when this bloke came up to the bar.

'You're a disgrace, you lot,' he said. 'You should be resting, not drinking.'

'What's your problem?' asked Bally.

'You shouldn't be here, you shouldn't be drinking.'

'Oh, give over. Shut up.'

'I'm fitter than you lot, anyhow,' he said.

Bally was never one to shirk a challenge or back down, so he announced, 'Come on then, put your money down. Let's see who's fitter.'

We'd been drinking all evening and it was midnight, one o'clock … I don't know what time it was. So we all went outside the bar, and Bally and this very sure of himself Evertonian set off for a run down Southport promenade and back.

'Come on then, show me how fit you are,' yelled Bally, and off he went into the night.

All you could hear was this heavy panting and Bally coming back in the lead taking the money and going up for another one.

It was just a fan wanting to have a go. It wasn't something that ever happened very much, but it was a reminder that our every movement was being watched and analysed by a fanbase that was desperate for us to encounter success again.

The new campaign opened on 9 August 1969 at Highbury. We were missing Bally through suspension and I was seeking to complete my first competitive match since 23 January. But I lasted just 36 minutes before limping off again with a knee injury. We took the game 1-0, controlling affairs, without ever fully dominating, which was the sign of a special team. Four days later we travelled to Old Trafford and, lining up against a team that boasted the famous Charlton-Law-Best forward line, won 2-0. 'With a start as blisteringly successful as this,' wrote Horace Yates in the *Daily Post*, 'the season could easily be the most fantastically successful in the history of the two Liverpool clubs.'

I didn't return to the team until the start of September. By then we were top having won six of the first seven league matches, drawing the other. I remained ever-present for the rest of the season, and our time at the top was virtually unimpeded. My team-mates in that famous Everton engine room fared less well, however. Colin was absent for two months with an eye complaint so serious that at one point we feared for his sight. Then, just as Colin was coming back into the team, Bally was suspended by the FA for five weeks after he was sent off yet again.

Bally could do daft things, but it was bound up in his character. He was firey. He'd run and kick someone and get himself sent off and then blame the rest of us.

'You don't care as much as me,' he'd shout in his distinctive high-pitched voice. 'That's why I did it.'

We did care; we cared passionately, we just articulated it in a different way.

When he returned, Catterick claimed to have pulled off one of his tricks. Brian Labone had been struggling with injury and so, in his place, he appointed Ball captain. 'It is a psychological move to give Alan more responsibility and make him more aware of referees' and players' problems,' Catterick told the press. What he was saying was that it was a move to positively channel Bally's aggression, but you'd never do that with Alan. He didn't need to be captain. It wouldn't raise his game, because it didn't need to be raised. It didn't change him because he was unchangeable and uncompromising. He carried on the same as he always had done: relentless, demanding, hot-headed, sometimes irresponsible. As a captain he was not a good example to follow, but his infectiousness rubbed off on us all the same. Claiming that making Alan captain was some sort of masterstroke was typical of Harry – taking credit for something that hadn't really changed anything.

Alan's ascent to the captaincy at the start of March 1970 coincided with the key games in that league campaign. We faced Tottenham in back-to-back fixtures and prevailed 1-0 at White Hart Lane and 3-2 at Goodison. It put us three points clear at the top ahead of the following week's derby encounter with Liverpool at Anfield. When we'd met in December, a calamitous 3-0 defeat had been rounded off with a spectacular own goal from the head of Sandy Brown.

Derby matches were something else. Although when you joined the club you became an Evertonian and an adopted Scouser, it was sometimes difficult to grasp what it meant to some of the lads, like Colin and Tommy Wright, who had grown up locally. The intensity of our play showed itself at different times. I think derby games reflected that. After the 'Sandy Brown' match you'd have had to have picked some of my team-mates off the ground they were that low. We all were in our own way, but you could see that it particularly hurt the local players. You could see how they raised their game when they played Liverpool and when it all came together we were magnificent.

Rarely were we better than in the return match at Anfield. It was a completely different story. We outclassed and outplayed Liverpool, beating them 2-0 with goals from Royle and Alan Whittle. It cemented our place at the top of the table and we practically knew then, with five games remaining, that the title was ours.

It's worth reflecting on the role of Alan Whittle, who came on to the scene that season and was absolutely brilliant for us. He was another to come through the youth ranks and was phenomenal at first. There'd be a little dart and a goal. He was a little quick lad, chock-full of confidence. However, his record of goalscoring wasn't maintained after the end of that first season. He later went on to Crystal Palace, where Malcolm Allison was the manager. Because it was Malcom and because it was London it was considered something of a glamour move. Alan, however, was insistent that he wouldn't change; he wouldn't be swayed. At the time there was a gulf in perceptions between the northern clubs and those in London – Harry Catterick used to warn me later in my career, 'Don't ever manage Blackpool and don't manage Chelsea, because you'll never be able to control the off-the-field activities.' London, like Blackpool with its bright lights and nightclubs, was considered a decadent place where young men would be led astray and that seemed to be the case with Alan, who I recall came back to Liverpool with a fedora on his head and a big cigar in his mouth. So much for not being swayed by Malcolm Allison!

We were now back on top form. We steamrollered the next visitors to Goodison, Chelsea, 5-2, including two goals in the opening three minutes. I scored after just 14 seconds – one of the fastest recorded strikes by any Everton player in the club's history. It was so quick, in fact, that my father missed it; he hadn't got into the stadium on time. A superlative performance in goal by Gordon West kept Stoke out two days later, who were seen off by a solitary Whittle goal.

It meant that a win at Goodison over West Bromwich Albion on 1 April would secure the club's seventh League Championship. Prior to the game, Catterick took us away for a two-day training camp in Cheshire. At that stage it didn't really matter what preparation we did; we knew we were the best. We were never going to let this one slip away; least of all because we faced our nemeses, West Bromwich Albion. Whittle sent us on the way with his 11th goal in 14 games on 19 minutes. It was left to my great friend Colin Harvey to score the goal which secured the title on 65 minutes. His strike has gone down in the annals as one of the finest Goodison has witnessed. 'First he moved towards goal, changed his mind and veered out, as though to bring Morrissey into play,' wrote Horace Yates in the following morning's

Daily Post. 'Seeing Morrissey was covered he doubled back to the edge of the penalty area and while on the run sent a crashing drive soaring into the net with Osborne leaping spectacularly, but vainly across goal … Everton sparkled in their play to the sparkle of their fans' applause.'

From then on, we knew the title was ours. The remaining 25 minutes were played out to nonstop chants of 'Ever-ton', 'We are the champions', 'We're on our way to Europe', 'Send our team to Mexico' and even a couple of choruses of 'When you're smiling'.

The sound of the final whistle was the prompt for thousands of supporters to run on to the pitch, chanting 'We shall not be moved'. We returned to receive the Championship trophy. The only thing I was disappointed with looking back on it – and I didn't think about it at the time – was that Bally was presented with the trophy and it should have been Brian, who was out injured. Bally had done well deputising in Brian's absence, but Brian was the captain, the one we looked up to, not Alan. It was typical of Brian's character that he never made a point about it, but I'm sure it would have annoyed him a little.

'They have won it by playing football, by applying their individual skills to the team as a whole,' said Catterick. 'And I would like to believe they have also managed to entertain spectators all over the country in the process … Our success has been a team effort and the effort must be shared all round.' Success was down to many factors. Joe had scored 23 goals, Alan Whittle 11 from 15 games, many of which were at critical moments. Johnny Morrissey's role was often overshadowed by our midfield partnership. As Catterick put it, 'When we are talking about those three, we mustn't forget the great part played by Johnny Morrissey – he was always available to receive the ball whenever one of the three was in trouble, and he played a great part in our style.' Many other players were underrated too: John Hurst was ever-present in the league and rarely got the recognition he deserved. Keith Newton, Sandy Brown, Roger Kenyon and Tommy Jackson all came in and did good jobs as well.

And who could forget Big Gordon West? As a goalkeeper he was undoubtedly one of the best in the game; as a character he was one of the biggest too. He was a truly great goalkeeper. When you talk about Neville Southall, very rarely can you think about a goal that was conceded and he was responsible for it and the same was as true for Gordon. He was absolutely brilliant in the dressing room too, which shouldn't be overlooked. He could lift us up with a laugh and a joke. We used to get the call to go out for training and he would be stood next to the dressing room door and booming, 'Nobody goes out until Westy goes out!'

After we sealed the title against West Bromwich Albion the celebrations went on and on and on. For too long. We won the title on the Wednesday, but still had to play Sheffield Wednesday on the Saturday. Wednesday needed to win in order to stay up, and in all honesty we gave them the best possible opportunity. Some of the lads had been out in Aintree since the Wednesday night and by Friday were in a bad state. Tommy Wright was suffering with heartburn as a result of his exertions so didn't join us.

On the night before the game, there was a knock on the door of my room. It was Bally.

'Come on,' he said, 'Let's go for a couple of pints.'

'I'll go and get Tommy,' said Colin, who roomed with Tommy.

But Tommy was in no fit state to go anywhere, so we left him and carried on drinking. The next day at Hillsborough it was a heavy ground; there were masses of supporters and the Match of the Day cameras.

Tommy looked at them with some disbelief.

'Oh hell! That camera's next to where I'm going to play,' he groaned.

It was by far the worst preparation for a game I'd had in my life and I'm sure I wasn't alone in that. We shouldn't have done it. But we were flying and we knew we'd won the league. I pulled a hamstring after about 20 minutes, and half a dozen of our players were running off beer. They hit the bar. They hammered us. But we still won and condemned Wednesday to relegation.

It'll forever stick with me Bally passing me on the pitch that day.

'What's it like to win it? What's it like to be the best?'

'It's brilliant, isn't it?' I laughed. 'It's absolutely brilliant.'

THE GREAT MYSTERY was not how we won the League Championship in 1970. It was how we didn't win more in the years that followed. 'I can see five great seasons ahead. This team is certain to get better,' said Bally with typical confidence after we'd lifted the famous old trophy. 'We have lots of skill and every player works hard for each other. With that behind us, how can we fail?' He was completely right. Really we should have had a dynasty, in the way that Liverpool under Bob Paisley later did. Instead we won nothing.

I don't know whether it was fatigue or complacency or the injury crisis that would soon engulf us, but we started the 1970/71 season as if we were preparing for a relegation battle rather than the defence of our title. Of the first six league games we drew three and lost three, and although form picked up a little we were hardly ever in the top ten, never mind challenging for honours. Brian Labone and Jimmy Husband were undermined by injuries, and Harry Catterick quickly lost faith with some of the stalwarts of our title win. Keith Newton was dropped and so was Westy after he was involved in an altercation with supporters during a European tie.

For a period it seemed as if Harry was questioning my value to the team too. In October he signed Henry Newton from Nottingham Forest for a club record £150,000.

Henry was a right-sided midfielder and it was clear to a number of observers that he was there to replace me. When he made his debut against Arsenal at Highbury it was John Hurst that dropped out and I moved to centre back – a position I'd never played in my life. Arsenal had John Radford and Ray Kennedy up front and slaughtered us. We got absolutely stuffed, 4-0, and I never played in central defence again, thankfully. But it was Henry to drop out, rather than me. When he returned it was at left back, in place of Keith Newton, and from thereon he looked the proverbial square peg in a round hole.

It was unfortunate for Henry, who was a good player. He had a tremendous long-range shot on him – they called it Henry's Hammer – but Goodison didn't see too much of it, to be honest. Why did Catterick sign him? I really don't know. Maybe he was building up a squad system and he perceived a lack of strength in depth.

Some of my team-mates were convinced that Catterick was determined to get rid of them for years before he finally did, but despite the arrival of Henry I never once felt like that. Indeed I never felt unwanted until the day that Harry left Goodison for the last time.

My own view is that Everton's decline in fortunes was linked inexorably to the way that Alan Ball changed after the title win. Bally had a tremendous goalscoring record, but after 1970 he went from 20 to two goals in a season. His father was very influential in his career and Alan hung on everything that he said. I think his father warned him that if he kept on covering the miles that he was he wouldn't last long at the top. So Bally started coming back deeper, not getting in the penalty area, but dropping back and taking the ball off Tommy Wright on the right and me on the right-hand side. I'd tell him to clear off, to get away. But instead of being a poacher and leaving the defensive bit he started playing in the wrong area of the pitch and would never go in the penalty area. It was inevitable then that his scoring rate dropped.

It's true that he contributed in different ways. He was always bubbly, he was always giving 100 per cent; but at the same time he was in the wrong areas. I had something similar with Peter Beardsley during my second spell as Everton manager. The first season he came to Everton he scored 20 goals; then I would look at him the following season and he had a poor goal return but he would be sprinting over to take corners. I'd tell him again and again, 'You need to get into goalscoring positions.' The crowd would love it – 'Oh, look at him, he's keen to take that corner, he's sprinting over there' – but my view was that he was one of my goalscorers and he was taking a corner. You can't take that many goals out of your team. At the beginning of a season you can virtually work out, or you should be able to work out, your approximate goal return from the players you have. Because you don't get somebody scoring five one season, and then they score 20 the next. You might see an improvement to eight. But you certainly don't count on someone going from 20 to two.

I think there was also probably a bit of staleness on the training ground too. It was still a lot like when I'd started out at Preston a decade earlier. Wilf Dixon knew the game, but he was a trainer first and foremost and would work us hard. On a Tuesday morning it'd be sprints: 8 x 80's, 4 x 40's, 2 x 20's, 100 yards. People would be sick behind a tree. I've seen Joe Royle absolutely spewing up behind a tree; Westy too. We had a running track at Bellefield with sand on it, and we'd pair up, and Wilf had the stopwatch; one player would go round and then his partner would go round, so you had a little bit of a respite. And Tommy Wright wasn't too good one morning, so he went round once – he was pairing with Colin – and he flopped behind a tree. So Colin went round and round and round. There'd be no Tommy, so Wilf would shout, 'Colin's got to go again … Colin, you're slowing up … Your time's not good enough.' Colin, who was a great trainer, was absolutely shattered, while Tommy was behind a tree.

I never liked the running side of the training ground routine. It's why, when I went into coaching and later management, I did most of it with a ball. The more interesting you make it the less the players know that they're working hard; even if they might be doing the same amount of exercise as on a cross-country, or 800 metres routine. It kept them fresh and it kept them motivated. I'm not saying we lacked motivation as players, but sometimes there's a need to freshen things up.

One of the things about Harry that worked against him after the League Championship success was his cool relationship with the media. When he was successful he didn't think he needed the press. He was naturally aloof, and wasn't forthcoming with information about the team or players, or anything like that; he just kept everything to himself. That's the way he was, whereas Shankly was a dream for the journalists. But when things started to go badly the pressure built up on the back pages. Harry didn't really have an outlet or a friendly face he could turn to. You could see the pressure starting to build up on him.

Although we struggled to build momentum in the league we progressed well in the cup competitions. The season reached a critical juncture in the last week in March when, within the space of four days, we had a European Cup quarter-final against Panathinaikos and an FA Cup semi-final against Liverpool.

Despite battering them we had somehow contrived to draw the first leg of the Panathinaikos game at Goodison 1-1, which meant we went into the second leg in Athens with an away goal against us. We faced the worst sort of intimidation on that trip. The plane was not able to land until the early hours of the morning. The hotel was circled by cars beeping their horns well into the following night. The club secretary, Bill Dickinson, received a death threat before the game. Things didn't get much better once the game got under way. We were spat at and all manner of abuse and missiles rained down from the pitch upon us. John Hurst had his eyes gouged by an opponent. It was incredible, really. We were absolutely robbed by the referee with a dodgy decision. The whole thing stank. Having seen Greek football as a manager and the corruption and fixing that goes on there, I think it's quite likely that someone manipulated the outcome of that match. We drew 0-0 and were out on away goals. Panathinaikos went on to reach the final where Ajax beat them 2-0, although I'm quite sure we would have posed a more significant challenge if given the chance.

Harry Catterick didn't exactly cover himself in glory afterwards. You'd expect him to come in and say, 'Bad luck, lads, it didn't go our way, the referee made some bad decisions.' Instead he came into the dressing room and announced, 'You bastards have cost me five grand tonight.' That was his bonus. It was also the extent of his post-match team talk.

We returned tired and dejected. However, there was no time to be downhearted as we were playing Liverpool less than 72 hours after the end of the match. Bally, Joe, Colin and Johnny Morrissey had all picked up injuries against the Greeks. He kept us away from home, which I think was a mistake, in the Lymm Hotel in Cheshire. We were bored, we were disappointed. We should have had a day's break and then met up again. Then he didn't turn up at Old Trafford. Catterick was nowhere to be seen. Health problems had already started to take their toll on him and would greatly affect him over the coming two years. He was too unwell to manage us, so it was up to Wilf Dixon to take charge.

We knew this was our final, final chance to redeem something from the season. It was a frenetic start, but Bally put us in front on ten minutes. The turning point came when Brian Labone went off injured with a thigh strain in the 50th minute. Soon after Alun Evans equalised and from thereon Everton were under the cosh. Liverpool's winner came from Brian Hall eighteen minutes from the end.

The defeat destroyed us. We only won one more of our remaining eight league games, finishing the 1970/71 campaign 14th. For Everton that was a disaster.

I think the fact that it was Liverpool was psychologically very damaging. It didn't take long for an outsider to realise what it means to a local lad on Merseyside. We had the likes of Tommy Wright, Colin, Joe and Andy Rankin who would take derby defeats far, far harder. But even for the rest of us it wasn't nice.

It was a catastrophic day for Everton Football Club. That was the day that we handed the baton of Merseyside football supremacy to Liverpool. We've had our moments here and there since then, but we've never challenged their supremacy for a sustained period of time despite our best attempts.

HOPES THAT THE 1970/71 SEASON was some sort of bizarre aberration soon dissipated as the new campaign got under way. In what seemed like some sort of bizarre nightmare the conquering champions of barely a year earlier would win just one away game all season and score only 37 goals, eight of which came in a single remarkable afternoon when we tore Southampton apart like it was still the good old days.

That afternoon Alan Ball scored his 79th and last Everton goal. A month later Catterick sold him to Arsenal in a shock £220,000 deal. In a lot of ways it didn't surprise me. Not long before, we were having a practice match that Wilf Dixon was in charge of.

I'll always remember Wilf stopping the play and saying, 'Alan, what's wrong with you?'

You could see Bally wasn't interested. He was sulking, or having a strop. He put his hands out and said, 'How can I play with this lot?'

Most of the players he'd not long ago won the league title with were standing there, looking on. And so too was someone rather unexpected.

Harry Catterick was standing behind the goal and I thought, 'What's he doing out here?' He'd come out to see Bally. He went straight back in his office and I'm sure the deal was done to sell him to Arsenal that day.

I found out about Alan's sale in the most unexpected manner. Very late at night I received a call from a supporter and good friend of mine called Joe Murray. He and his mates had got word of the deal and were devastated by the news.

'My boys can't sleep, Howard,' he said. 'Bally's gone. They can't sleep.'

It said much about the esteem Alan was held in that he prompted such mournful reactions.

Alan's departure left a huge void in the Everton team. One of Catterick's biggest problems was how difficult it was to replace Bally. He brought in Mickey Bernard from Stoke the following summer, who was a totally different type of player. Being classed as the replacement for Alan Ball was a burden for him. He wasn't of the same standard as Alan. No one I ever played with was.

Mick wasn't the only one who didn't live up to the standard of his illustrious predecessors. It wasn't his fault, it wasn't any of their faults. Many were good players. It was really just a case of wrong place and wrong time for a lot of them.

Things also weren't right behind the scenes at the club. After a build-up of health problems Harry suffered a heart attack and was never really the same again. I was made captain and did my best to pull things together, but it wasn't always easy. Over the next 18 months a succession of the old guard – Westy, Labby, Tommy Wright, Jimmy Husband – were sold or retired. Colin and Joe suffered long-term injuries. Harry – or those around him – made a series of bad signings.

Probably the most notorious of these was Bernie Wright. We played Walsall in the FA Cup in February 1972, and I think the scouting report had gone in and said, 'Big strong lad, the centre forward, have to be aware of him on the day.' Somewhere, somehow, down the line this was translated as 'We must buy him.' Catterick was having one of his spells of ill health and the decision was taken by the board in his absence. It wasn't Harry's signing, but it was an indication of how the club was becoming disastrous.

He wasn't, frankly, the brightest of players, and our perceptions of him weren't exactly helped by his thick Brummie accent.

'What are you going to do when you finish playing?' we'd say to him.

'I'm going to be a dropout!' he answered, deadly serious.

The end for Bernie wasn't long in coming. Every year all the players got Christmas hampers from Littlewoods. There was an A and a B hamper, and the first-team squad got the A hampers and it was bottles of port and bottles of sherry, and biscuits and sweets.

The next day Bernie came into the dressing room with his bottle of port. He'd clearly been working his way through the hamper since the end of training the previous day.

'When Bernie drinks, everybody drinks,' he announced in his thick Brummie brogue.

This was before training! So we told him to piss off and went outside to warm up. Bernie joined us with his bottle of port and began trotting around with it, taking swigs. Before Harry Catterick caught wind of it, Westy went after him and tackled him to the ground. He was then seen on the back of a lorry going into Liverpool with his kit on, still swigging from his bottle. That's the last any of us ever saw of him.

Westy was in and out of favour, but Everton – not just Harry – struggled to replace him. In fact no one really did until I became manager and signed Neville Southall. I do think Everton suffered because they lacked a great goalkeeper between Gordon and Neville. It's the number one position. I think it was very difficult for anyone to come in and match the qualities of those two; very difficult indeed. It's not easy for the manager to go out and find them either.

Harry brought in David Lawson for a lot of money from Huddersfield. He was no Gordon West. He had no shoulders. The comment from the dressing room was that they'd have to nail his braces on to keep them on. He was an okay keeper but it's who you're following that you're judged by; if you're following somebody exceptional it's very difficult for a lower-league player to come in and immediately be a success.

Then there was Dai Davies. The fans dubbed him 'Dai the Drop'. I think by the players Dai would be remembered as not being consistent; liable to make a mistake every now and again. Because of this the players in front of him lacked confidence in him. I remember the ball going into the penalty area and Dai calling 'keeper's ball', but he left it and the defender left it and a goal was conceded. According to Dai that was the defender's fault. But it happened so often. Dai certainly had some good attributes: he was a big lad and could be commanding. He was just prone to some terrible errors.

There were some other big signings that didn't come off. Joe Harper had a tremendous goalscoring record in Scotland. He was signed from Aberdeen as another replacement for Bally, but like Mike Bernard it never worked out for him. He was a smallish striker, an individual on the pitch; he had a great reputation in Scotland for scoring. But then you look at the opposition up there and it's certainly not as strong as down here. In any case he faced the perennial problem: who can step into Alan Ball's footsteps? It was a difficult ask for most players.

We also had some good young players come through but, perhaps because they didn't have the stability a previous generation had enjoyed, they didn't make the same impression. Mick Buckley came into the side towards the end of my time at Everton. He was smallish, talented, with a good brain; a neat player really. Like a lot of the young players at the time, they all had something to offer or they wouldn't have been at Everton Football Club. But, like the situation with the goalkeepers, it was just a case of them being compared with what had passed before. It was unfair on them. Some of the players couldn't live up to what was expected. The crowd could be very demanding, as indeed they still are. On the other hand, I think they do give the local lads a chance; they don't really set about criticising if you've come through the ranks. But if you've been bought for a certain amount of money and you're disappointing, they're more likely to get on your back.

Roger Kenyon was a really good player; good enough to make it to the verge of the England team at a time when it was very hard to even get that far. He didn't get a cap in the end, which was unfortunate because he had everything: he had pace; he was tall, good in the air; he was a very good centre half. Later, off the field, he had a very serious car accident and was lucky to survive, which impacted severely on the end of his career. But he played his part in a difficult era for Everton, as he had at the end of our title-winning season when he was an able deputy for Labby.

Others fell short of their potential. Gary Jones was a phenomenally talented winger; he really had it all. Right-footed, left-footed, quick; he had everything apart from concentration. When I returned with Birmingham, he was up against the full back Terry Darracott and Everton were attacking the Gwladys Street. Terry was moving forward and Jonesy said to him, 'Hey, Terry, I didn't realise how big that main stand was.' He was looking up wide-eyed at what was towering above us as the game was going on! He was just vacant, Gary, and he wandered off. But what a talent he could have been.

AS EVERTON'S FORTUNES NOSEDIVED, SO MINE ROSE. I was club captain and playing well even amid the decline of a once great side. Some said that I was responsible for keeping Everton in the First Division during this time. I wouldn't go that far, but in 1973 – a year in which Liverpool won the league title and UEFA Cup – it was not Kevin Keegan or Emlyn Hughes named Merseyside Sports Personality of the Year, but me. I took that as an enormous personal compliment, even though I would have swapped it for Everton to be doing better.

What was, however, missing from my curriculum vitae was an England cap. At the time Sir Alf Ramsey was manager, and he had a reputation for standing by his players; of being unstintingly loyal to them. He didn't change things around much and openings were few. If you were in, you were normally in for a long time. His substitutions were few and far between too. I was involved in a few squads and got near on one occasion, in October 1972.

We trained at the Bank of England ground in Roehampton, and we were playing Yugoslavia the next day. We got on the bus after training and Alf got up at the front of it. 'For tomorrow's game I'm going to announce my twelve players,' he said.

I was about the fourth name mentioned, so Bobby Moore – and I'll always remember this – just winked at me from the other side of the bus.

Alf sat down, but then got up again straight away and said, 'Rodney Marsh, have I named you?' Rodney answered 'no'. He said, 'You're my twelfth man.'

As soon as I was back at the hotel I was on the phone to my wife and parents, telling them to get down to London, that I was in. The next morning at breakfast I picked up the newspapers but they told a somewhat different story. The line was that if Colin Bell failed the fitness test Howard Kendall would play. But I knew Colin Bell was fit. I was gutted.

It was frustrating but Alf, give him his due, told me that if he made a substitution I'd definitely go on. I sat next to him on the bench. Joe Royle and Alan Ball were both playing, as was Rodney Marsh, supposedly the twelfth man. But I never got a look-in; Alf never made a substitution all night.

Although full international honours continued to elude me I was called up for the English League versus the Scottish League in March 1973. Bobby Moore captained England and I played in midfield alongside Colin Bell. But besides those seasoned internationals, these games – which were coming to an end – were considered stepping stones for aspirant internationals. One of the English League players was Peter Shilton, for example, who was at the start of an international career that would see him claim 125 caps. This particular game was a nightmare for me. I was always a team player and the team that Sir Alf Ramsey selected was a side full of individuals. We had plenty of big names among us, but no cohesion. I was playing out of position, wide right, and I probably helped earn Danny McGrain his first full cap because he kept racing past me all the time. He absolutely slaughtered me. He hadn't played for Scotland at that stage but he turned out to be an absolutely magnificent full back; but I just couldn't get near him. And I wasn't getting any help, because the players who were playing in our team, in the Football League team, were individuals and trying to impress. I just didn't feel comfortable at all and in the end Tony Currie was brought on in my place. It was, frankly, a sobering experience.

Was I disappointed by this? The short answer is yes. I found it frustrating that someone like Peter Storey was brought in as Nobby Stiles' replacement when I felt I had more to offer at that time. But other good players were overlooked or never given a proper chance. Colin Harvey, for example, got just one cap.

The long answer is that there was some virtue in being overlooked. Subsequently I was very kindly classed as the best player never to be capped by England. In many ways I'd rather have that outcome than talk about going on for five minutes as a substitute and being able to say, 'I've played for England.'

ON 11 APRIL 1973 CAME THE NEWS we had all been expecting for perhaps two years. Harry Catterick, at the age of 53, would be stepping down as manager and moving to an unspecified executive role. His illness was well known and it was really just a matter of time. The 1972/73 season was a transitional year – we'd finish 17th in the league – and we were really just waiting for him to go.

He was an unhappy figure in the shadows and not treated very well. The club would send him his money by post so that he wasn't seen at Goodison. Everton could be ruthless like that. I remember him cornering me once and telling me, 'They're waiting for me to die.' Eventually they stopped paying him under some pretext or other. The end for Catterick was inevitable and it didn't surprise me one bit the way that he was treated.

It was never clear what sort of 'upstairs' role he was supposed to have, but whatever it was it didn't work out. He had started to go a bit strange. He claimed that the club reneged on his pay-off because they didn't receive a scouting report from him. Later in the decade he managed Preston but that didn't work out either. His eccentricities got worse and he had his office soundproofed so he wouldn't be disturbed.

Bill McGarry, then manager of Wolves, and Don Revie were the names in the running to replace him. Revie came close, but the appointment never came, and Billy Bingham was the surprising choice as successor over the summer. He had managed Southport and Plymouth and had a spell in charge of the Greek national team. He was considered a progressive manager and was fondly remembered for his stint as the Everton winger in the 1962/63 League Championship winning side, but had no real experience at the top level.

I was captain at the time and drove down to Bellefield to wish him all the best. I knocked on his office door and was beckoned in.

'Congratulations, Billy,' I said. 'I hope things go well.'

He cut me short and hissed, 'It's boss, not Billy.'

There was nobody else in the bloody building! I backtracked, and said: 'When the lads are here I'll call you boss; but we've met before and I called you Billy then ...'

'It's boss now,' he said, 'okay?'

I knew at that moment that my time at Everton was drawing to a close: Bingham was going to sell me.

CHAPTER FIVE

BIRMINGHAM

BILLY BINGHAM WAS THE FIRST TRACKSUIT MANAGER THAT I WORKED WITH. He was far more hands-on than Harry Catterick or Jimmy Milne. Great emphasis was put on our fitness and conditioning, and new training ground techniques and routines were utilised. But for all his time spent with us at Bellefield he was no less distant or enigmatic than Harry Catterick.

The local journalists, with whom I always had a good relationship, used to ask me, 'What have you done to Bingham?' He was, I was told, always complaining about me, telling them that he didn't rate me. I was the club captain and had just won the Merseyside Sports Personality of the

Year so I can't have been that bad. Newspaper speculation started to appear linking me to a move back to the Northeast. Bingham, the stories said, wanted to part-exchange me for Sunderland's Dennis Tueart.

Presented with the 1973 Merseyside Sports Personality of the Year Award.
(Author's Collection)

Everton were a team in transition and the 1973/74 season was a personally frustrating campaign for me. I picked up a nasty knee injury just five games in and spent nearly five months on the sidelines. I was just coming back to fitness and had returned to the team in February 1974, when I was summoned to Bellefield on my day off. I knew, straight away, that something was up.

'A club has come in for you,' announced Billy in his thick Belfast accent. The papers had been full of stories about Tueart coming to Everton and there had been contact from Bob Stokoe, the Sunderland boss. I was certain I would be moving to the Northeast. 'It's Birmingham City.'

To say I was surprised was an understatement. The reality was that I was a chip in a complicated deal, which involved the Birmingham centre forward Bob Latchford coming the other way. Everton had made a cash bid for Latchford, but with Birmingham fighting relegation their manager Freddie Goodwin needed bodies that could lift the club from the mire. As such he held out for a players-plus-cash offer, and with Archie Styles I was one of the two players he wanted. With Everton offering £80,000 on top, the deal was worth £350,000 – a British record fee. Everything hinged on my decision.

Because of the passion that football generates, there tends to be a lot of sentiment attached to relationships with clubs. I had become an Evertonian and had grown to love the club. But actually, as a player, there's little room for emotion. It's your job, and the same factors apply to your work as a footballer as they do in most other workplaces. If you're unwanted by the boss, there's no place for you there. So while it was sad to have to leave a club I had served for seven years and a wrench to uproot my young family, the decision was actually an easy one. I wasn't wanted at one club, but another team sought me. I would become a Birmingham City player. The swap deal that brought Bob Latchford to Everton and sent Archie and me down to St Andrew's was a British record that stood for three years.

I was sorry to go, but at the same time I wasn't beset by any great disappointment at leaving Everton. There was, nevertheless, an element of culture shock on arriving at Birmingham. The first day I went there it was a real eye-opener. Birmingham trained at Elmdon, which was near the airport. Because of the height of the ceiling, the changing room resembled an air-raid shelter. It was a real dump. The kit was passed out to the players, filthy dirty, ready to put on for training.

John Roberts, the centre half, came up to me and said, 'You're the biggest signing here, why don't you go to the manager and complain about the kit?'

I looked over at mine and it was new as it was my first day.

'I don't think so, John,' I laughed. 'Mine's all right.'

I soon knew it was a different ball game altogether at Birmingham. If you were back in the afternoon after a morning session and it was muddy, the kit was put in the dryer without being washed and came out with congealed mud on it.

But I was there to do a job and amid the dilapidation and struggles at the wrong end of the First Division there were some positive aspects. Having dealt with enigmatic managers at Everton in Bingham and Catterick I got on well with Freddie Goodwin from day one. He made me captain and started to make me think beyond my role as a player. Although we were struggling in the First Division we had a good squad. We had the centre back-cum-centre forward Kenny Burns, the prodigious young striker Trevor Francis, and Bob Hatton, an experienced campaigner and fine centre forward.

After Alan Ball, Trevor was probably the best player I ever played alongside. He was still only 19 when I arrived at St Andrew's, but the sense that he could do anything was palpable. He was fast and skilful and could finish with deadly accuracy. He could also create as well. I felt then that in the right team he could be a world-beater, and of course he was. Five years later he became English football's first 'million-pound signing' and a few months after that deal he scored the winner in the European Cup final. He would star in Italy and have a decade-long England career, although his full potential possibly went unrealised owing to the blight of niggling injuries.*

One of the first dates in Birmingham's upcoming relegation battle was at Goodison Park. Naturally it was going to be an emotional day for me when I returned to the stadium in which I'd enjoyed so many memories. The suddenness of my departure meant that there had been no proper farewell. On the day fans were coming up to me, giving me so many things – plaques and other mementoes – telling me they missed me, thanking me. It was tremendous.

But I also had a job to do and that was to save Birmingham. I had my role as a player, but as a senior member of the team too it was my responsibility to instruct my team-mates and make sure they did the right thing. I knew plenty about my old team-mates, but I also knew that Everton's danger man was their old colleague, Latchford.

Bob was a terrific player, but there were times when he played within himself. Because he is by nature placid and laid-back, sometimes his personality would be reflected in his play. As an opponent you wanted him

---

* Jim Smith, who was by then Birmingham manager, had fallen out with Trevor and was determined that Trevor wasn't going to be the first million pound signing. So he made sure the transfer went through at £999,999.99.

to be calm, because you knew you stood a chance with him. If he was wound up he was a different man. He was like the Incredible Hulk. On a nice day he'd be a real gentleman and he wouldn't even think about it. But if you wound him up or upset him, he was a monster.

He knocked the teeth out of Malcolm Page when he came back down to St Andrew's. He even kicked his brother, Dave, who was our goalkeeper at Birmingham.

That day at Goodison we had Joe Gallagher, who was a Liverpool-born centre back, marking Bob.

'Joe, when you go out there with Latchford, just ask him how he's settled in, where is he living and how's the family,' I said. 'Be nice to him. Don't for Christ's sake kick him.'

'Okay,' replied Joe.

In the first minute, Joe whacked him from the back.

Latchford was like an animal after being wound up. He ran us ragged that afternoon and scored twice as my old team won 4-1; their biggest win of the season.

That result put us in serious danger of relegation, but we turned things around. A week later we beat Manchester United – themselves in danger of the drop – 1-0 at St Andrew's and we would lose just two of the last ten games. Victories over Queens Park Rangers and Norwich City in the final two games of the season elevated us to safety, after we'd sat in the three relegation places since the day of my arrival. As I've said, we were a good team and had some decent players; the margins between the catastrophe of relegation and respectability were slim. Just eight points separated Southampton in the last relegation spot and my old club Everton in seventh.

On the final day of the season, with safety secured, we were ordered out of the dressing room by Freddie Goodwin to go and applaud the waiting fans. A few years earlier I'd done the same at Everton. Then, we'd won the title. Here, avoiding the drop was considered a triumph.

⊖

FREDDIE GOODWIN was someone who I respected and liked. He would have a profound effect on my career. He was a shirt-and-tie manager, like Catterick, but dissimilar in almost every other way. He started to make me think about coaching and what life after football held for me. I was now in

my late twenties and I always assumed I'd finish up playing and then do my badges, but realised that I had to be ahead of the game. Freddie encouraged me to take my coaching badges while I was still playing. A few years later this would give me a crucial head start.

The coaching qualifications then were very different. I remember at the FA training centre at Lilleshall that a schoolteacher would have the same qualification as me, if we both passed. Nowadays it's changed – you've got your A licence, B licence or whatever – but back then the professional footballers trained with the schoolteachers, Sunday League coaches and anyone else who put their name forward. I remember one guy I was training with who polished his boots and put his new tracksuit on as if he was living the dream. He was first on after lunch, and would organise the drill among the rest of us. Then he made a big mistake. He started to try and move the goalposts, thinking they were portable. But they were rooted to the ground, and he was completely flummoxed. He just collapsed and couldn't cope with the mistake.

I also came into contact with other young coaches and up-and-coming managers. One of them was Malcolm Allison, who had formed such a well-known partnership with Joe Mercer at Manchester City. We

I was lucky enough to play for England Schoolboys, a game which didn't go so well for me, but helped attract the attention of a number of clubs. (Author's Collection)

With my England Schoolboys teammates.
(Author's Collection)

The FA Cup goal for Preston against Nottingham Forest, which brought me to national attention for the first time. (Author's Collection)

Inspecting the great expanses of Wembley Stadium the day before I became the youngest player in a Wembley FA Cup final. (Author's Collection)

*We encountered a simply unbelievable reception both at Wembley and
on our return to Preston, where we were greeted as if we'd won the FA Cup.*
(Pictures courtesy of Lancashire Evening Post)

Despite losing the FA Cup final we were treated like heroes on our return.
(Pictures courtesy of
Lancashire Evening Post)

With my mother sorting through the reams of fan mail that came after the FA Cup final appearance. (Author's Collection)

With my Young England teammates. Our reward for winning the Little World Cup was a trip to Gibraltar. (Author's Collection)

Liverpool were the longstanding favourites to sign me; I never knew of Everton's interest until the day before my transfer. (Author's Collection)

On my debut for Everton v Southampton, a less than successful experience. (Colorsport)

Preparing for extra time in the 1968 FA Cup final. Defeat that day was devastating. (Colorsport)

*Playing against
Stoke City in 1969
in Everton's famous
white-hooped shirts.*
(Colorsport)

*Goodison's Holy Trinity:
The most famous
partnership in Everton
history.* (Colorsport)

'You don't care as much as I do!' Alan Ball was the most brilliant player I worked with, but his determination sometimes became hard to deal with. (Colorsport)

With my great friend Colin Harvey as 1970 League Champions. (Colorsport)

*Our away goals defeat in the European Cup against Panathinaikos was
a turning point in Everton history. I remain convinced that the outcome of the
match was manipulated.* (Welloffside / L'Equipe)

*At the unveiling of Billy Bingham as manager. Even though I was captain
I knew from the start that he wanted rid of me.* (Colorsport)

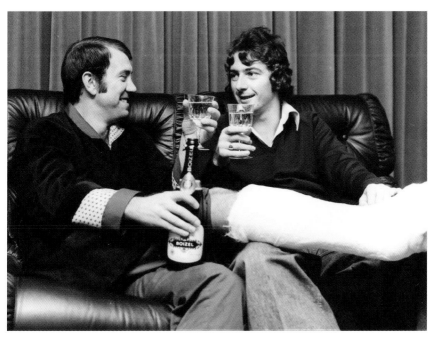

*With Trevor Francis, who, after Alan Ball was
the most talented player I played with.* (Author's Collection)

*I was still winning playing awards during the veteran part of
my playing career at both Stoke and Blackburn.* (Author's Collection)

In a smokey back room I was unveiled as Blackburn Rovers' player manager.
(Author's Collection)

Celebrating promotion with the late Noel Brotherstone. (Author's Collection)

were having a practice match under the supervision of the FA technical director Allen Wade when all of a sudden this Rolls-Royce comes over the top of the hill, and a sheikh, dressed in robes, got out. Malcolm had been linked in the press with a move to the Gulf and the fortunes promised in the Middle East. The sheikh solemnly beckoned him as if to say, 'Malcolm, I want to see you up there.'

Malcolm went running up the hill to meet the man who he hoped would make him a very rich football manager. Of course, it was no Saudi prince but one of the lads dressed up. Down on the pitch everybody was rolling around the floor laughing.

At St Andrew's Freddie also welcomed me over the threshold into the manager's office. Back then this was a closed world to most players and we had little notion of what went into the running of a football club. At Everton Catterick was completely remote from us and we had no idea what his thinking or principles as manager were. The world Freddie showed me was intriguing, but you became aware of some of the idiosyncrasies and odd things a manager had to deal with.

Take Kenny Burns, who had a strange contract. He was contracted to play in defence and attack but whenever he played up front he got £5 a week extra, as an encouragement for doing something he didn't want to. Kenny was a bit of a lazy sod, and at Birmingham, anyhow, he just wanted to play at the back. But it showed you some of the unorthodox things a manager had to do to squeeze a bit more from one of his players.

The money issue was one that would resurface at Birmingham, to my distaste. At Everton it had never been an issue. We were all pretty much on the same money, except Alan Ball, who got more since he was a World Cup winner. We accepted that and it made for a more harmonious experience. But at Birmingham there wasn't that equilibrium and it caused problems for the manager and problems in the dressing room. I found people fighting for more money or flaunting their wealth unedifying. Years later, when I was a manager, I sold a player because he dropped his wage packet deliberately on the floor so that the others could see how much he was on. I hated that sort of thing.

The pettiness over money and other issues bubbled to the surface in my first full season at St Andrew's – 1974/75. We were floating around the bottom third of the league table, but without any imminent threat of relegation. I was playing well and there were calls in some newspapers for me to be selected for England. We had also progressed well in the FA Cup. We beat Chelsea at Stamford Bridge and were handed a favourable fifth round draw at home to Walsall, which we won 2-1. In the quarter-finals we beat Middlesbrough 1-0 in front of 47,000 fans at St Andrew's.

Although I became disillusioned under the management of Willie Bell, I enjoyed some good times during my three years at Birmingham City and got my first real thirst for a career in management. (Author's Collection)

It set up a semi-final tie with Second Division Fulham at Hillsborough. They had Bobby Moore and Alan Mullery playing for them in the veteran stages of their careers, but we felt we had the beating of them. Our form

running up to the tie was unconvincing and it rained and snowed on the morning of the match. It was a tight, competitive game and when John Mitchell volleyed Fulham into the lead shortly after half-time, it left us reeling. The atmosphere was tremendous and our supporters outnumbered the west Londoners. They spurred us on, and eventually our pressure paid off. Joe Gallagher collected Kenny Burns' flick-on near the penalty spot; he lost his marker and swivelled a shot home to earn us a replay the following Wednesday.

It was here that the difference in mindset between Birmingham and Everton exposed itself. On the Monday morning, the first topic at the team meeting was not about how to overcome Fulham in the replay. Instead it was about parking arrangements for the wives' bus and how far they'd had to walk to get to the ground. Apparently the Fulham coach was in the main car park and ours was up the road.

As captain I was infuriated.

'Let's concentrate on the bloody game, get to Wembley and we'll find a car park that's near Wembley for them.'

I just couldn't believe it. The wives had to walk I don't know how far – 100 metres? Catterick told me once to keep women out of football. It seemed, even then, a little outmoded, but at times like that it's not a bad idea.

In the run up to the first match we'd encountered something similar. Willie Bell, the trainer, Goodwin's assistant, had come in and said, 'There's a boot company want to sign you up, it works out £110 each to wear their boots in the semi-final.'

'We'll have a bit of that,' we all said, rubbing our hands together. Boot deals were far from the norm back then, and it was an unexpected bonus.

'I'll have a bit of that too,' said Trevor Francis.

'Hang on, you've got your own boot contract, haven't you?' someone else pointed out.

'Yeah.'

'Well, this has got to be split between the lads, hasn't it?'

So another squabble broke out and Trevor got his way and the £110 became £95 (Kenny Burns, who likewise had his own deal, didn't want anything). Little things like that would never have happened at Everton. I hated squabbles over money and petty issues. It was infantile.

The replay at Maine Road was a catastrophe for Birmingham. We were unable to stamp our authority on the game, and it drifted into extra time and seemingly towards a second replay with the scores goalless. But then, with virtually the last kick of the game, a long ball was pumped into our area. John Mitchell met it on the volley, but it was saved by Dave Latchford's face. The ball could have gone anywhere, but it deflected back off John and crept over the line for Fulham's winner. I'm sure neither man knew much about it.

I'd lost semi-finals twice before, as I had two finals, but I was really choked by that defeat. I was captain; I'd have been leading Birmingham out at Wembley. We were miserable having come so close. It was one of the biggest disappointments of my career. We'd booked to stay overnight in Buxton in the expectation of a big celebration. Instead it was a wake. We sat there drinking with Freddie and the staff until about five o'clock in the morning, when he'd had enough. So I had to go round all the lads and tell them, 'Come on, we're getting on the bus; we're not staying.' Freddie was totally devastated.

We got back to Birmingham at around 9am and I said, 'I've got a mate who's got a pub round the corner, anybody fancy a shandy?' The drinking continued for some time after. I think there was a hunt on for about half a dozen players that day from the wives.

Freddie's managerial reign never really recovered from that defeat. It took us until the eighth game of the 1975/76 season to record our first win, by which time Freddie was on his way. He was replaced by his assistant Willie Bell, who had been one of his team-mates at Leeds when he was a player. I didn't like Willie at all. One of his first acts as manager was to drop me and Terry Hibbitt for a game away at Liverpool. We were Freddie Goodwin's two big signings and he left us out to say, 'I'm my own man.' I thought it was a joke, and although I swiftly returned to the side that was me – to all intents and purposes – done with the man.

The change of manager did not dramatically revive Birmingham's fortunes. We missed relegation by a single place that season and were eliminated in the early rounds of both cup competitions. We continued to be well attended – crowds averaging just below 30,000 – and I was proud to be captain. But as a player you want to be wanted, and I never felt that with Willie in charge.

As the 1976/77 season drew to a close, with the comfort of a mid-table finish in store for Birmingham, speculation abounded about my future. I was linked with another part-exchange deal for Burnley's Brian Flynn. Harry Catterick, now in charge at Preston, wanted to buy me and there was talk of fans raising money to fund the transfer. I'd have absolutely loved to have gone back to Deepdale, even if I wasn't fussed about a reunion with Harry.

We ended the season with a 2-2 draw at Queens Park Rangers. I scored in the 11th minute with a 'killer drive' that, according to the local press 'was magically put away'. With Hibbitt, they said, I 'controlled the midfield brilliantly'. We finished the season 13th, one of the club's best showings since winning promotion five years earlier. As captain, senior professional, and a midfield general I had played my part. But by then I knew my time was over: Willie Bell had placed me on the transfer list.

CHAPTER SIX

STOKE

AS A PROFESSIONAL FOOTBALLER, you have an inherent need and desire to be wanted. I did my best for Birmingham and performed well in an improving team. But for my final 20 months at the club there was a great psychological void. I felt unappreciated by the manager. I knew I was playing well, but sometimes you need someone to tell you that. I wasn't quite going through the motions, but there was something lacking. It was unlikely that we'd win anything, unlikely that we'd do anything better than aspire for mid-table; but I could live with that. It was playing for a manager who didn't want me that was the issue. Moreover, the progress I had made towards my managerial and coaching ambitions under Freddie Goodwin had stalled too.

Everything that was lacking at St Andrew's was made good at my new club, Stoke City, whom I joined in the summer of 1977 for £40,000.

I'll always remember the medical ahead of that transfer's completion. It was probably one of the more straightforward I encountered in my career. The doctor was a gynaecologist and simply asked, 'Are you pregnant?' 'No!' I replied. 'Well then you've passed!'

Instead of Willie Bell, my new manager was George Eastham, the man who had been my boyhood hero. George had been a skilful and visionary inside forward, who had shone for Newcastle when I stood on the terraces as a fan in the late 1950s. Later he had a key involvement in a court case that brought an end to the maximum wage and precipitated an era in which footballers were well – and sometimes lucratively – paid. He was part of England's World Cup winning squad and ended his career at Stoke, where he became Tony Waddington's assistant. Waddington had overseen success at first, winning the 1972 League Cup, but in March 1977, with the club doomed for relegation, he stood aside and George succeeded him.

It was exciting to be working with someone I had so admired in my boyhood, more so that he and his assistant, Alan A'Court, treated me with the same openness and encouragement that I'd encountered under Freddie at Birmingham. No longer was there a great threshold at the manager's office door as had existed under Willie Bell; it was open to me again. They recognised my desire to learn, my thirst for knowledge, and took me in their confidence. Mentally I was starting to make the transition from playing to managing, and my questions about coaching, preparation and tactics were probably never-ending, but always dealt with patiently and generously.

I was fit and I was happy as a player. Although we lost Peter Shilton to Nottingham Forest early in the 1977/78 season, we had a good team with lots of experience. Players like Alec Lindsay, Denis Smith, Terry Conroy and Viv Busby were supplemented by some talented young players, the pick of which was probably Garth Crooks. A teenage Adrian Heath was on the fringes of the first team.

But seemingly the hangover of relegation weighed heavily upon the club. Our away record was particularly poor – we won only three times on the road all season – and we just couldn't seem to string a run of results together. The nadir came when we faced Blyth Spartans in the fourth round of the FA Cup. They were a distinguished amateur team in the Northern League, but on home soil we should have beaten them easily.

The game had been postponed twice, so we were forced to play on a Monday night. Although Spartans took a tenth-minute lead, quick-fire goals by Viv Busby and Garth Crooks soon after half-time appeared to have settled it. Then, with ten minutes to go, we threw it away. A free-kick spun off the wall at a daft angle and bobbled against the left post, the ball pinballed around the area and after hitting another post ended up in the back of the net. In the last minute, we were unable to adequately defend another free kick and – to gasps of horror around the Victoria Ground – Spartans had their winner.

It was a disgrace losing to a non-league club. Thankfully it was an evening game, so we could slink away in the dark and contemplate the horror of our humiliation on our journeys home.

Unfortunately, that was the end for George Eastham as manager. I was sad because he had been my hero and had brought me to the club. Managerial changes always threaten uncertainty to players, particularly a squad that is underperforming. At this stage relegation to the Third Division remained a possibility. The danger – as I'd encountered at Birmingham – is that the new manager wants a clean sweep in order to impose himself. At 31 – while I still felt I could play in the top flight – that could have posed me with a tricky situation. I didn't want my career to peter out amid transition.

Change can be good as well, though, and this change was a good one for Stoke and me. George's successor was Alan Durban, an experienced former Welsh international midfielder who – after a fine career with Cardiff City and Derby County – had become Shrewsbury Town's player-manager. At Gay Meadow he had worked very closely with Richie Barker and he wanted to bring him with him. Had Richie followed him things may have turned out very differently for me, but Richie was offered the Shrewsbury job so he stayed there. This meant Alan was looking for a coach and so he asked me if I wanted to be player-coach.

It was a fabulous opportunity and offered me further insight into the running of a club. Alan was great with me; he took me into his office and I became something more than a player who was keen to learn the ropes, I became a key component of his managerial team. I think he wanted somebody on the pitch to put his ideas over on the field at the time, rather than simply shouting and screaming from the sidelines. If somebody was out there he thought it would help. I enjoyed that.

I was impressed by how quickly Alan laid out his ideas and principles and imposed them upon the struggling squad. Tactically he was very astute and as his lieutenant I was able to carry his instructions onto the field of play. Results very quickly picked up, but then they had to. Although we would finish the 1977/78 season seventh, we were just five points clear of relegation. That's how tight that league was.

*Sliding into action for Stoke on a mudheap of
a pitch.* (Author's Collection)

One of the best signings Alan made was Mike Doyle from Manchester City that summer. He was absolutely tremendous for us and would be central to our progress over the following 12 months. In his handling of the old veteran, I learned an important lesson that would stand me in good stead. Mike lived in Manchester, and Alan didn't expect him to drive him down to training every day. He trusted him to get on with it himself and didn't see the need for a long commute, which would be tiring or unsettling. Mike was a player who looked after himself. He played squash regularly, and he would come down two or three times a week, and then turn up on match days. But it was the way that the manager handled him, which was a lesson to me later on with the likes of Andy Gray and Peter Reid. He knew how to handle and look after the older players. It followed on from what Tom Finney once told me, 'It's not how many games at the end of the season you play, it's how many seasons.' All the way through those years I was picking up tricks I'd utilise later.

Mike was absolutely magnificent for Stoke. The uncertainty and inconsistency that had plagued us through the previous campaign was eradicated. We lost just six league games through the 1978/79 season and reached the quarter-finals of the League Cup, where we lost to Watford. We were organised and disciplined and played some good football.

We went into the final game of the season away at Notts County needing a win to be sure of promotion. A draw would have seen Sunderland edge it on goal difference.

Yet with two minutes remaining the score was goalless and Stoke – having come so close – were destined to spend another season in the second tier. I hadn't had the best of games and as player-coach I'd perhaps been too wound up to impose myself on the game. I'll always remember Alan Durban yelling from the touchline, 'We need to win it!'

We were backed by 14,000 of our own fans who'd made the journey to Nottingham and the noise was terrific. Many of those present say that what happened in the 88th minute was the best moment of their lives.

Wave upon wave of attacks had been made, and two minutes from the end Paul Richardson's header won us the match and secured us that precious third promotion spot. It had been a fiercely tight finish at the top. Had we beaten Newcastle United in our penultimate league game we would have won the title as it turned out, but could only manage a goalless draw at home.

I had played well all season. I was free from injury throughout most of my time in the Potteries and that definitely helped me. With Mike Doyle and Brendan O'Callaghan I was named in the Second Division's PFA divisional team. It is nice to receive any honour in football, but it is particularly gratifying to be recognised by your fellow professionals – the people you play against week in, week out. Years later, the full back Jackie Marsh would see me when I went back and tell me, 'You're the second-best midfield player that Stoke have had. Alan Hudson's just ahead of you.' It was a lovely compliment, because Alan was a fabulous player and Stoke probably had him in his prime.

Alan Durban knew that I wanted to play in the First Division again, that I wanted to test myself against the best once more. I told journalists during this period that I'd love to grace the Goodison turf for one last time. Earlier that year Alan had paid me the following tribute: 'Howard is a model for every youngster. He's a complete professional with a wonderful grasp of the game. Nothing will please me more than to see him finish his playing days where his skills belong – in Division One.'

He was never one for platitudes, but come the end of the season he was frank about my chances of stepping up a level. 'I don't think you'll be able to play in the top flight,' he told me.

Of course, I was hugely disappointed at this and the likelihood that I'd be looking for my third club in two years. But events were moving quickly. Tommy Docherty had just been sacked as Derby County manager and Alan's former club wanted to hire him as his successor. For a while it looked like he would be heading back to the Baseball Ground and the

Durban–Kendall partnership would be broken up anyway.

But by the time Alan had decided to reject Derby and stay at Stoke, another managerial opening had opened up. This one, however, had my name on it.

CHAPTER SEVEN
BLACKBURN

AS GOOD AS THE 1978/79 SEASON HAD BEEN FOR STOKE CITY, so it was awful for Blackburn Rovers. The club had never really recovered from the departure of their manager, Jim Smith, to Birmingham City in March 1978. From a side pushing for promotion to the top flight, they had plumbed the depths the following season. Jim Iley hadn't made an impression as manager and was sacked six months into the job. His assistant, John Pickering, was appointed as his replacement, but he wasn't able to save Rovers from relegation to the Third Division and he too was sacked.

Rovers were thus looking for their fourth manager in 15 months and I was on a shortlist of two. I was recommended to Blackburn by Jimmy

Armfield, who was a paid advisor to the Rovers board. He had come to a training session ahead of a game at Blackpool. I didn't know at the time what he was doing there, but looking back I suppose he had come to weigh me up. I wasn't the only prospective manager in the running, but they were getting a player as well with me, so I think that swayed them a little bit, as did Jimmy's recommendation.

On 7 June 1979, just weeks after securing promotion with Stoke City, I was unveiled as the new player-manager of Blackburn Rovers. There was a nice symmetry that my playing career had started in Lancashire and now, nearly 20 years later, my managerial career would be starting there too, not ten miles away from Deepdale.

Blackburn paid £20,000 for my playing registration, and I was given an annual salary of the same amount, with a £10,000 bonus if we achieved promotion to the top flight. That seemed a distant prospect back then, but I was clear – when I met journalists for the first time – what the club's priority was. 'Promotion is the aim,' I said, 'whatever the method.'

I was under no illusions about how hard managing Blackburn Rovers might be. But at the same time I entered the dressing room with plenty of confidence. I knew I could still play at that level and I think I had the self belief, having worked with a very confident manager in Alan Durban, that I was ready. I had picked up and absorbed many things in the five years since I'd left Everton. I wasn't going to try and be someone else or copy the style of another manager. The likes of Alan Durban, George Eastham, Freddie Goodwin and even – for all his flaws – Harry Catterick had taught me a great many things. I took on board and adapted many of those lessons, but I knew I had to be my own man. I had to put my own stamp on things. I think that's where Alan Ball later fell short. He tried to be like Brian Clough, but it was beyond him. It was beyond anybody. Clough was such an icon; there was only one of him.

As well as developing my own style, there were, nevertheless, many challenges I would face. I was only just past my 33rd birthday and knew that

33 years old and raring to go. My first job in management. (Author's Collection)

as a young manager, of a similar age to some of my players, I needed to show who was the boss. There were people at Blackburn lurking in the background who represented a challenge to my authority. I don't think it was done in a malevolent way, or that they purposely sought to undermine me, but I think among some players their input might have begged questions.

I'll always be grateful to Jimmy Armfield for his role in bringing me to Ewood Park, but once I was there he inadvertently posed problems. Jimmy had been England captain and had also managed Leeds to the European Cup final, so he was a man of some influence. He was – and is – a lovely man, but there was also a sense that it wasn't doing me any favours having him around. He was recommending players to the board and various other things. He had a reputation for indecision when he was manager, but it seemed to me at the time as if he was going to make all my decisions for me. One day we went out for training, I came back in, his feet were on the desk and he was in my chair smoking a pipe. I don't think it was a challenge to my authority, but I did have to say, 'Sorry; my chair, and I make the decisions.' After that I had a word with the chairman and they came to an agreement and Jimmy left the club and let me get on with it.

You've also got to get the players behind you. I had one instance where I'd not had a day off from training for some time. The former Newcastle manager Richard Dinnis was working as an assistant at Blackburn when I arrived. But he wasn't to everyone's liking. He'd only played as an amateur and had risen as a coach under Gordon Lee. This particular day I wanted a break and to catch up with some paperwork, so I asked Richard to take the players for training.

At eleven o'clock there was a knock at my door. It was centre half Glenn Keeley.

'Boss,' he said, 'can I have a word with you?'

'Yes,' I answered, 'but why aren't you training?'

'I've walked off the training ground,' he replied. 'He's a bastard.'

'Calm down, calm down; what's going on?'

I'd told Richard to keep it light, have a bit of fun, keep the lads ticking over.

'He's had us sitting down and talking about what we didn't do and what you didn't do last Saturday.'

'What!?'

'He's a bastard.'

'Thanks for telling me,' I said.

It was good of Glenn to be so upfront. Of course, I had to let Richard go; I mean, you can't have people talking behind your back, can you? In his place I promoted Mick Heaton from reserve coach. He had been Blackburn's captain in the early 1970s and was well respected and liked by everyone in the town. I'd done my homework on him, and although I didn't know him, I knew he'd do what I asked him to. Little did I know then just how long and enduring our working relationship would be.

I showed early on to the players that I was no pushover. In the first league game the left back Micky Rathbone got sent off, and the report came through that he had called one of the linesmen something he shouldn't. So I suspended him for two months. For me it was the perfect opportunity to show discipline to the dressing room. After a month out in the cold I needed him, so I got all the players together on the training ground, including Mick.

'Have you served enough time for what you've done?' I asked.

'Yeah, yeah, boss. I won't do it again. Lesson learned.'

'All right, Mick. It's okay now, your place is out here.'

What he didn't know at that moment was that I didn't have any other fit right backs. When he found out he named me the 'Mad Monk', on account of my receding hairline.

Things were tight at Ewood Park. There wasn't a great deal of money, although the £300,000 we took from the sale of John Bailey to Everton certainly helped. I'll always remember that at every board meeting John's transfer was discussed. We'd taken a £200,000 downpayment, with the rest to come after a certain number of games. They were literally counting the remaining games until we got the remaining £100,000. We had a high wage bill and some players, like Duncan McKenzie, were on top-flight money. Barely a year earlier he'd been a star part of an Everton side that was pushing for the League Championship. Now he was in the Third Division on top-flight wages. Duncan did very well for me, but I wasn't the type of manager that likes that sort of player. I'd rather the team play than the individual.

I was very conscious of the financial limitations we had because I sat in on board meetings. Compared to Everton, which was run by Littlewoods executives, it was highly amateurish, but its old-fashioned ethos was also endearing. Money, in this pre-Jack Walker era, always came up.

There was an old director named Arthur Fry and he raised his hand at one meeting I was at.

'I've got the solution,' said Arthur.

'What's the solution, Arthur?' asked the chairman.

'I think we should send out second-class stamps instead of first-class stamps.'

'Yes, good point Arthur; on to the next item.'

Arthur put his hand up again.

'I'm telling you,' he said. 'I came in yesterday and I walked behind the corridor and there was two bottles of milk there from the previous day; that's a waste. We can save on that.'

The chairman put his pen down and said, 'Arthur, it's players' wages that we're in trouble with; we've got to get rid of our highest paid to sort the financial situation.'

The exchange was indicative of the old-time thinking at the club. It was old-fashioned, but at the same time it was a lovely place to work. Everyone gave me their full support. We were all pulling in the same direction. What money they did have they made available for player signings and salaries. The board supported me and didn't question my dealings.

My first signing was the goalkeeper Jim Arnold. I was taking a chance, because he was non-league and he was already in his late twenties. But the way we played, we kept a certain system at the back where we were allowing Jim to come out into the penalty area wherever he wanted; and his hands were brilliant. He was absolutely terrific for me. I always remember when I signed him for Everton; we drew 0-0 at Old Trafford, drew 0-0 at Anfield, and Bobby Robson came up to me at Anfield and said, 'I like your young Welsh goalkeeper.'

'Pardon?' I laughed. It was a classic Bobby blunder and he'd mistaken Jim for Neville Southall. Who knows; perhaps if England hadn't been so overburdened with good goalkeepers at the time he may have made the transition from non-league to international football.

I signed the forward Andy Crawford from Derby County. He was a brilliant finisher and scored some very important goals for us. He had a tremendous goalscoring record. I'd be playing with him and I'd go and support him and be calling for the ball: 'Andy, Andy – I want it here.' He'd turn his head to me, ignore my instructions and then belt it in the back of the net. You couldn't help but laugh and tell him, 'Well done, lad.'

But what a frustrating person he was to deal with. After his first spell in the team, I received phone calls saying he wasn't coming back in and wanted to play at a higher level. I told him, 'You will be playing at a higher level next season!' But he wanted a higher level than the Second Division. Of course, it was beyond him; his head had been turned. He came back from his strike, but my trust in him had been lost, and he played in the lower leagues before dropping out of the professional game in his mid-twenties. Crazy.

When I was signing players at Blackburn, I'd always be very specific about giving players directions. On the M6 you come off at Junction 31, where there's a pub called the Tickled Trout. But there's a quicker way through Darwen, which is a grimy, post-industrial town. I always used to send the players to the Tickled Trout and come into Blackburn, because it was a lovely, picturesque drive. I knew if they came the other way that their wives would take one look and rule it out.

As a young manager I think I made fewer mistakes than I did later on. There was less pressure, and you're on an even playing field at that level because nobody else has got anything either. I think senior players, experienced players, are important down there, rather than kids. Someone like the full back Jim Branagan, who I bought from Huddersfield for £20,000, was absolutely brilliant in the dressing room.

On a Monday morning, win, lose or draw – we didn't lose or draw many either – Jim would be walking down the corridor calling 'Viva L'Espana, Viva L'Espana'.

He had a building society account and the lads would put a couple of quid or a fiver in; spending money to go to Majorca at the end of the season. He brightened the place up, and would warn, 'If anybody's sold, there's no interest on your savings!' It was a great atmosphere he helped create.

Tony Parkes was another one who was absolutely superb. He was the archetypal one-club man and after his playing career would serve Rovers for 25 years as a coach, stepping in as caretaker manager on no fewer than six occasions. As a player you knew inherently that you were guaranteed a performance from him. I was right midfield and he was left, and it was a perfect combination. You didn't have to tell him to do anything.

We had a slow start to the 1979/80 season and won just one of the first ten games. It was disappointing, but people were patient. You look at Blackburn of late and the pace with which they've gone through managers, but people could see what I was trying to do and gave me time. We were playing okay, but giving away silly goals and missing gilded opportunities. It was clear that there were certain players in the team who didn't deserve to be down there, so I had a good starting point. I could play myself and added something to the team. I had something to work on. We had the odd bad result but didn't deserve it. Sometimes we played some really super stuff. 'They absolutely murdered us out there,' said Jack Charlton after we beat his Sheffield Wednesday team 3-0 at Hillsborough. 'If they can maintain that sort of form, few teams in the division are going to be able to contain them.'

On the other hand, I had a rude awakening in that first month or so as manager. Drawn against the European Champions Nottingham Forest in the League Cup, they hammered us 6-1 at the City Ground. Afterwards I had my first proper encounter with Brian Clough, who I would come face to face with often over the next 15 years. I'd just come out of the shower and into the corridor outside the changing rooms, and there was the great man walking towards me.

'Congratulations, Mr Clough, I thought your team were magnificent tonight.'

Clough paid no attention to my platitudes. 'I saw you play a ball to-night, thirty yards without looking right to left,' he said. 'How old are you?'

I was 33 at the time and told him.

'Oh,' he said. 'Too old, just too old,' and walked off shaking his head without saying another word.

I think the biggest test I had was when I was on the field with the players and things weren't going according to plan. I found it strange at first because if something is going wrong your team-mates look at you as if to say, 'You're the manager, you put it right.' At other times some of them seemed inhibited by my presence. But I was on the field with them. I had to convince them – and it took a little bit of time to convey this – *I'm one of you out there; if I can help you, if I can see something out there I'll tell you. But I'm a member of the team.* Once I got that through to them it was all right.

Sometimes playing was more challenging than I hoped.
My teammates looked to me for guidance constantly, but on the
field I was simply one of them. (Author's Collection)

The lack of consistency was primarily a case of us getting to know each other. It was also, partly, players getting to grips after the shock of relegation.

But then the wins started to come and they didn't stop. It was a hell of a winning run and we broke all sorts of records. Eight successive wins was a Third Division record. The loss of just a single league point in a run of 15 games was the best in the Football League since Tottenham Hotspur's famous double season of 1960/61. In April *Match Weekly* named me player of the month and Bell's Whisky simultaneously named me manager of the month. By then we were in the midst of another formidable run. We won 16 of the last 20 league games and were promoted as Third Division runners-up to Grimsby Town.

'I've got a good side and I know I have players who won't be content with just this past season's success,' I said at the end of the season. 'They want more, they want to keep going forward.'

They weren't the only ones with higher ambitions.

AS A MANAGER I used to remember the advice my father gave me, which was that players have a standard: some games they'll go above that, but they should never drop below it. I never liked players that could reach a high standard, but would then sink below their par. I always watched for the ones who could maintain a steady level, who you knew you were guaranteed a performance from. Now and again it would be higher, but never lower.

Wherever and whenever I was manager it was that sort of consistency that I sought in my squad. At Ewood Park I knew I'd assembled a squad of players and a backroom staff that I could rely upon, even as we stepped up a level.

Like my dad, I was never forthright in handing out praise. I think the players themselves know when they've done well. Naturally you congratulate them; but I tended not to pick out an individual and say, 'Oh, you did great today, mate; and by the way, the one sitting next to you, he wasn't so good, was he?' That wasn't me. The players knew themselves when they'd done well. They also knew that I wanted better; I wanted promotion out of the Second Division and back into the top flight, a place Rovers hadn't been since the 1960s.

We were never out of place in Division Two. We were unbeaten until October and lost just twice in the league after Christmas. For periods in the first half of the season we topped the table. More bottles of Bell's Whisky came my way from winning manager of the month. Again, I simultaneously received the player of the month award. When we played Notts County at home in March, the Football League secretary, Graham Kelly, made the short journey from their Lytham headquarters to present me with a silver salver to commemorate my 600th league appearance.

I was, at that stage, a wanted man. In October 1980 Crystal Palace approached me with a view to succeeding Terry Venables, who had taken over at Queens Park Rangers. Palace were in the top flight and they were willing to meet all of Blackburn's demands for compensation. I was allowed to meet with them, and they were prepared to offer me more money than Blackburn could ever have afforded. But there was just something not right about the move that I couldn't quite put my finger on.

My wife wasn't keen on uprooting the family, as two of our three children were of school age. As a football manager you're constantly on the go and you have to sacrifice a lot in terms of your family. One of the biggest disappointments for me was that I couldn't put the same time in with my lad – or for that matter my two daughters – as my dad did with me. That is my great regret; because he was not a bad little player, and I wished I'd had the time. On a Sunday, my day off, he'd want to go and play football in the garden, but I was shattered and it was the last thing I wanted to do. What I could offer, in lieu of time, was a semblance of stability, a place they could call home, and a move to London would have challenged that.

Perhaps that played on my mind, but I remember sitting up in bed in the early hours of the morning and deciding that I wasn't going to take it. There and then I decided to phone the Blackburn chairman David Brown and tell him that I was staying. It was a ridiculous time to discuss business with him, but I don't think he minded at all. I wanted to get Blackburn over the line. That's why I gave full backing to Blackburn when there were approaches coming in; I didn't want to concentrate on anything other than the end of the season and trying to get promotion.

Blackburn continued to progress well and we remained near the top of the table. However, the club's limitations were exposed and would cost us dearly in the end. The day before the transfer deadline, which was still in March in those days, I was trying to get Brian Marwood in from Hull City. I could go to £28,500 but Hull were asking for £30,000. The Hull manager Mike Smith, who went on to manage Egypt and Wales, was pushing for the deal to go through. It went up until the last minute before the deadline, but the Hull board wouldn't take any less and the deal fell through. It was costly because in the next game Noel Brotherston was injured and ruled out for the rest of the season. So we were now a midfielder down and had lost out on Marwood for the sake of £1,500: who knows how that might have paid off? (In the long term Brian went on to win the title with Arsenal and also played for England, and clubs paid a lot more than £30,000 for him over his career.)

The game that cost us most dearly was when we played Swansea City at the start of April. Had we won that we would almost certainly have been promoted. In the second minute I chipped a free kick into the Swansea City penalty area. Glenn Keeley was left with virtually a free header, but unfortunately he put it wide. That was as close as we came and Swansea went on to beat us 2-0.

Our fate was still in our own hands, but we didn't quite recover from that setback. In our next three games, against Newcastle, Bolton and Preston, we couldn't buy a goal – but didn't concede any either. Three goalless draws, three points. We played Newcastle again, this time at Ewood Park, and beat them 3-0.

It meant we went into the last game of the season at Bristol Rovers needing a better result than Swansea City, who were playing at Preston. We needed my old club to do us a neighbourly act, or else score eight or nine goals ourselves. Blackburn fans came down to the West Country in their droves to cheer us on. It was a fantastic atmosphere, and we edged the game 1-0. All sorts of wild rumours were flying around the ground that Preston had scored, that Preston were leading. Mickey Heaton was sat on the bench, listening to these rumours, but they were false. Swansea were 3-1 victors at Deepdale and promoted ahead of us on goal difference.

It was tough for the players to take; for many of them it was as close as they'd get to top-flight football. 'Hey, we can't do any more, lads,' I told them afterwards. 'We've won today.' Even now, I still think the

Brotherstone injury and not being able to bring in Marwood – a good winger, a good supplier of balls from the flank – cost us dearly.

I knew then that my time at Blackburn was at an end. I'd taken the club as far as it could go. I hadn't taken the Palace job, which wasn't for me. There was, however, another club whose attention I had captured.

CHAPTER EIGHT

HOME

BLACKBURN'S SEASON – and promotion hopes – ended on 2 May 1981. Two days later my old club, Everton, finished a disappointing season 15th, following a 0-0 draw at Wolves on the May bank holiday. By the end of that week my new world had collided with my old one: I was back at Goodison Park, this time in the manager's seat, charged with the task of restoring Everton to former glories.

In reality I knew I was coming home months before the end of the 1980/81 season. It was a done deal irrespective of whether Blackburn were promoted or not. Gordon Lee's contract was coming to an end and the Everton board were not going to renew it. He had done well in his first two years at the club, and although Everton progressed to the latter stages of cup competitions after that, league form had dropped off alarmingly.

The Everton board acted honourably throughout this period. There was no tapping up or covert meetings. The Everton chairman Philip Carter dealt only with his Blackburn counterpart David Brown, who in turn kept me abreast of developments. He was keen for me to stay at Rovers, to see out the job – as he saw it – of restoring Blackburn to the top flight. Part of me would have liked to have achieved that, but I knew that the opportunity of managing a club like Everton wasn't one that arose every day. Indeed, the chance of managing *your* club was one that came to few players, and only then once in a lifetime. Everton, I should be clear, were *my* club at that stage. Once you're bitten by the Everton bug, nothing is ever the same again.

When the contract negotiations came, they were seamless. Everton agreed compensation with Blackburn for my playing registration. I went in in the morning to meet with Philip Carter and came out in the afternoon as Everton's manager, having signed a four-year contract. I think a lot of the preparation and homework had been done long before that meeting with the chairman. I'm pretty certain Everton vetted me. I'll always recall one Sunday morning when a gentleman turned up on my doorstep claiming to be representing an unnamed First Division club. I invited him in and we had a short chat, but I think the purpose of the visit was to check on me; see what sort of person I was; make sure I had a stable, family background – which, of course, I did.

When I became Everton manager I was 34 years old, ambitious, hungry and fearless. I had no doubt I could do the job. My age and relative lack of experience did not concern me. I'd learned a lot at Blackburn and under Alan Durban at Stoke. No one was more aware of how big a job – and club – Everton were than someone who had played for and captained it. Perhaps looking back I didn't show my joy at being back at the club I loved, but I certainly felt it. My wife probably expressed what was going on in my mind most accurately: 'It's like a fairy tale come true,' she said in a newspaper interview. 'It's the fulfilment of Howard's ambition. When he was an Everton player he used to live for the next game. He loved the bones of the place. Everton was everything to him and still is.'

Philip Carter, who led negotiations to bring me back 'home', would be a crucial ally throughout my first spell as Everton manager. (Author's Collection)

But the task I faced was huge. Everton had not won a trophy since that wonderful season 11 years earlier, when myself, Colin and Bally had captured so many plaudits. A lot had changed since then; indeed a lot had changed since my own departure seven years previously. The trophyless years had gnawed away at every fan, but had been worsened immeasurably by the fact that Liverpool had comprehensively overtaken their great rivals. Since 1970 Liverpool had won the League Championship five times and an FA Cup, but had also started to dominate in Europe, winning the European Cup and UEFA Cup twice apiece. They also had a third European Cup final against Real Madrid in Paris looming. My intention, I told the press, was to match Liverpool. I knew if we were to achieve this we'd be one of the best teams in the world. The newspapers, in turn, were well aware of the size of the task and weight of expectations facing me. 'They're not asking much from Howard Kendall,' wrote one newspaper. 'Only a three-minute mile, a century before lunch and a successful assault on Everest.'

Although I had the entire summer to prepare for the 1981/82 season, there was no period of bedding in. There was an end of season tour to Japan to oversee and wholesale changes that needed to be made to the squad and also to the coaching staff.

I was told by the board when I was given the job that they wanted a clean sweep of Gordon Lee's backroom staff. There was a sense from them that a 'jobs for the boys' culture had permeated, and they wanted a cull. The chairman said to me, 'Take your time, do it when you're ready.' It was something that I accepted unquestioningly and, looking back on it, I think it was totally wrong. There were people on the payroll that were loyal, good workers and didn't deserve to leave the club. But I took the job knowing I had to do it.

On my first day I could sense an atmosphere in the backroom. So I followed the chairman's advice and did it in my own time – I did what needed to be done on the first day. I can't stand talking to people and telling them what I want to do and what my plans are, knowing they're going to be out in two or three weeks. So I did it the first morning, and telephoned the chairman and told him it was done. But I think mistakes were made, Eric Harrison being a prime example. Eric wasn't long out of work and joined Ron Atkinson at Manchester United a month later as youth-team manager. His record over the next two decades was nothing short of stupendous, and he oversaw the development of a host of players that included Norman Whiteside, Ryan Giggs, Paul Scholes, David Beckham, the Neville brothers, Wes Brown, Robbie Savage, Keith Gillespie and Nicky Butt.

My own backroom staff throughout my managerial career would be small. I brought Mick Heaton in from Blackburn as my assistant manager. I'd developed a very close relationship with Mick at Ewood Park, promoting him from reserve-team coach to first-team coach. He knew the way my mind worked and brought tremendous enthusiasm to the training pitch and dressing room. One member of Gordon's backroom team who was going nowhere was Colin Harvey, who was initially in charge of the reserve team. Together we would reprise our old partnership with enormous success.

Colin was such an intense presence. If you ask many of those players who wrote their name into Goodison lore just a few years later, they will point to Colin's coaching as being integral to their success. When he came into the coaching room to talk to you on a Monday, you knew he'd been deliberating and thinking about things all weekend. We didn't have modern technology in those days and he would play the game again and again on a VHS player. He'd stop the tape, write the counter number down, make a note and start again. I had words with the players after the game but he used to get them in individually on a Monday morning and go through it again. 'What were you told after the game?' he'd ask. 'Have a look.' He would stop the tape at that particular point, and show them where they'd gone wrong, or how they could improve. He'd watched the game all weekend long; he knew it inside out, and the players too. He was a great worker, an absolutely fabulous grafter, and would be crucial to me and Everton Football Club.

I arrived at Everton without any preconceived ideas about the squad I was inheriting. My first task was to fly out to Japan for the end of season tour that was to last three weeks. We left literally days after my appointment and I had a completely open mind. As a manager I don't think you can have a fixed idea on who is staying and who is going at that stage. I think you can have a broad opinion before you get there, because you're watching games and you know the individual players, and you know as a team they're not good enough – or else I would never have been appointed manager. But you don't know for sure about your inheritance. Nevertheless, it didn't take long for me to realise that many things needed to change at Everton.

One of the things I learned from Harry Catterick was about balancing a team. He was very clever because all his squads had that symmetry and if injuries happened he had versatile players who could step into the breach. When I took over from Gordon Lee there were about eight centre halves, six centre midfield players, one left winger, one left-sided player, one right-sided player, and two strikers; something like that. It was totally unbalanced.

I also looked for players who inherently knew and understood their positions. Catterick didn't have to really say that much to Colin Harvey because he knew that position from being a youngster. He didn't have to say much to Alan Ball; Bally was just full of enthusiasm and went up and down the park. He didn't have to say much to me. We all knew our positions, and what we had to do. But I looked at that squad and there were a number of players who, although talented, were the proverbial square pegs in a round hole. If they didn't know where they were best deployed, how as a manager was I to know?

There were also one or two strange characters in the dressing room, players I knew I needed to move on. One thing I never had time for as a manager was oddballs. I remember in Japan, the taxi driver couldn't understand English, but we got into this American bar. The place had a model train that did laps of the top of the bar.

Our goalkeeper Jim McDonagh was a Yorkshireman, but of Irish parentage, and had recently been called up to the Ireland national squad. He'd also taken to being called by the Irish equivalent of his name, Seamus. Anyhow, we were having a good time, but Jim sat muttering darkly towards this model train: 'IRA target.'

'Hey, Jim,' I said. 'This is the only place they speak English; we're having a nice time.'

'IRA target,' he muttered. I didn't really know what he meant. I suppose he was drunk or joking, but it was a strange way to behave.

The train went around and around. Jim went off to the toilet and as he was going past it he stuck an ashtray on the rail tracks and derailed the train. 'IRA target.'

We went back the next night and I warned Jim, 'Hey, calm down, lad; this is the only place we can speak to people.' We were having a nice night, a few beers and a chat and the train was derailed again. This time it had become an incident, the police were arriving and out we went, Jim still muttering, 'IRA target'. I couldn't be having that sort of behaviour at the club and resolved to sell him as soon as I got back.

Wherever I managed, I always thought the first signing was the most important one. It was a statement of intent, and as it turned out at Everton my first signing was the best one of my career – eventually. But when I first went there my number-one objective was to sign Bryan Robson from West Bromwich Albion. He was a magnificent, energetic midfielder, end-lessly brave and a contributor of goals for whichever team he played. He was also a leader, and captained both his club and country. I fancied his team-mate, Remi Moses, too. But I had formidable competition for both of their signatures. That same summer Ron Atkinson left the Hawthorns to become Manchester United manager. Hard as I tried to sign both players, there was an inevitability about Robson following his boss to Old Trafford. How might Everton in the mid-1980s have been different with Bryan in the side? It couldn't have been better, but it would have been different. It would have been just as successful.

There was lots of transfer activity that first summer. One of Everton's biggest names – the man whose arrival seven years earlier had precipitated my departure – was first to leave. I'd have liked Bob Latchford to stay at Goodison and later I considered bringing him back. But with his contract expired his transfer to Swansea City was already a done deal and so that went through. Asa Hartford followed him early the following season.

I got some stick about my signings, dubbed the 'Magnificent Seven'. Perhaps some of it was fair; but Neville Southall was my number-one buy, so how can you criticise me on the other six? I needed a goalkeeper because, of the two goalkeepers I had, Jim McDonagh I didn't rate, and Martin Hodge was out with a long-term injury.

I first got a whisper about Neville a year earlier from a very good friend of mine called Norman Jones, who had a public house in Llandudno. Neville was playing for Winsford United in the Cheshire League at the time and

Norman told me that he was a local phenomenon and that his father drank in his pub. I asked him what the pub was called, and he said it was The Neville. I knew then that we were fated.

I went down to Cheshire to see Neville play. It's very rare that you see a goalkeeper that you're impressed with so much when watching them for the first time. I was fortunate this particular night as Neville was busy: coming out for crosses, shot-stopping. I could see his kicking was good, his positional play was a little raw – but that was to be expected. He had all the qualities you love to see in a goalkeeper. There aren't many times you see a goalkeeper for the first time and think 'he's the one'. So I contacted my chairman and told him that I'd found a goalkeeper. But the £6,000 fee was too much for Blackburn at a time when the club already had two senior keepers, and Bury signed him instead.

I continued to monitor Neville at Bury and he didn't let anyone down. He won their player of the year award, and his price had inflated a bit too by the time I inquired about him at Everton. But at £150,000 he proved one of the best bargains ever. Neville became the world's best, for me and many others, but it never changed him.

I knew Neville wasn't quite ready for the first team, but that it was only a matter of time. So I signed Jim Arnold from Blackburn as well, who I knew I could depend upon. I knew it would be a bit much to jump from non-league to the First Division in barely a year and I saw Jim as a short-term answer to my problems. But I never doubted Neville.

Having four goalkeepers in an age before they sat on the substitutes' bench was a luxury I couldn't afford, so Jim McDonagh was on his way out back to Bolton from where Gordon Lee had signed him. Bolton, however, didn't have enough money to buy him back, so they offered me a player. I needed a centre back to balance things up, and while Mickey Walsh would not have been my number one target, he was what was on offer and I felt he could do a job, so he became my third signing.

Then there was Alan Biley. I was on the lookout for a goalscorer who could play on the right and had done some asking around. His scoring record at Derby County was very good and I knew Manchester United and Liverpool were both interested, so I went for him. On his debut he looked like a world-beater, scoring in a 3-1 win over Birmingham. Afterwards I always remember Denis Law appearing on TV, proclaiming, 'I don't know what Bob Paisley's doing missing out on him.' It took me just a few weeks to realise that Bob Paisley knew far more than me. Alan had these little short steps, and was always nearly getting to the ball but never quite managing it. I think it was also the blond hair that did it for me; I was always wary of blond and bald players – I thought they stood out in a bad way. Thankfully I could never watch myself play or I might have taken action! As for Biley, I sold him to Portsmouth a year later, and he prospered again in the Second Division.

I also bought Mick Ferguson from Coventry City. I spoke to my old Preston team-mate Gordon Milne, who was Coventry boss, about him and – looking back – I should have known there was a catch with what he said to me. 'He's unstoppable if he's on the pitch,' he said; 'if' being the key word, it emerged. Mick was very rarely on the pitch for me. He was six foot two inches tall and wore size 6½ boots. Every time he jumped and landed his ankle gave way. He didn't tell a lie, Gordon. Whenever Mick was on the pitch he was unstoppable; he just wasn't on the pitch that often, that was the problem.

Winger Mickey Thomas came to Everton from Manchester United as part of a deal with John Gidman going to Old Trafford. He was full of enthusiasm; you couldn't fault him. He nearly failed a medical after we found an enlarged heart, which I thought was a good thing, but apparently not. I liked the lad in a way, but there was no discipline from him at all; he just did his own thing and ran all over the place. He couldn't play in a position and follow your instructions. I was quite prepared to try him, work with him, but Mickey had other ideas.

A couple of months into his Everton career he had an injury, and Paul Lodge had taken his place at Coventry in a League Cup game, and done well. And I thought, 'Mickey, have a run-out with the reserves before I call you back in'. The reserve game was at Newcastle, away; the longest journey of a reserve-team season. Mickey wasn't happy at all.

'I'm not going up there,' he said. 'I came here to play for the Everton first team.'

'No, you joined Everton Football Club to play in the team that I select you for,' I said.

'I'm not going,' he answered.

We left it at that, but when it was time to meet up to go to the North-east Mickey didn't turn up for the coach. I wasn't happy at all.

Mike Bailey was the manager at Brighton, and had been interested in Mickey when he'd been at Man United, so I phoned him and asked, 'Do you want him?'

'Why, what's happened?' he asked.

'No, look, do you want him? I've got somebody else in mind.'

So we agreed a deal and there was a £25,000 profit in it for Everton as well. Mike Bamber, the Brighton chairman, sent his private plane for Mickey and his missus. She went shopping while he had his medical and agreed terms. He came back on the private plane with everything sorted and everyone was happy with the deal.

On the Monday morning, however, the club got a call. It was Mickey.

'How do you get to Brighton?' he asked. When the journey was explained to him he was completely taken aback. He'd signed without knowing where it was. 'But it only took about 45 minutes in the private jet,' he protested.

'Mickey,' we explained. 'Forty-five minutes is only to New Brighton by road!'

I brought in Alan Ainscow because, as I said, I felt the side lacked balance. There was really a shortage of wide players. Joe McBride was the only naturally wide player and Alan had a good record at Birmingham from a wide position scoring goals. At that time it was just a case of making some changes to get a balance in the squad. Not that it was ever going to win the championship or anything like that, but it was just a case of achieving a balance.

When pre-season started, as I had at Blackburn, I wanted the routines to be fun. If the players were engaged they were focused and my job became a lot easier. There was an emphasis on doing as much as possible with the ball. I remember how I disliked the endless running of my Preston and Everton-playing days. Under me there would be no slogs up and down the sand dunes at Ainsdale. I'm not really envious that I don't manage in the current era, where there is so much emphasis on training ground tactics and working out moves and so on. I'm a firm believer that you can get to a stage where players become bored if you're stopping and starting and concentrating on one particular player, or movement. I wanted training ground routines to be sharp, focused and continuous, involving as much ball-play as possible.

The FA, on the other hand, had their own way of doing things. We went down to Lilleshall, where the FA's centre of excellence was located at the time, ahead of a game against one of the Midlands teams. Charles Hughes, a somewhat controversial figure who advocated playing to percentages and was a proponent of the long-ball game, was the FA Director of Football at the time and giving a coaching course at the far end of the field.

Charles had some interesting ideas, but they were far removed from the sort of football I knew and advocated. I recall going on one of his courses and all he would talk about was 'POMO', which was apparently an acronym for 'Position of Maximum Opportunity.' 'Oh,' piped up one of the lads that was on the course, 'You mean the far post.' Later on that day, Jim Smith could be seen hopping around on a corner flag. 'It's my POMO stick!' he laughed.

Anyway on this particular occasion, Colin and I always liked joining in with training, and passing on information while we were working rather than stopping play. Going up to a player to instruct him while everybody else is stood around waiting, especially in the middle of winter, is not what I'd consider good management.

I was later told by my old Preston teammate Alan Spavin who was on the FA course, that Charles Hughes stopped everything and gathered everyone around.

'Come here, everyone; look at them down there, those Everton lot down there,' he said. 'They're doing it all wrong. They should be on the sidelines spotting the problems, then stopping it, then going in and informing the players.'

*Back home again, although my first years as Everton
manager would be replete with challenges.*

Alan told me about this a few weeks later. We went on to win the league that year. But it was our way of doing things at Everton and was from the start. So long as the legs were ready, the quickest way of informing players of what you wanted was as you went along.

THAT FIRST SEASON AT EVERTON was one of quiet evolution. I learned a lot about the players that I inherited and the ones that I bought. None of the 'Magnificent Seven' barring Neville lasted more than a couple of years at Everton. I was always quick to move players on if I could see that they didn't have a role to play. I was never one for having players toiling endlessly in the reserves; it didn't do them, their market value or the squad any good at all. Far better to move them and bring someone else in.

The manner in which Everton was run was very different from Blackburn. It was professional. The board were mostly comprised of the directors of the Littlewoods corporation. They were top business people, running the football club as a business. That came from the very top: the old man, Sir John Moores, wouldn't have it any other way. The Financial Management Committee of the board would set targets and my budget would be set accordingly. For example, there'd be a target of an average gate of maybe 18,000, and I'd be told that. And then they would decree that that covered all the expenses and wages and everything else. Anything over that would be given to the manager to spend on the players, and anything beyond the third round of the FA Cup was given to the manager. As long as the fundamentals of the club were run on an even keel, any extra income was given to the manager. It was so much simpler then than it is today. In fact it was a lovely way of running it.

Other clubs were different and had 'characters' on the board. Luton Town, for example, had the entertainer Eric Morecambe on its board. I was told a lovely story about Eric by Viv Busby when he was a player at Luton, about how they'd been on a run of about five games unbeaten. Then all of a sudden they lost a game at home. So they're all in the dressing room, heads down, and all of a sudden the door bursts open. There's Eric Morecambe coming in and doing one of his little dance routines. 'Don't worry, lads,' he said, to universal silence.

'Piss off, Eric,' they said as one.

It must have been the only time that he's done that routine and nobody's laughed.

Ipswich Town were another club that had eccentric board members. They were owned by the Cobbold family, aristocratic brewery owners, who were another bunch of characters. At Goodison in the 1980s there were separate directors' rooms, one for the men and one for their wives. When we played Ipswich that season the Ipswich plane had been delayed due to fog at Manchester airport, so they brought the ladies into the main directors' room. We were hanging around – Ipswich manager Bobby Robson was there – and Philip Carter and his wife, Lady Carter. She had sent for coffee and when it came back, Ipswich chairman Patrick Cobbold offered her some sugar, which he kindly dropped into the cup. I could tell by the look on Bobby's face that he knew exactly what his chairman had done. To the complete

horror of Lady Carter the sugar melted to reveal a plastic penis and two balls, which floated to the top of her cup!

But there was none of that at Everton. It was very business-like. If I wanted to buy a player I'd contact the secretary, Jim Greenwood. The two of us vir-tually ran the club together and we'd be talking constantly. Jim

I had very few dealings with Sir John Moores, although his influence was felt throughout the club. (Author's Collection)

would then notify the chairman and he would go around the directors, and they'd sanction it. Philip Carter was managing director of Littlewoods at the time; it was a huge job in its own right, but if I ever wanted to speak to him I'd simply have to pick up the telephone. He was always there when I needed him. But, as I say, I would know the financial position and wouldn't ask if I didn't think there was a realistic chance of getting.

One of the people I got to know early on in my time back at Goodison was Bill Shankly. His house was on Bellefield Avenue, beside the training ground, and he used to pop into the training ground for a cup of tea in the morning. Bob Paisley had told him to stay away from Melwood after he had retired. Shankly had been going in and the players were saying 'Hi, boss' to Bob and then 'Hi, boss' to Bill. It was a situation that couldn't continue. I think Shanks always regretted leaving the manager's job at Liverpool. It was true what they say about them reacting very quickly to him putting a resignation in. He'd done it before – including after not signing me – and not meant it, and maybe he didn't want them to take this one either. But the Liverpool board had accepted his resignation and he really didn't know what to do with himself. It was sad to see, and sad for everyone when he passed away in September 1981, aged just 68.

When I moved from Blackburn to Everton I retained my player's contract and Everton paid for my registration. Playing for the first team wasn't on my agenda. Ideally I wanted to play in the reserve team to help the kids; because although I might be taking a young player's position – a young lad who could be playing in the reserve team – I was getting more out of the others on the field by helping them out there. We had the core of Everton's great mid-1980s team at the time – Neville, Gary Stevens, Kevin Ratcliffe, Kevin Richardson, Graeme Sharp – playing alongside me. I enjoyed being out there among them, helping them. I was the playing link between Harry Catterick's Championship winning side and the ones I myself managed to success.

I didn't want to make a playing return to the Everton first team, however. I wanted Evertonians to remember that I could play as I had in my twenties. But then a selection crisis necessitated my return. Asa Hartford and Mickey Thomas had moved on and I think Trevor Ross was injured. Mickey Heaton suggested I step in, but I resisted at first, despite having played the previous two seasons at Blackburn. But then we lost 2-1 at home to Sunderland in a poor performance on 21 November 1981, with the midfield lacking discipline. Mickey's powers of persuasion paid off and I felt compelled to act.

I made my playing return in a 2-2 draw at Notts County three days later. I knew I'd done the right thing by playing and it went quite well on the night. But I was so nervous ahead of each of the six games I played. There was always a fear that I'd go out there and be a laughing stock. But once I was out there I found something of my old rhythm and quite enjoyed playing because I didn't let the team down. A couple of weeks later I made my playing return at Goodison, where we won 3-1 and I was voted man of the match, but was left needing eight stitches in a gash to my mouth. Four weeks later, against West Ham, I made my last senior professional appearance in a 2-1 FA Cup third round defeat.

Playing for the reserves was different. We played at Goodison, which was always a privilege even when it was nearly empty, but there was none of the pressure accompanying me. I was there to help the young players in our ranks, and what a bunch we had. The most naturally gifted among them was Neville. I could tell he was going to be phenomenal. Some of the saves he made were superlative. Contrary to what he and other people say I don't think he's ever been shy. He used to ask me for a lift back from training because he couldn't drive at the time and I lived near his home in Ramsbottom. You wouldn't have asked Harry Catterick for a ride, but you could ask me; I was more of a players' manager than a manager upstairs in an office. You'd congratulate Neville after a reserve-team game where he'd had probably one save to make and he'd reply, 'Bored; I'm bored,' and slouch off back to the dressing room. Some keepers do work harder in training than they do on match days, but it's the decision-making on match day which is most important. Neville at that stage perhaps didn't have that; he lacked experience. But it was only really ever a matter of time.

We finished my first season as Everton manager in eighth position, having been as high as fifth mid-season. We fared poorly in the FA Cup, losing in the third round to West Ham, and reached the League Cup quarter-finals, which we lost at home to Ipswich. Crowds hovered around the 20,000 mark and sometimes dropped below. They were witnessing progress; but I'm sure some of them expected and needed more. Liverpool won the League Championship again that season.

What did I learn from those first days in the Goodison hot seat? That pressure and expectations were high. That many of the players I'd bought and inherited were not talented enough to take the club to where I wanted it to be. But also that we had some good young players, who were going to mature into-top class professionals. Neville, who played in just over half our league games, was the prime example, but there were others too.

Kevin Ratcliffe was someone I had admired since my Ewood Park days. I first saw Kevin when he was playing in the Everton reserve team at Blackburn. I tried to sign him in an exchange deal with a centre forward I had called Kevin Stonehouse who Harry Cooke was ringing me about fairly often. Everton came back and said no, but my loss as Blackburn manager was to be my own long-term gain. Kevin was a fabulous captain and centre back. He was initially playing left back but wasn't making an impression as he was more technically suited to the centre, where he had more space and options. He had tremendous pace; I was trying to build from the back with the change of pace in Gary Stevens and Ratcliffe, and I thought it was really vital for the way I wanted Everton to play. He was a great leader as well, although our relationship wasn't the commander–lieutenant type that I'd encountered under Alan Durban at Stoke. I didn't really need that after the first season at Everton. You see enough in the ability of a side to see that they know what they're doing and know what they want; and they're doing what you asked them to do. You can't ask for any more than that. I'm glad I didn't sign him for Blackburn.

Sharpy had done really well in my first year at Goodison, but his second season was slower to pick up. You could tell that he felt under pressure because he was trying shots from impossible angles as he was short of goals. He scored seven goals in the last eight matches of the season to give him a very respectable tally of 15.

Adrian Heath was someone I had signed after I'd missed out on Bryan Robson. I'd played with Adrian at Stoke and he was a record signing for Everton. I looked constantly for what the paying public would consider an 'Everton type of player'. By that I meant men who liked to go forward, have a crack at goal and entertain the fans. Adrian was one of those players but, perhaps mindful of his price tag, not every supporter took to him straight away. He had a bit of a slow start and took time to develop, but he was still only 21 and although he wasn't scoring bagfuls of goals he was getting into some tremendous positions. It was all about learning, progress and attuning to the pressures of the First Division.

At right back I alternated between Brian Borrows and a young converted winger called Gary Stevens. Brian was very good on the ball; he was very intelligent and had great technique, but he was not really strong enough and nor did he have enough pace. Gary on the other hand was a left winger when I joined the club. I was a great believer in pace at the back, and I thought he was worth a go in the full back berth. I tried him there but he had to learn the position. He was caught out quite a number of times when I first switched him, but at least the signs were promising. And what an athlete he was too.

MORE TRANSFER ACTIVITY FOLLOWED over the summer of 1982. Graeme Sharp's emergence enabled me to sell Peter Eastoe, which in turn freed up money to bring Andy King back to Goodison. Peter was a fine player, technically very good in the area; but I liked Andy and I knew the fans would welcome him back. He'd been phenomenally popular in the late 1970s, before joining Queens Park Rangers and then West Bromwich Albion. He had stayed living in the area and trained with us and I was impressed with the way Andy was performing at Bellefield. He looked fit enough and I thought it was worth a go. He proved a good signing and was outstanding at times, but got very badly injured at Sunderland; I think that was virtually the end for him at Everton. It was a really bad knee injury.

Another player who returned to Goodison was David Johnson, who I'd played with in the early 1970s. Harry Catterick had sold him to Ipswich and exchanged him with Rod Belfitt. It represented a poor bit of business for Everton: Johnson later joined Liverpool, won a multitude of trophies and played for England, while Belfitt never fitted in. He was now in the veteran part of his career but at just £100,000 I thought I was getting value for money. At the same time, the fans don't look at the cost of the players as much as they do these days; they just look at the performances of the players. I'm not saying he was a failure, but he disappointed a little bit.

That wasn't the only bit of business I did with Bob Paisley that summer. Their reserve midfielder Kevin Sheedy was a player that Colin Harvey had spotted. I went to Preston to see him play for Liverpool reserves with Colin and you could see his potential. His left foot was like a wand; his technique glorious. But I still didn't think he had what it took.

'Superb effort, but I think he's lazy, Col,' I said.

'Take him,' he said. Colin was only ever forthright about the very best players. It was an important part of our partnership; me appreciating his opinions and knowing when he was right, even if doubts crossed my mind.

'All right,' I said. 'We'll take him.'

But when I met Kevin the doubts resurfaced.

'Can't you run about more than you do?' I said to him when we met.

Sheeds was phlegmatic.

'Yeah, in the first team I will, yeah.'

'Well, that's all right then, because I want to sign you and play you in the first team.'

'Yeah, okay,' said Sheeds. I still wasn't really convinced.

We went to Israel on an end of season tour and Harry Cooke, who was handling negotiations, phoned me at the hotel.

'Sheedy's willing to sign,' he said. 'But he wants a house included as part of the deal.'

A house! He was a good player, but he was still just a Liverpool reserve; he wasn't exactly a star signing. I just laughed and told Harry 'no chance'. A short while later I got another call from Harry.

'Sheedy's changed his mind,' he said. 'He'll accept our terms.'

I told Harry to wait for half an hour and make him sweat a little bit before getting him to confirm the deal.

Looking back, he was worth a house, a car and whatever else he wanted. He was one of the best signings I – and Everton – ever made. When you look at the goals he was involved with and scored himself he was fantastic. There's just something about those natural left-footed players. Like Liam Brady or Juan Riquelme, they seem like they have an extra-special gift. When you see the old footage of Everton in the 1980s, the times Sheedy's involved as the creator of goals is incredible.

Before and since my times as Everton manager there has been some sort of unwritten code proscribing transfer deals between Everton and Liverpool. I never bought into that, and as well as Sheeds and Johnson I later bought Alan Harper, Peter Beardsley and Gary Ablett from Liverpool. But there was never any great bond between myself and my opposite numbers at Anfield. We'd do some photo-calls together but although my relationships with the various Liverpool managers – Bob Paisley and Joe Fagan; later Kenny Dalglish, Graeme Souness and Roy Evans – were cordial they remained largely distant.

I'd first properly met Bob when I was a player at Birmingham, around the time Kevin Keegan was leaving Liverpool. A friend of mine had a pub in Malton in Yorkshire and I went up there now and again. We were in there this night, some time in 1977, when someone came up to me and told me Bob Paisley and Frank Carr the racing trainer (Bob was into horses) were in the bar and would like a word.

So I went back in there. Bob Paisley, Frank Carr and two ladies were sat at a table.

'I'm undecided; can you help me?' asked Bob, straight to the point. 'I don't know who to replace Keegan with – Trevor Francis or Kenny Dalglish.'

I was playing with Trevor at the time and thought he was an absolutely fantastic player and told him so.

'What about his injuries?' asked Bob.

'Well, yeah, he's prone to them, but he's a fantastic player.'

Bob caused me some significant anxiety that 1982/83 season. We had started the campaign inconsistently, but were doing okay. We lost to newly promoted Watford on the opening day, but then beat Aston Villa – the European Champions – 5-0 the following Tuesday. We then beat Tottenham – the FA Cup holders – but lost at Manchester United. It was that sort of start to the season.

By November we were mid-table, but at that stage of the season you're never too far from either end of the league. We were facing Liverpool in the Goodison derby and were all desperate to make an impression. We'd lost both encounters 3-1 the previous season and Everton had actually won only two derby matches since we'd won the League Championship. Liverpool were the measure by which every Evertonian marked my team. I knew how important winning the derby was.

In the week before the match we were unsettled by an injury to Mark Higgins. In his place I brought in Glenn Keeley on loan from Blackburn. He was a good centre back, who I trusted, and he'd had some big-game experience while playing for Newcastle in the mid-1970s.

What followed was a football catastrophe. Glenn was sent off after 32 minutes with Everton trailing to an Ian Rush goal. Rushy scored another three times and Mark Lawrenson added a fifth. It was a shocking afternoon.

People ask me if the 5-0 defeat to Liverpool was the lowest point in my managerial career, but I can truthfully say that it wasn't. Of course you want the final whistle to blow about half-an-hour earlier but we were down to ten men, and Liverpool had a fabulous side at the time. As a manager you had enough of a challenge playing against them with eleven men. To be down to ten men so early was a killer, you just want to get home. It was a low point and you could say it was one of my mistakes in management, bringing in Glenn Keeley from Blackburn and putting him straight into the team like that. But he'd already played for Newcastle in the top flight; and I knew him. I'd managed him and played alongside him. I knew he would give his all.

Luck also conspired against us. I believe that was the first weekends that the ruling whereby someone is sent off automatically for denying a goalscoring opportunity was enforced. Just my luck that the first incident would involve Glenn and Ian Rush.

The challenge that you face after losing a game in such a fashion is how to deal with the players afterwards. One thing I'd learned from my own playing days was that you don't 'run' them. That was how it was with some managers: 'A bad result, run the bastards; bring them in tomorrow, run them again.' But what good does that do? The next day you're not going to be as bright going into training as you were, so doing a load of running is not going to lift anyone's mood. Harry Catterick would try a bit of reverse psychology. When things were going well Catterick ran you. Jesus, he worked us hard. But after a couple of defeats he'd change his tune; he'd send us for a lunch and a sauna and a massage in Southport. That was his philosophy. So he was lifting us after defeats, but working the balls off us after winning.

I tried a bit of that myself. If we lost we'd go out for a Chinese or a few drinks; we'd try and build some team spirit where it had lapsed. On the field I tried to change things around after the derby. I sent Neville on loan to Port Vale, dropped Brian Borrows – who never played for Everton again – and brought Kevin Ratcliffe and Gary Stevens back into the team. Neither man ever looked back, and Neville certainly benefited from his time at Vale Park.

But I still realised that my squad wasn't right. I always looked for a bit of devilment in players. I think that was from my early days. I never liked a wimp. That's possibly why I didn't like wingers, because most of them were! If somebody shirked a tackle, my upbringing was that he's a wimp; and I didn't like people who were jumping tackles.

There were issues about fitness as well at the time, and I wasn't convinced by some players. Our centre back Billy Wright was a good player; he was the nephew of my old team-mate Tommy Wright and honoured at England B level. We expected him to go on and do great things, but his career was starting to get stuck in a rut. It was very disappointing. He put on weight and I told him to lose it, but then he put more on. I had to have a showdown with him in the end, not long after the derby humiliation.

'Listen,' I told him, 'you're not going to be considered for the first team until you get down to your playing weight.'

We were playing Ipswich away when the news broke that he was dropped and Mark Higgins and Ratcliffe – who had been playing left back – were instead partnering each other. I wasn't delighted about the prospect as they were both left-sided and there wasn't a balance, but we needed a change.

Anyhow, I was lying in bed at the hotel in Ipswich and the local radio station was on. 'Everton are at Portman Road today and the team news is, Everton have made one change: Billy Wright has failed a fatness test.' I shouldn't have, but I doubled up laughing so hard. Then the newspapers dubbed him 'Billy Bunter'. I felt sorry for the lad, he had a problem; and it was harsh of them to make jibes like that. But he had to look after himself and sort himself out. He was a good player but he didn't play again for me.

We won that day at Ipswich in December 1982, our first victory in ten games. We won 5-0 against Luton a week later, but our lack of consistency was manifest. In the space of 24 hours at Christmas we lost at Stoke and then beat Brian Clough's Nottingham Forest, 3-1 at Goodison.

We lacked experience and guile in the centre of the park. I was no longer playing and I was never entirely convinced by Steve McMahon. I sought to change things again, but there was a lack of money. Just 13,707 people had attended a league match at Goodison at the start of December, and at a time before big TV or marketing deals that impacted on my ability in the transfer market.

One man who I knew wouldn't shirk from anything was the Bolton Wanderers midfielder, Peter Reid. I played against Reidy when I was at Stoke and I thought he was a good player even then. I could see it and I could feel it when he tackled me, and he stuck in my mind. Gordon Lee had tried to sign him before I became Everton manager for £600,000, but the deal broke down. Then Reidy suffered a bad injury – ironically against Everton – at a match that had to be abandoned at Burnden Park because of a frozen pitch. The injury almost ended his career, but Reidy was nothing if not resilient and fought his way back.

I knew about his injuries and I sent Colin Harvey to watch him on his return for Bolton. Colin came back and was firm in his admiration. 'Best player on the field,' he said. It was always black or white with Colin. He was either good enough for Everton or he wasn't; there was no in between. And I knew what Reidy could do because I'd played against him; there's no better knowledge than that.

I signed Reidy just before Christmas 1982, but it was a struggle. The club's financial predicament was such that we had to change banks from the Midland to the TSB so that they would extend our overdraft to cover the deal. We weren't talking vast sums either: just £60,000 secured a player who would be vital to the club. It was a fine show of faith, but we weren't initially convinced of the dividends.

We were still a long way off challenging Liverpool at the top of the table. These were still the days that preceded the Champions League and there was little glory in finishing fourth, or third, or even runners-up; and certainly not mid-table. But the cup competitions did offer a chance of glory.

We reached an FA Cup quarter-final tie having knocked out the holders, Spurs, in the fifth round. Facing us was an away tie at Manchester United. We had lost Andy King to a bad injury the week before at Sunderland and David Johnson was forced to pull out with a back injury. United were vying with Liverpool at the top of the First Division and strong favourites against my young team, every outfield member of which was aged under 25. We were magnificent and brave, and outplayed United for long stretches. The young Scottish winger Alan Irvine, who was a late addition after Johnson's withdrawal, tormented United all afternoon long. But for all our quality, we just couldn't score. The game seemed to be heading for a replay when, in injury time, Frank Stapleton struck the winner.

'The brave young men from Everton were holding their heads in their hands in anguish at the finish,' recorded one newspaper report. 'They'd been stunned. They'd looked disbelievingly at the screaming, jumping, near 60,000 crowd when the final whistle blew. For they'd played United with a spirit and adventure which deserved more than the cruel punishment they suffered.' There is no glory in defeat and the game is ultimately about taking your chances and winning. But I do believe my young team served a notice to English football that day. 'Everton were beaten, but they will be back,' reported another scribe. 'Their talented youngsters demonstrated clearly that Howard Kendall is now close to building a side that will bring that long-awaited success back to Goodison Park.'

Yet at the time it was difficult for some people to see this, including our own fans. Liverpool won the title again that year and any sense of progress tended to be seen through red-tinted glasses. Yet I was as aware as anyone else of the need to build a better side and acquire the players that would enable us to challenge our neighbours. I was still on the road a lot, scouting players, desperately seeking out the men who could change Everton's fortunes.

You learned tricks off other managers in the game. I remember meeting Jimmy Sirrel, the Notts County manager, early on. I went to watch Watford reserves at Sunderland as I had a couple of the players on my radar, and Jimmy was there. He was in the toilet before the game and I said hello.

'Which way did you come?'

'M6, across to Scotch Corner, up the A1.'

'Ah,' said Jimmy in his thick Scottish brogue. 'Naughty road that; naughty road. How long did it take you?'

'Three, three-and-a-quarter hours, something like that.'

'Aye, about the same time as me.'

So we sat down to watch the game, but after ten minutes I looked over to his seat and he was gone.

The next night I travelled down to Port Vale and he was there again. So I decided to have a little bit of fun because he wasn't the handsomest of fellows.

'Jimmy, rumour has it you've got a bird in Sunderland,' I said.

He made this confused growling noise at me and muttered, 'Got a bird in Sunderland?'

'You only stayed for a quarter of an hour of the game.'

'Aye,' he said. 'If you see something you don't like, don't wait for ninety minutes to finish waiting for something you do like.'

It was good advice and important advice. Nothing is more precious to a manager than his time, and it told me there was no point waiting around longer than necessary for lost causes.

One of the players I knew straight away that I would do anything to sign was Trevor Steven. I went to Burnley a number of times to watch him and he always shone for me. He looked an Everton player, and when I say an Everton player I'm talking about an Alex Young-type player – that standard, that level of class. Whatever club he went to fans would love him, but especially Evertonians given the tradition they enjoyed with such players.

What I couldn't believe was that I was the only one in for him. John Bond, who was manager at the time, was wanting to change Burnley, have some money in and bring players in that he knew from other clubs. I wanted Trevor badly. The fee was £300,000, which was a lot of money, and I knew I'd have to trade one of my more saleable assets, which in the end turned out to be Steve McMahon.

Although he would become something of a hate figure later, Steve was a lifelong Evertonian and had served as a ball boy during his teenage years. There was a determination to him which was good, but a 'professionalism' too. He was no Johnny Morrissey, but I was never a believer in or fan of those players that boasted a nasty streak. I didn't think a player needed that. My belief was that you outplay your opponents rather than kick them. The trouble we had with Steve was that he wanted a better contract than we were willing or able to offer him. In the end it became an easy decision to let him leave for Aston Villa, where he spent just a year before returning to Merseyside with Liverpool. I don't think I could have anticipated the success he later enjoyed or the England recognition bestowed upon him.

Expectations were nevertheless low going into the 1983/84 season. I'd seen it at the end of the previous campaign where, despite winning four of the last five home games, chasing a UEFA Cup place and ultimately finishing a respectable seventh, attendances for those games had been roughly 15,000, 22,000 (against Manchester United, who always brought a large following), 16,000, 13,000 and 17,000. Terry Curran, who we'd had on loan the previous campaign, and Alan Harper were my only other new acquisitions.

Alan, like Sheedy, was a player I spotted in Liverpool's reserve team, playing in different positions. I watched him at Bury playing right back and made my mind up. Technically he was very good and read the game well. He wasn't the quickest, not the strongest, but played very good football and was very versatile. I don't think Evertonians were too excited at the time about another Liverpool reserve joining the club, but they soon saw what I'd seen – and continued to see. I signed him for Everton, I signed him for Manchester City, then brought him back to Everton again. When he signed for City we had a bit of lunch at a place called Harper's and I said to him, 'Look, you've even got a restaurant named after you now, and you've only just arrived!' He was a cracking lad and a good pro and he served me and Everton well for many years.

I'd looked at bringing in two players I'd later be able to buy – Paul Bracewell from Stoke City and Maurice Johnston from Partick Thistle – but the money wasn't there. I'd also had to let other players leave, such as Trevor Ross, Billy Wright and Mike Walsh – in order to cut the wage bill.

It was a difficult start to the season. We won just one of the first five games and were struggling to score goals. Peter Reid had made just ten appearances since joining the previous December and got injured again in pre-season, missing the opening of the campaign. I recall, vividly, sitting in a hotel room in Carlisle with Colin soon after. We'd been to see a game up that direction and were waiting for the team coach to pick us up on the way to a friendly in Scotland.

'Sorry about Reidy,' he said.

'Colin,' I said, 'we all make mistakes.'

The two of us were convinced he was finished.

Pressure was mounting and it was understandable. We lost another derby, comprehensively, at the start of November. It was a year to the day since the 5-0 annihilation. This time it was only 3-0.

Things were difficult and supporters were making their unrest known. Before one game photocopied leaflets were distributed bearing the message 'Kendall and Carter Out: Bring Back Attractive Winning Football to Goodison Park'. Gates were really low and some of the media were on my back. I fell out with the now-disgraced broadcaster Stuart Hall, who wrongly reported that the Wales manager Mike England was sat in the directors' box ready to step into my job.

However, I just got on with things, even though it was hard. If you can't see the good signs, you can be despondent – but I was never despondent even if the criticism could be hurtful. What I didn't like was when my family became involved. I got home one day and my garage had been vandalised with the words 'Kendall Out'. That was particularly hard; I could take the flak, but it was now hurting my family too.

At the same time, you're never going to stop Everton fans supporting their club. They're not supporting the manager, they're supporting the club. The manager appreciates that and I appreciated that on the day. You select a side and you live and die by it. Was it particularly hurtful because of my record as a player? At times, yes, even though I was usually unemotional when it came to such matters.

I think I got more time because of my record as a player at Everton. I said to Philip Carter, 'If you want to change, I will understand.' Gates were down to 12 or 13,000, but the chairman was unequivocal in his backing. He refused at point blank my offer of resignation.

'Listen, Howard,' he said, 'I've given you a vote of confidence, and I mean a vote of confidence.' Usually that was a hangman's noose to a manager, because they'd be gone the next week. 'I mean that,' he said. 'I really do.'

Throughout all this time I remained confident that we'd turn things around. I had utmost confidence that some of the players I'd brought in – Southall, Steven, Sheedy – were class acts, and that others would come good too. The atmosphere in the dressing room was good as well. And I'd see things on the training ground that weren't being translated on the pitch.

I remember one morning at Bellefield bringing Harry Cooke, the chief scout, to the window. I wasn't out on the training ground that day, and I said, 'Harry, have a look at that quality.'

We were flying on the training ground but it just wasn't happening on match days.

'Have a look at that quality,' I repeated. 'We're not far away, are we?'

Harry had been at the club man and boy and seen everything. His grandfather, also Harry Cooke, had played for Everton and served as trainer for more than 50 years. Nobody knew the club better. I suppose as much as anything I needed a member of staff to turn around and reaffirm my belief. In front of us were players like Kevin Sheedy, Trevor Steven, Neville Southall; some of the finest players to ever wear an Everton shirt.

'We're not,' agreed Harry. 'We're not at all.'

CHAPTER NINE
WEMBLEY

AS A FOOTBALLER it's inevitable that you strike a chord with your supporters. The nature of the game propels you into people's lives and their homes via the medium of TV or radio or newspapers or magazines. Some supporters take a special liking to certain players. Indeed most top players can name a fan who takes a particularly close interest in them. I had Lynn, a young Birmingham City fan who, for whatever reason, had taken me to her heart. She'd come and see me play, long after I'd left St Andrew's, even coming to see training at Bilbao once.

For years she meticulously logged my progress as player and manager in notebooks, copying in longhand match reports, interviews, anything that was associated with me. They are an incredible testimony of a large chunk of my life and after filling up each 160-page notebook she would faithfully present them to me. I must admit that these lay in storage, with much of the rest of the paraphernalia of my playing career, until I sat down to work on this book. But flicking through them, one of her own reflections at the end of the 1983 volume stood out. It read:

'The belief in Howard's ability as a top manager has never wavered. He has the potential to be the best and people at the top let him manage his way. I know it's not much comfort at the moment, but I'm PROUD OF YOU. You'll be alright. You'll make it to the top.'

It was dated Wednesday 9 November 1983.

She would not have known the significance of the date when she wrote that, but a few things were happening around that time that would have lasting significance for both my and Everton's fortunes.

Earlier that day it was announced that Colin Harvey was to be promoted to assistant manager. It was important because Colin had the complete respect of the up-and-coming players, many of whom he'd nurtured through from their apprentice years. He didn't need to prove himself because of his fabulous playing career. I just felt the first-team lads would have liked to work with him; and that's why I made the change. It was a difficult one for me because of the personal relationship I had with Mick Heaton but it was the right one. I didn't want to demote Mick; he was naturally disappointed, but at the same time I felt it was the right decision for the club.

That evening Everton were ten minutes from exiting the League Cup at home to Coventry City. Trailing to Dave Bamber's opener, Adrian Heath levelled the scores before Graeme Sharp headed an injury-time winner to put us through to the fourth round. Barely more than 9,000 people were present, one of the lowest attendances in Goodison history. Who knows what might have happened had we lost.

The next day I signed Andy Gray from Wolves. The acquisition of Andy was a little bit fortunate, but his effect on the club was seismic. We were struggling for a striker and the board had told me to make a shortlist for our next meeting. I wasn't exactly sure how much they'd let me spend. So I made a few enquiries and drew up a shortlist: Ipswich Town's Paul Mariner was available at £600,000, Andy Gray was £300,000 and Bob Latchford was available on a free transfer. I then did a cross-section of the pros and cons of bringing Bob back from Swansea or signing Andy Gray who'd had well-documented injury problems but had played in twenty-odd games the previous season, and the one before that as well. Mariner, I knew, was a quality player and a regular part of the England squad.

I went into the next board meeting and presented the options to the directors. Bob coming back didn't feel like the right move. We didn't have £600,000 to sign Mariner, so the board suggested I went for Andy. I progressed with the transfer, but when it got to the medical his knees were an issue. We got a specialist in who looked at the number of games he had played over the previous two years and said that if he developed his quad muscles in his legs and kept them strong to stabilise the knee joints then there was no reason to fail his medical.

We met Andy and it was straightforward enough to agree the transfer; he agreed everything but he had things to sort out financially at his end. This was on the Thursday and I wanted him to play against Nottingham Forest on the Saturday. We needed to get his registration into the Football League that night, so I pushed with Jim Greenwood, but Andy was adamant that he needed to sort out his affairs. So I thought, 'How can I get round this?' Then I had a brainwave. I called the Wolves chief executive Derek Dougan and said, 'We want to take him on loan for three days. Everything's agreed: the fee's agreed; the terms are agreed; he just wants to sort things out.'

Derek was a little bit perplexed at first, but he went with it. We signed Andy on loan on the Thursday. He played on the Saturday and we won. Then he signed permanently on the Monday.

I'll always remember Andy meeting the press for the first time. He was asked why he had come to Everton. 'To win things,' he answered without hesitating. When they told him that they'd heard that sort of thing many times before, he told them: 'You've never heard it from me.' Such self-confidence had a great effect on the dressing room. He was loud, cocky, always spurring his team-mates on. On the field he was brilliant, leading by example. He was absurdly brave, putting his head in places where others would have shirked at putting their boots. I'll always remember the goal at Notts County when he was virtually on the ground when he headed it in. Possibly that was because his legs were knackered!

It's true that he had knee problems, and I used to have to stop him in the week training so hard. 'Save yourself for match days,' I'd tell him. I mean, he used to be blasting balls in the back of the net and things like that, on his own. Kenny Dalglish, by then in the veteran stage of his career, used to make the tea for the Liverpool lads on a Friday morning. I'd give that as an example to Andy. 'You take it easy; you're playing tomorrow,' I'd say, but sometimes there was no stopping him.

My team was continuing to evolve, sometimes more through accident than design. It's often overlooked that at this crucial time I lost my captain, Mark Higgins. Mark was fast, composed and formidable in the air, but was struck down by a serious pelvic injury that ended his Everton career that autumn. I suppose the fact that his demise is often overlooked is credit to Derek Mountfield's ascent into the first team in Mark's place.

It was really just local people talking about him that brought Derek to my attention. We got permission to play him in a reserve game at Preston and for the money Tranmere were asking – just £30,000 – we saw enough in him to take a chance. Derek was a good defender but not up with the Labones or that standard, which is a high one, but he scored an incredible number of goals. He was a bit like John Hurst – a magnet – or years later, Joleon Lescott. I was always a believer that the best teams were those that spread the goals around; where you weren't relying on one player. As I've already written, I'd look at my squad at the start of the season and have an idea of how many goals each player was going to score. With Derek you'd get at least seven or eight, which is phenomenal really for a defender. When we won the title he would get 14. That lay in the future, of course, but during that difficult year preceding our success, my bargain buy from Tranmere never looked out of place.

We also had another couple of good additions to the first team who would serve us well. When I promoted Colin to first-team duties, one of the additional jobs I gave Mick Heaton was to work with the full backs. That was Mick's position when he was a player and I knew his experience playing there, combined with his excellence as a coach, would benefit the players. The one to profit the most from Mick's input was Gary Stevens. He had been a left winger or left-sided midfield player when I went to Everton and I transformed him into a right back because of his pace and his athleticism. Mick worked with him after training and gave him special coaching for the full back position. He'd been in and out of the team during my first two seasons as manager, but now seemed set to make the number two shirt his own.

Having written him off some months earlier, Peter Reid was also seemingly starting to put his injury problems behind him. Reidy was clever; he adapted his game so he would be less vulnerable to injury. He learned how to go about playing football without going into crunching tackles. He intercepted balls. He used to close down opponents, and then read where the ball was going. He never went into a block tackle because he knew of his knee. Not sliding tackles; not crunching tackles; he looked to intercept the ball instead. In evolving his game he was very, very clever, and Everton would soon reap the full benefit.

THESE DEVELOPMENTS, TWEAKS, CHANGES – call them what you will – didn't reap immediate dividends, but they would serve us incredibly well over the next few years. Indeed things got worse – much worse

– before they got better. Our results over Christmas 1983 were desperately disappointing: goalless draws at home to Sunderland and Coventry City and a 3-0 defeat to Wolves, who were bottom and hadn't won at home all season. The Boxing Day crowd – typically one of the biggest of the season, irrespective of the opposition, was less than 19,000. Just 13,659 saw us play Coventry at Goodison. I think if I hadn't been connected with the club before my managerial career I may have been sacked by then. I think there was more patience because of my playing record with Everton; it was something I was forever grateful for.

A week after the Coventry game we went down to one of my old clubs, Stoke City, for an FA Cup third round match. If the Goodison crowd had shown their indifference to my team over the Christmas period there was no doubting the passion of these supporters that had travelled down the M6. It was like their last stand. The noise was ferocious.

In the Victoria Ground dressing room I didn't really have to give a team talk. The atmosphere among the players – despite the shaky form – was great. It was increasingly vociferous and full of character. In Reidy, Rats and Andy I had some real leaders. There was the bubbly, wisecracking Bails (John Bailey); the dry wit of Big Nev; and players like Sharpy and Adrian Heath always made their feelings known. On this day I went around the changing room and all you could hear were Evertonians singing and chanting. I opened up the windows and simply said to my players, 'Just listen to that. Are you going to let them down?' They knew what they had to do.

Andy put us in front with a spectacular diving header that soared into the roof of the Stoke net on 67 minutes. Alan Irvine added a second with six minutes remaining, drilling an angled shot into the roof of the goal. Did the supporters and their passion rub off on the players? It always does. But I think it was more important in those days than it is now. I think the fans were closer to the players than they are today.

Some people say that the Stoke match was the turning point in Everton's history. But to my mind it came a couple of weeks later when we played Oxford United in the quarter-final of the League Cup. I think there would have been a lot of pressure had we not won it. Although they were in the Third Division they were a good side and had beaten Manchester United in the previous round. The Manor Ground was a difficult place to go; it had a sloping pitch and Oxford were on the rise. Within 18 months they'd be in the First Division.

We were missing the cup-tied Andy Gray and fell behind to Bobby McDonald's goal on a cold night. We tried, but we just couldn't seem to break down our opponents. Then, with just nine minutes remaining, a miracle. Kevin Brock passed the ball back to his goalkeeper, Steve Hardwick. He was actually under a lot of pressure from Peter Reid, which tends to be overlooked, but nevertheless Adrian Heath read it superbly, ran on to the loose ball, took it past Hardwick and, from a tight angle, struck the equaliser.

On the coach on the way back to Merseyside we kicked back and talked about the game over a glass of wine and a beer. There was no celebration – why would you celebrate drawing at a Third Division team? – but a sense of relief that we'd skipped that hurdle and got them back to Merseyside. Even now I'm not sure if that goal saved my job or whether I'd already passed into a position in which I was safe. It certainly helped me, anyway. When we met Oxford in the replay at Goodison the following week we beat them 4-1 on a snowy pitch, Goodison's biggest crowd of the season so far rising in delight each time the orange ball was plucked out of the back of the Oxford net.

The confidence that we had in the dressing room, and that I witnessed in training matches at Bellefield, was starting to be replicated on match days. That isn't to say there weren't struggles. Gillingham took us to two replays in the FA Cup fourth round and may have won, before we beat them 3-0 at Priestfield. But after that, winning was starting to become habitual.

We faced Aston Villa in the League Cup semi-final first leg at Goodison on 15 February. It was seven long years to the day since Everton had last reached Wembley when they beat Bolton Wanderers to reach the final of the same competition. Kevin Sheedy put us in front with a goal on

28 minutes after a mix-up in the Villa area, but it was the unsung Kevin Richardson who was the key man that night. Early on he had fallen and hurt his arm quite badly. He was insistent that he wanted to play on, despite being in considerable pain. It said much of the spirit we had engendered by that time that his bravery overcame his common sense; nobody wanted to let anyone else down, or give up their place in the team lest they lose it long-term. Eight minutes from the end Kevin struck a fantastic second goal sweetly on the volley. Even then Kevin wasn't done, and he blocked a shot on the goal-line with a couple of minutes left. The Villa players said he handballed it, but the referee saw it differently.

A week later at Villa Park in the second leg we played tremendously well, and our passage to Wembley may have been easier had an effort by Graeme Sharp not struck the crossbar. Andy King handed Villa a lifeline when his poorly struck backpass was seized upon by Paul Rideout, who scored, and for the final 30 minutes on it was a stern defensive test. But we were resolute and Wembley bound. Afterwards we saluted the thousands of ecstatic Everton supporters, fists raised in triumph. So much had happened over just a couple of months, but a team that had appeared to the world to be on its knees at Christmas now had its first major final since 1977.

That would be against our great rivals Liverpool, a club that had contested 11 major finals in that same period. When I was first appointed Everton manager I said that my target was to match Liverpool, and over two games and 210 minutes of football I felt that we did just that. In the first game at Wembley, which ended in a 0-0 draw, we had enough chances to have won 3-0 – sentiments voiced by Joe Fagan after the game. In the first half Adrian Heath stole the ball off Bruce Grobbelaar on the edge of the penalty area and hooked a goal-bound shot that was heroically blocked by Alan Hansen. Well, Alan's hand, anyway. Even *The Times* reported, Hansen 'handled so blatantly that the offence was clearly visible from 100 yards'. It was a clear penalty but play carried on. Everybody in the ground had seen it except the referee, Alan Robinson. He was perfectly positioned and there should have been no excuses. Richardson and Sheedy both went close with volleys that hit the side-netting and Lawrenson's outstretched boot, but the crucial goal wouldn't come.

We played the replay at Maine Road just three days later. It took a superbly struck goal by Graeme Souness to beat us, but once more there was not much in it. We were disappointed to lose, but the fact that we'd matched the best team in Europe told us how far we'd come. The belief that we had in ourselves, we felt, was starting to be matched by the fans. They were the important ones, who we needed to impress. They'd seen enough in those two games to recognise we could compete with the best.

Our disappointment was also tempered by the knowledge that we'd have another chance of glory that season. Just over a fortnight later we were due to face Southampton in the FA Cup semi-final at Highbury.

Southampton were a really good team and only narrowly missed out on the league title that year, finishing runners-up and just three points behind champions Liverpool. We knew we'd have to be at our best. I dropped Graeme Sharp to the bench and played Terry Curran on the flank. My instructions to him were to get the crosses into the area as often as possible and see what either Andy Gray could do, or hope that one of Peter Shilton's punched clearances would fall kindly for us. The tactic worked reasonably well, and we enjoyed a lot of domination, but Southampton had the best chances. Fortunately Neville, as he was on so many days, was in inspired form. Nothing was going to get past him.

The tension was incredible. The crowd at Highbury, like Goodison, was very close to the pitch and there were no security fences at Highbury during that time. Deep into extra time, Peter Reid's free kick was nodded on by Derek Mountfield – only on as a substitute for Trevor Steven – and Adrian Heath headed past Shilton.* The crowd roared and streamed onto

---

* For me the goal was a personal victory. Southampton would send their forwards back to mark our defenders, and having seen them in the past I didn't think that Frank Worthington was too interested in his defensive duties. So I instructed our set piece takers to target Derek and on this occasion it came off.

the pitch, and the last few minutes were played out with hundreds of Evertonians lining the sidelines, watching the club that they and I loved so much confirming their path back to Wembley.

On the way back to Merseyside we told the coach driver to take it easy, as we savoured every moment of our victory. We watched car after car of jubilant Evertonians, scarves hanging from the windows, head north. The beer flowed, our joy was uncontained. It's a big thing being responsible for bringing so much happiness to so many people.

In the weeks leading up to the final, against Watford, we played some lovely football. We were peaking at just the right time, and the potential that I'd watched during those hard winter months on the training ground was now being replicated on match days. At times our football was exuberant. Players like Trevor Steven, who had had a slow start to his Everton career, were starting to show their ability. Goals, previously a problem, were no longer an issue. Until New Year we had scored just 11 league goals; in the second half of the campaign we managed 33.

Wembley wasn't always a happy place for me, but success in 1984 was sweet. (Author's Collection)

Because of what I saw, I was so optimistic about our chances in the final against Watford that I had to contain myself. I didn't want this to seep through to the players and breed complacency. Although John Barnes and Les Taylor both missed early chances, my confidence was never seriously misplaced. On 38 minutes we seized control of the game and never looked back. Richardson's cross from the left looked aimless until Gary Stevens met it with a shot. Sharpy in a single movement stopped the ball, turned, and shot off the inside of the post into the Watford goal.

With the team before leaving for Wembley. (Author's Collection)

After that Everton's dominance was never seriously questioned. Six minutes after half-time Trevor Steven's deep cross was reached for by Steve Sherwood – who was groping backwards – and Andy Gray seemed to make contact with the back of the goalkeeper's hands as he rose to head the ball home. Watford appealed for a foul, and I looked to the referee and then the linesman, and they signalled a goal. After a gap of 18 years the FA Cup would be coming back to reside in the Everton trophy cabinet.

I was very happy and very emotional after our win. These were the days before the managers received winners' medals and I stood on the Wembley pitch, looking up as my captain Kevin Ratcliffe took the trophy from the Duchess of Kent and raised it aloft. Having been up those famous steps twice before to collect losers' medals and experienced that agony, I was so happy my players were going up as winners.

The first trophy is always the best. It's something no one can take away from you. You've made an indelible mark in the history of Everton Football Club, that you were the manager when the FA Cup has been lifted. Whatever else happened in my life and career I was the manager when we won something. Joe Royle would feel the same way too. Nothing would ever feel as good as that first trophy, but more were to come.

CHAPTER TEN
ROTTERDAM

WHEN ROTHMANS PUBLISHED THEIR ANNUAL FOOTBALL
ALMANAC at the start of the 1984/85 season, I was listed among the
recipients of their annual awards. The citation is worth quoting in full, for it
neatly encapsulates the extraordinary confusion of emotions and fortunes I
encountered during the course of the 1983/84 season:

> *In 1983–84, Everton came out from the Merseyside darkness*
> *which had shrouded Goodison Park since their last major*
> *honour in 1970 when they won the League Championship, a*

trophy which has since appeared to have become the property of their great rivals at Anfield.

It was not an easy transition and often painful in execution, but manager Howard Kendall kept faith in his ideals and persevered to a point where the second half of the season produced a respectable league position and a place in two major cup finals. On top of this, the club's youngsters won the FA Youth Cup.

In finishing as runners up in the Milk Cup, Everton more than matched Liverpool over two absorbing games. In the FA Cup, they deservedly won the trophy for the first time in 18 years, marking a tribute to Kendall's honest and endearing approach to the rigours of management.

It was nice to know that you're suddenly one of the best. I don't think there's a better feeling than that. People ask you the question about management compared to playing. I think the playing side was absolutely brilliant and I loved every second. But being responsible for being the best, I think that just goes above it, because you've put together something. You're not part of it, you're responsible for it.

My challenge as Everton manager was to continue to draw on the tremendous momentum that had carried us through the second half of the 1983/84 season. As a player, like I've already mentioned, I'd always disliked the pre-season routines, road-running in Preston and pelting up and down the sand dunes in Ainsdale. I could never see the point. As a manager I wanted it to be more interesting, less painful. I still did exercises; I just mixed them all up. The kids mixed in with the senior players and would be the butt of our jokes. Some couldn't take it: Gary Parkinson, who had a good career with Middlesbrough, couldn't handle the stick that he got and left Everton and went back home to the Northeast. For most of the others, however, keeping it fun and interesting bred desire. They wanted to be on the training ground each day, and by being there they became better and better at something that would become habitual – winning.

The squad I had assembled didn't need a lot of strengthening. It was almost there. But I wanted to add a little more quality, so I brought in two players that would be crucial to me and Everton Football Club. Paul Bracewell was a player I'd encountered near the end of my playing days. When I was at Stoke as a player-coach, they didn't have an apprenticeship scheme, didn't have any youngsters coming through at all. Reviving their youth scheme was something that Alan Durban started off. What he did was contact local amateur leagues to ask them about their best young players, and he brought in about 12 players in the summer for us to have a look at. It was essentially to start off an apprenticeship scheme and we agreed that we'd sign six out of the dozen. From the trials we picked out five of the six players and then there was a vote on the last one. The youth-team coach and myself voted for one, but Durban disagreed. But because we had two votes, we won and the young kid was given an apprenticeship at the Victoria Ground. That player was Paul Bracewell.

Bracewell made it as a professional and when Durban went to Sunderland, Paul followed him up north. He progressed well, was short-listed for the PFA Young Player of the Year and was part of the England squad that won the European Under-21 Championship in 1984. I signed him from Roker Park for £250,000 and, as with Trevor Steven, it was a great bargain. All Paul had needed was just that little bit of luck to get him started, but he was a great player for us. For 18 months or so he was absolutely magnificent with Reidy. They were on the same wavelength. If Reidy went in and closed down, Bracewell followed him. If Bracewell did the closing down, Reidy was following him. I think it was a superb partnership. Peter later spoke of a 'telepathic' understanding between them and he was right. 'If he went forward I was always in behind him, we had it worked out to a T,' he said. 'As a midfield partnership we played against all the top teams and I don't remember us coming off second best to anyone.'

Another player I encountered from my own playing days was Pat Van den Hauwe, who was someone I knew from Birmingham. As a kid he came up with Mark Dennis, from the same youth club in south London to Birmingham, so I knew them both from an early age. I loved the bones of John Bailey; I think he's an absolutely fantastic character. I've employed him, I've sold him; I think he's absolutely brilliant. He was constantly cracking jokes. We were playing Liverpool and Craig Johnston ran down the left-hand side and crossed the ball; Rushy nipped inside Bails, past Neville and scored. Neville, in his typically blunt manner, yelled, 'Where did Rushy come from?' Bails replied, 'I think it was Chester.' That was the type of character he was. But I felt that he wasn't as good a defender as I wanted. I felt I needed another left back, so I sent one of my coaches, Terry Darracott, down to Birmingham to double-check on Pat. My reason for sending Terry was that he was a full back, so knew and understood the position, which I felt was something very important. Terry came back and reported, 'Not too sure about the left foot; but he can defend, there's no problem on that.' That was good enough for me.

It was at the time that Ron Saunders was doing the clear-out of the so-called 'bad boys' at St Andrew's so I had no problem agreeing a deal for him. I brought him up from Birmingham, took him to a place called Tree Tops in Formby, had a meal with him, and said, 'You have a medical in the morning and everything's done. How much do you think I'm paying for you?'

'Thirty thousand?'

'Sixty thousand.'

It wasn't a huge sum, but he was absolutely shocked.

'I'm paying a lot of money for you so be ready in the morning.'

Unfortunately Pat didn't heed my advice. He went out drinking and was absolutely rotten going for his medical. I was furious.

'You've been at it all night?' I asked him.

'I couldn't sleep; excitement.'

'Listen, mate; you're talking to me now. I know when you've had more than a couple.'

But he turned out to be an absolutely fabulous player. His nickname was Psycho, but his reputation as a hard man was overstated. There were some tough players at Everton then, but none had a reaction like Pat. It was his reaction that got him the nickname, rather than doing something dirty or crude or something like that; it was his look.

He could also do some daft things. We were travelling to Asia on tour and were having a couple of drinks on the way when all of a sudden Philip Carter appeared from First Class with a grave look on his face. There had been an announcement, which we'd been oblivious to.

'Howard, didn't you hear the captain?' said Philip. 'There's been an incident. We're in trouble. We're going to have a meeting, we'll be stopping off somewhere; we have to have a meeting.'

At the stopover we were ushered into a room and I tried to get to the bottom of this unspecified incident.

'Come on, lads, what's the problem? Who's misbehaved? What's happened?'

There was silence.

'It's a very serious problem,' said Philip. 'There'll be no more drinks on board until we arrive.'

'Okay, fair enough. What's going on here?' I asked, trying to find out what had happened.

The lads still said nothing. We flew on, completely dry.

It wasn't until about two years ago that I found out what the problem was. Midway through the flight Van den Hauwe had gone to the toilet and there was an attractive young woman sat behind him, with an empty seat next to her. In the bathroom he'd stripped off and gone and sat next to her, stark bollock naked. The flight crew were outraged, but in that room the players had stuck together: they never gave me any information about what had gone on. That sort of story would be on the front cover of every newspaper today. But the *omerta* from the lads, who were protecting Pat, said much about the team spirit we had at Everton.

Despite his disappointment at dropping out of the team, Bails never stopped with the wisecracks. Of course, when he wasn't in the side he was always first to complain in the morning. It was hard when I brought in Pat because I loved John to bits, but we started trying to move him. One offer came from South Africa. 'I've had a great offer to go to South Africa; couple of years' contract, free flights, few bob in the hand,' he told us one morning. And one of the lads said to him, 'But what about that apartheid over there?' He replied, 'Oh yeah, it's a two-bedroomed one on the beach!'

WE REAFFIRMED OUR BELIEF that we were close to achieving something special by beating Liverpool in the Charity Shield, the 1984/85 season's curtain-raiser. But despite starting the season full of confidence, the league couldn't have gotten off to a worse start. We took an early lead in the opening game against Tottenham Hotspur, but contrived to lose 4-1. Two days later we went to the Hawthorns and lost 2-1 to West Bromwich Albion.

This wasn't the start that we'd hoped for. But then a win away at Chelsea on the last day of August set in motion a run of just one defeat over the next 13 games spanning the opening rounds of the League Cup and European Cup Winners' Cup, in which Sheffield United and University College Dublin were disposed of respectively, and took in an incredible 5-4 win over Watford.

I think the point when everyone started to take notice of our credentials was after we played Liverpool in the Anfield derby in October. They were the team that set the standard by which every club measured themselves in the 1980s. We were without a league win over them in six years and we dominated the game. The only goal came from Sharpy and was a worthy winner of *Match of the Day's* goal of the season competition.

Gary Stevens had hit a long ball up the field and Graeme got a lovely touch over Alan Hansen and volleyed it past Bruce Grobbelaar. The Everton end exploded. It was a great moment for Evertonians after years of coming away from Anfield with nothing. Even Joe Fagan admitted, 'It would almost have been a shame for us to score after a goal like that.'

Arguably Everton's finest performance of that season came a week later, when we faced Manchester United at Goodison. United were tipped as one of the title favourites and had a team that cost six times what I'd spent on my Everton team. What followed that afternoon wasn't so much a win, but a rout. It began on five minutes with a rare headed goal from Kevin Sheedy, who bravely outjumped Kevin Moran to angle home Everton's first. His effort left a gash across his forehead, which was stitched and bandaged up but continued to bleed, eventually becoming so bad that I had to take him off. Before I could there was time for him to add a second: on 23 minutes Heath played him through and he drilled home with unerring precision. As the crowd shouted 'Olé', Heath added a third himself 12 minutes later from close range. A fourth goal came in the final ten minutes, when Stevens drove home from 20 yards via the post, and Sharp added a fifth with a near post finish.

The great Joe Mercer, who was watching from the directors' box, described it as the greatest Everton performance he had ever seen. Invariably the display evoked comparisons with the great side I had played in with Colin and Alan, although I was always reluctant to make them. Sheedy, however, was incredible that day, and across the team you really couldn't have asked for anything better.

Trevor Steven was a player that was now living up to his full potential in a royal blue shirt. He didn't have the best of starts when he joined from Burnley, but his technique was always there; it was just a matter of time before he showed his pedigree. It wasn't just match days, it was every day in training with Trevor; he was a dream, absolutely superb. By the time he started producing the form I knew he was capable of and was really one of the outstanding players in British football, I remember Bob Paisley saying to me, 'You were right about Steven, by the way.' Bob said: 'I went to watch him a few times and he never finished a ninety minutes; I thought he was weak.'

What used to happen was that Trevor took a little extra touch to go past people back then. He wasn't as direct. If his opponents were slower, they'd be clashing with him and he would get hurt or injured. I never had any doubt, however, that he'd make it into a top, top player and I told that to Bob then.

Bob had by then retired from the Liverpool manager's position, but there were still plenty of great characters among my fellow First Division bosses. None of these were bigger than Brian Clough, who was larger than life; the ultimate one-off. I don't think anyone was particularly close to him, or knew what went on in that mind of his, but I was closer than most – or at least I was invited into the Nottingham Forest boardroom, which is more than most people were.

I think my camaraderie with Clough stemmed from an incident in December 1984 when I saved him from a massive FA fine. It was a tough, bad-tempered game. Gary Mills had had his leg broken early on, and there were running battles between Graeme Sharp and Chris Fairclough, who was sent off after going through Sharpy. At half-time Cloughie went absolutely mad. He was apoplectic and kicked the referee's door down.

We won 5-0, and by full time he was somewhat more contrite. 'Can you come and help me?' he asked. He wanted me to go with him into the referee's room after the game to smooth things over, so I agreed.

'These things happen,' I said. 'We get emotional; we get disappointed. You're not going to take any action are you?'

The referee was surprised at my intervention. 'No, that's the end of the matter, seeing as you've come in.'

Later that season we played at Forest and I got invited into Cloughie's office after the game. No other manager as far as I know ever crossed that threshold.

'Hey, young man,' he said. 'You saved me a lot of money. Have a drink!'

Clough was one clever bloody thing. On another occasion at the City Ground Sharpy had a head injury in the first half after clashing heads with Justin Fahsanu. At half-time we were looking to get him stitched up, but Forest had put our doctor in a seat right on the other side of the stadium – not in the boardroom, not in the directors' box – the other side of the ground, so he couldn't get to Sharpy. Forest's doctor said he'd tend to Graeme, but he was taking his time. In the end we ordered our physio, John Clinkard, to bandage Sharpy up and get him back on the pitch, and we put the stitches in later. I had no doubt Cloughie had done this deliberately and I was angry that he'd put a player at risk in the name of gamesmanship.

Afterwards Cloughie came up to me.

'Well done, young man, for sending him back out,' he laughed.

'You weren't exactly helping,' I said.

'No, no,' he said with a smile, knowing he'd been rumbled. 'Well done for sending him back out.'

By November 1984 we were top of the First Division and besides a brief spell over Christmas we remained there until the end of the season. I had a similar problem as I experienced at Blackburn five years earlier: we just couldn't stop winning. How do you motivate players when they're winning? Send them out there. Don't bore them. How do you stop them from getting complacent? Other players stop them from getting complacent. It wasn't down to me.

To be honest, it was easy to manage in the second half of the 1984/85 season. You knew what you were getting; you knew who was going to be on your teamsheet. Every Monday morning, there'd be a 'knock-knock' on my door. I'd say, 'Come in, Kevin.' Because I knew exactly who it would be. Richardson.

'What have I got to do, man?' he'd ask. 'What have I got to do?' He scored two at Southampton and I dropped him; left him out, for Sheedy. Sheedy was safe. The other one was Harper. 'What's happening?' he'd ask.

I said, 'I've got to pick my best eleven. You're a very good player and I want you; but I've got to pick my strongest team, I'm sorry.' I think they got the chances though; they played the games because it wasn't a 20-man squad or 22-man squad; it was 14 or 15, and that was enough back then. They knew they were going to get the chances.

Winning the League Championship was down to so many factors. People ask me what the key component was in that team, and the answer is simple: goals. Without them you won't win anything. It's fine having a tight defence, but you need to do more than simply shut out your opponents; you need to beat them. Five players – Trevor Steven, Derek Mountfield, Graeme Sharp, Kevin Sheedy and Adrian Heath – scored more than ten league goals, while a sixth – Andy Gray – scored nine.

Our midfielders were athletic, technically excellent and controlled many of the games we played. We had a hard defence that was blessed with good pace, allowing us to keep a high defensive line. Pace was a crucial factor for us as well, as we were able to squeeze our opponents and put them under pressure. Quite often they'd resort to long balls over the top, but when they did so no one could outpace a Ratcliffe or a Stevens. It was always a losing battle.

I think Kevin Ratcliffe's role in that great side is sometimes overlooked a little bit. He wasn't the most technically gifted player, but he had pace, character, aggression; plus he was left-sided, which is always an asset to a manager. As a captain he controlled the dressing room. When someone stepped out of line he made my job a little bit easier by imposing discipline upon them. He used to be in charge of distributing the players' tickets and I remember an occasion when Van Den Hauwe turned up late to get his. He was suspended at the time and so Rats told him to get lost as he'd let the team down. At times like that he was doing my job for me. Reidy, Sharpy and others were big personalities, but Kevin was my main man. I could rely upon him completely.

What had started out as a team of unknowns would end up a team full of internationals. Andy Gray was the only full international that I signed; the rest of them – Southall, Ratcliffe, Reid, Steven, Stevens, Bracewell, Van den

Hauwe, Sharp, Sheedy – would represent their countries by virtue of their excellence in Everton shirts.

At the end of the season Neville Southall was named the Football Writers' Association Player of the Year and Peter Reid won the PFA award. Evertonians used to sing, 'He's fat, he's round, he's worth a million pounds,' about Reidy, but as one of the fanzines wrote a few years later, Reid was worth 'much, much more than that to Everton'. He was tough and tenacious and a winner. They were all winners, but during the dark days of late 1983 players like Reidy maintained that mentality. It helped the less experienced players flourish.

And where do you begin with Neville? Neville became the world's best, for me, but it never changed him. He was still grumpy and down to earth. There were none of the things that you associate with a famous footballer and he still cycled to training from his home in West Derby. But his success and recognition were all fully deserved.

Although he seemed shy in many ways, he was also very vociferous on the training ground. He was a great example of a player helping me as a manager. He'd dictate how he wanted the defence organised for set pieces. 'I want someone on the back post, I'll deal with anything that goes anywhere else but I can't do both,' he'd say. 'I can't protect my near post as well as my back post.' So we got a defender to go back when the ball was about to be taken, to go on the back post so the goal was protected. And the rest of it was down to Neville. To be honest, that wasn't my idea of coaching; that was the goalkeeper telling me what to do. But if he's telling me what to do and he's comfortable about that, then you do it.

On Saturday afternoons he was magnificent. He made a wonderful and crucial save against Imre Varadi in a game against Sheffield Wednesday that was played on the opening credits of *Match of the Day* for several years. But nothing ever surprised me with Neville. I remember playing with him for Everton reserves against Nottingham Forest reserves when I was starting out as player-manager, and he was every bit as good. I just stood there and thought, 'Have we got a keeper here.' After that nothing ever surprised me in terms of what he saved.

Although we won the title at a canter, 13 points clear of Liverpool and Spurs, it was a save by Neville that probably pulled us over the line. Tottenham had been neck and neck with Everton virtually all season and, as they showed on the opening day of the campaign, were a team packed with quality. When we met at White Hart Lane in early April it was a tough, scrappy sort of game, but when you're in the habit of winning that doesn't matter. We capitalised on a couple of defensive mistakes, Andy Gray volleying home a poor clearance. Then in the second half Trevor Steven, who I'd pushed up front in place of the injured Gray, showed great skill and composure to rob Mark Bowen of the ball, then take it around Graham Roberts and Ray Clemence in the Tottenham goal before rolling the ball into the empty net.

The game changed on 73 minutes when Roberts pulled a goal back from 30 yards. Suddenly we were under great pressure from the Londoners. On 87 minutes came the moment that is still talked about today in gasps of astonishment. From a left-wing cross Mark Falco, positioned on the edge of the six-yard box, bulleted a header towards the roof of the Everton net. It looked like a goal all the way until Southall somehow turned in midair and managed to tip the ball over the bar. At the other end of the pitch it brought Clemence to his knees in despair. After the game had been won, my opposite number Peter Shreeves said, 'The talk in our dressing room was all about the save near the end that stopped us getting the draw. It was world class.' Neville, typically, was more circumspect. 'Everyone went on about it,' he said, 'but it was straight at me.'

WINNING THE FA CUP the previous May meant we were eligible for the European Cup Winners' Cup. There was none of the elongated group stages that predominate now in European competition; it was a straight knockout tournament and when the competition started in September our first round tie was against University College Dublin. The expectation was that we would get a cricket-sized score against what was essentially a student team. In many respects what should have been by far our easiest tie was our hardest. In Dublin they lined up their defensive ranks in what seemed a damage-limitation exercise, but the reality was that they defended extremely well and probably deserved their goalless draw.

At Goodison it was an even more frustrating experience because we played poorly. Graeme Sharp's goal won it, but we had some anxious moments and they grazed Neville Southall's crossbar near the end. A score draw would have earned them an away-goals victory and seen us fall at the first hurdle.

Next was a trip to Czechoslovakia to meet Inter Bratislava. Crossing behind the Iron Curtain was really like stepping into the unknown. I wasn't able go and see them and was reliant on Jim Greenwood, who had been out there to arrange the logistics of the trip. We had a video, but that was it. We did a job, though, and won thanks to Paul Bracewell's first goal for the club – a sixth-minute header from a Trevor Steven cross. It gave us an excellent chance of victory when the two teams were to meet at Goodison two weeks later. Afforded the cushion of an away goal, 25,000 fans turned out to watch us walk to a 3-0 win through goals by Sharp, Sheedy and, in the second half, Heath.

We then had a four-month wait until we faced the Dutch Cup holders Fortuna Sittard in the quarter-finals. Coming amid a blizzard of league matches and FA cup ties, the temptation these days would be to rotate your team and take one competition less seriously, but there was none of that with my team. We played eight games in March 1985 and wanted to win every one of them. I always fielded the strongest team possible. We were at home in the first leg, which placed us at a disadvantage, but I had nothing to worry about as Andy Gray struck a superb hat-trick without reply. There was no easing of the pace in the second leg and goals by Sharp and Reid secured an emphatic aggregate win.

It set up a semi-final tie with Bayern Munich. Of the three clubs left (Dynamo Moscow and Rapid Vienna being the others) they were by far the strongest, and not who we wanted to play. The consolation was that we would be playing the first leg at Munich's Olympic Stadium, meaning the second leg was on home soil. Bayern were a magnificent team and their ranks were replete with outstanding players. Lothar Matthaus, Jean-Marie Pfaff, Klaus Augenthaler, Wolfgang Dremmler, Soren Lerby – the names dripped off the tongue. Our task in Bavaria was made more difficult after Sheedy and Gray failed fitness tests on the morning of the match. Instead I opted to play Kevin Richardson and Alan Harper in wide midfield positions and play Trevor Steven off Graeme Sharp. Neither Kevin nor Alan let anyone down, but we wouldn't have expected them to because they were good players. It was a brilliant performance and we restricted Bayern to long-range efforts. The exception was when Michael Rummenigge beat Southall with a shot only to see Richardson clear it off the line. It wasn't tactical genius from me, it was circumstances that worked in our favour. All I remember of the press conference afterwards was Udo Lattek, their trainer, saying, 'No problem, they haven't scored away from home.' That was all he was concerned about. But what I was bothered about, when I look back on it, was that we had kept them out. That was the best way of playing against them.

What followed in the second leg is considered by many Evertonians as the greatest night in Goodison Park's history. It was an unforgettable, balmy April night and 50,000 Evertonians crammed into the old stadium. The atmosphere was breathtaking. I have never heard such noise. The return to fitness of Gray and Reid meant that we had a full-strength side to face the Germans.

The danger, however, when playing amid such enthusiasm and passion is that you lose your heads and make an error. A slack moment in the 38th minute saw Kogl played in behind the Everton defence by Matthaus. One on one with Neville, Southall blocked his shot only for Dieter Hoeness to put in the rebound past two defenders on the line. It was unfortunate for we had played much the better football and held a level of dominance. But such is the danger of European football. One slip and your dreams are over.

Disappointment and tension marked the dressing room at half-time. I told the players to maintain their tempo and continue to take the game to Bayern. Just because Bayern had scored from their one attack didn't mean that the game was over. In the second half we would be kicking towards the Gwladys Street goal. I felt that we had to play in a way that Bayern couldn't cope with. We had to overpower them in the second half. My half-time talks were always brief. Fifteen minutes is a long time to fill, but I never spoke for more than a couple. I told them that the Gwladys Street would help 'suck it in'. That they had to be direct. It was not the most attractive way of doing it – long throws, aggression – but it worked. I didn't tell the players to rough up their opponents, or do anything like that; they knew what they had to do themselves. Fortunately I had players who were capable of inherently understanding what I and Everton needed.

If anything, falling behind had made the crowd louder, more passionate if that were possible. 'The crowd never normally affected me in any way, but on this night – the only time in my life – they worked as twelfth man,' Neville Southall would remember. 'I don't think I've ever been overcome by so much noise and you could see that Bayern was suffering,' was Andy Gray's recollection. They were right; it was electric. We were abundantly aware of the size of the task facing us in those 45 minutes: two goals to overcome the Germans who now had a crucial away goal.

Three minutes after the break we got one back. Andy Gray flicked on Gary Stevens' long throw-in and Graeme Sharp glanced home to an explosion of noise. Goodison roared us on. We had to maintain the attacking tempo, but not make another slip. Losing another away goal could have been deadly. On 73 minutes Stevens launched another long throw into the Bayern box. This time Sharp flicked it on and Gray headed into the back of the net. The noise was unbelievable.

Andy seemed to go to war in that second half. The Germans just couldn't deal with him. At one stage a Bayern defender was off getting treatment for a bloodied nose and Udo Lattek leaned out of his dugout and screamed, 'Kendall, this is not football.' The reaction from me, the coaching staff, the substitutes, the physio – there must have been about 18 people who stood up – was unanimous and instant: 'Fuck off!'

Andy was at the heart of our third and final goal. Paul Bracewell played a ball to him just inside the Bayern half. Andy played the ball first time, without looking up, into the path of Trevor Steven who raced clear and calmly drew Pfaff out of his goal as he advanced unchallenged, then stroked the ball past the exposed goalkeeper and into the bottom corner of the net.

At the final whistle the scenes were incredible. I stood there trancelike as 50,000 supporters cheered and celebrated and sang the name of the club we loved. I have never experienced such a high from a football match. The Bayern staff and players couldn't seem to believe what had happened. Inside the tunnel the Bayern general manager Uli Hoeness complained, 'That was not football, you are crazy men.'

Afterwards I headed into Chinatown with some of the journalists that had been covering the game and reflected on a hugely momentous night in my life and career. I'm not sure if anything has ever lived up to that experience. Back at home when my children came downstairs the following morning they found me and the *Daily Mail's* Colin Wood replaying a video recording of the game and drinking brandy and coffee. There was no way I could have slept that night, with the adrenalin surging through my veins.

It's funny looking back because we had still not won anything other than the right to play in the final. Rapid Vienna had won the other semi-final 4-2 on aggregate, meaning we would meet in Rotterdam three weeks later. I immediately flew out to Austria to run the rule over them and on my return to Bellefield had to suppress my delight from the players. I was almost certain we would win the final, but I couldn't betray that confidence.

There was a carnival atmosphere in Rotterdam. The confidence that seeped from that dramatic win over Bayern Munich was shared among every Evertonian present. Nine days earlier we had secured the League Championship at Goodison Park. We were the best team in the country. Now we wanted to prove those credentials on the European stage.

It was a performance in which we showed the world glimpses of all the unity, panache, style and brilliance that had characterised our play for the previous 15 months. I think the only surprise on the night was that it took us 57 minutes to break the deadlock. Gray, who'd already had a goal disallowed, scored the opener after Sharp had intercepted a back-pass and pulled the ball back for him to volley home. Fifteen minutes later Everton doubled their lead through Steven's tap-in at the far post, after Vienna failed to defend a Sheedy corner. Our only nervous moment came with six minutes to go when Hans Krankl scored an unexpected goal. About 30 seconds before that a UEFA official had approached me on the bench asking me to appear at the press conference after we had been presented with the cup. At the exact moment he finished speaking, Krankl scored. He was clearly a bad omen, so I told him to clear off. He was walking away with his tail between his legs when Kevin Sheedy broke up the pitch and scored Everton's third goal. I shouted after him: 'It's okay! You can talk to me now!'

The win was richly deserved, but all of us considered that the trophy had been won at Goodison 21 days earlier against Bayern. 'Everton were the better team and we could not cope with their speed and aggression,' said the Rapid manager, Otto Baric, afterwards. 'Even on our best form we could not have lived with Everton tonight.'

I was thrilled at Everton's first European success. 'It was something special tonight, a truly tremendous performance,' I told reporters. 'We showed everybody what a good side we are. In terms of possession football you will see nothing better. Everyone in the side was magnificent. We deserved every bit of our win. I think the treble is definitely on.'

⊖

THE THIRD PART OF THE TREBLE I alluded to in that press conference was the FA Cup, the final of which was kicking off at Wembley just 64 hours after the final whistle in the Netherlands.

Our defence of the FA Cup had been defined by the same mixture of defiance and élan that had driven us all season long. We were the club that would not be beaten. Our early-round ties were relatively straight-forward. We beat the once mighty Leeds 2-0 at Elland Road, Doncaster 2-0 at Goodison and in the fifth round non-league Telford 3-0 at Goodison.

It was at the quarter-final stage things started to get interesting. We met Ipswich Town at Goodison and it was in many respects the perfect cup tie. The drama began after just five minutes when Kevin Sheedy scored twice from the same free kick. With the first kick he bent the ball over the wall into the right-hand side of the Ipswich keeper Paul Cooper's net, but unfortunately the referee hadn't blown for the kick to be taken. Sheedy kept his cool and chipped another shot over the wall to Cooper's left! But Ipswich battled back quickly. Neville Southall had conceded just once in the previous 17 hours of FA Cup football, but in the space of 16 minutes he let in two goals.

For the next 50 minutes we tried to get back into the game, but Ipswich were equal to us. With 13 minutes remaining Steve McCall was sent off by Alan Robinson for a late high tackle on Trevor Steven and we bombarded the Ipswich penalty area with attack after attack. Five minutes from full time our pressure paid off when Derek Mountfield, who had wandered up front of his own volition, touched home his ninth goal of the season after getting on the end of a right-wing cross from Pat Van den Hauwe. Two players totally out of position had saved us. We won the replay at Portman Road thanks to a Sharp penalty.

That set up a semi-final tie with Luton Town at Villa Park. It came in the middle of our epic two-legged semi-final against Bayern Munich. We had only been in the country since the early hours of the Thursday morning and so the players were tired. The Luton manager, David Pleat, was a wise head and had done his homework. They knew to capitalise on our fatigue and threw everything at us in the early stages, and Ricky Hill put them in front after 36 minutes.

Our tiredness showed and it seemed as if Hill's goal was going to be enough to put them in the final. With three minutes remaining we got a free kick after a foul on Derek Mountfield, who we'd pushed up front to give us some physical presence. Sheedy stepped up, and with his deadly left foot curled a shot wickedly around the Luton wall and it bobbled beyond the grasp of Les Sealey. We were ecstatic on the bench and as I celebrated I said to Colin, 'That'll do. When's the replay?'

Colin was perplexed. 'We've got extra time, Howard, there's still another thirty minutes to go.'

In the excitement and fatigue I'd slipped into a state of confusion and forgotten what we'd been through 12 months earlier at Highbury.

The late equaliser gave us a psychological advantage and seemed to re-energise my players going into extra time. After 115 minutes Brian Stein fouled Reid, and Sheedy again took the resulting free kick. This time he crossed it and, as he had been so many times that season, Mountfield was on hand to head home the winner.

What this meant was that five weeks later we were given the opportunity of winning a historic treble when we faced Manchester United at Wembley. Only Preston North End, Aston Villa, Tottenham and Arsenal had ever won a domestic double of League Championship and FA Cup before, and no club had matched it with a European trophy.

It was our 60th match of the season and our sixth in a fortnight. We were tired after our exertions in Rotterdam. We had flown back in the small hours of Thursday morning to Merseyside and travelled to London a day later. It was a hot day. We needed some rain or an early goal, something to ease the tiredness that slipped over us and give us a final bit of momentum. We almost got it when Peter Reid's volley was deflected off the line by John Gidman and onto the post.

The game swung Manchester United's way when Kevin Moran was sent off for a foul on Peter Reid. It was a foul, but lacking malicious intent, and because he caught Reidy off balance it looked worse than it was. I don't think it was a sending-off and I don't think Kevin deserved to be the first player to be dismissed in an FA Cup final. His sending-off seemed to galvanise his team-mates – as so often happens when a side is reduced to ten men – and it became even harder for us.

The game entered extra time still goalless. It was lost as it looked as if it may have been heading for a replay. Norman Whiteside turned Van den Hauwe on the right flank and unleashed a shot from just inside the area that curled inside Neville Southall's post. We had been defeated at the last.

It was a disappointment, but not a crushing one like the time we'd been defeated in the 1968 final when I was a player. In the context of a wonderful season, it was a slight slip-up. I was still able to leave the Wembley pitch with my head held high and enter the dressing room in the bowels of the stadium where I delivered my four-word post-match team talk: 'You're still the best.'

The FA Cup ended up in the hands of my rival,
Ron Atkinson, in 1985, but I was still able to tell my
players they were the best. (Author's Collection)

CHAPTER ELEVEN

BARCELONA

HOOLIGANISM WAS A PROBLEM that beset English football throughout the 1970s and 1980s. Domestically it was a huge blight on the game, contributing to declining attendances and dilapidated stadiums. Internationally it brought shame on the country. Seldom did an overseas England international pass without major disturbances, which dominated the press not just in this country but far beyond.

Everton, like all clubs, had a tiny minority of troublemakers, but wherever we travelled in Europe there were no real concerns about anyone misbehaving or bringing shame upon our great football club. Wherever we went our supporters followed us with passion and good behaviour. The final of the European Cup Winners' Cup in Rotterdam was a case in point. 'From the moment the Dutch police, with good humour and astute diplomacy, zealously took part in impromptu football matches organised in the market square here by Everton and Rapid supporters, we knew the day was bound to end happily,' reported *The Times*. 'The behaviour of Everton's followers was impeccable from sunrise to sunset and a credit to Britain.'

Two weeks later our neighbours visited Brussels to play Juventus in the final of the European Cup. What should have been a great day for Liverpool and English football turned into its nadir. A combination of heavy drinking, bad policing, an unsuitable stadium and supporters bent on wreaking havoc conspired to make a hugely volatile situation before the match started. Hails of bottles and missiles were thrown by rival supporters at each other. A mob of Liverpool supporters broke down the Heysel Stadium's inadequate fencing and charged across the open terraces towards the Juventus section. The Italian fans panicked, turned and ran towards an exit. In the ensuing chaos many supporters were trampled in the rush to escape. A wall then collapsed under the weight of fleeing supporters. In the terrible crush 39 supporters – 32 Italians (including two children), four Belgians, two French fans and one from Northern Ireland – were killed. A further 600 people were injured.

The match should never have been played at that venue. It's worth noting that the Liverpool chief executive Peter Robinson raised concerns about the choice of venue and arrangements on the day, but was ignored. That proved very costly. I was watching the match at home, completely incredulous. The loss of human life was just dreadful.

In the days that followed, condemnation was universal. 'Enough is enough and we cannot put up with these problems any longer,' said Prime Minister Margaret Thatcher. The FA, under pressure from her government, withdrew English clubs from European competition for one year. A few days later UEFA issued the ultimate sanction: an indefinite ban for English clubs from European competition. Could Everton have done more to escape this censure? I don't think – given the political atmosphere – there was anything that the club could possibly have done.

When you look back on it, it was a horrific punishment for English football – and only English football, despite other countries having a culture of hooliganism – and terrible for the game that our country had been made an example of. In the five years that the ban stood, Everton missed out on qualification to the European Cup in 1985 and 1987; the European Cup Winners' Cup in 1986; and the UEFA Cup in 1988, and probably 1990, when reduced entry meant that sixth place was no longer high enough for qualification.

I wasn't at Everton when the ban was lifted, but I felt that the club should have been the first to be invited back, irrespective of where they had finished. I don't think that the club pushed enough for that then.

It was a horrible feeling knowing we wouldn't get a chance to compete with the best. The fans had enjoyed Europe, the players had enjoyed Europe, and so had I. It was particularly hard to take because Everton were considered not just the best team in England or even Europe, but the whole world. Later that year I would travel to Zurich, where the FIFA president Joao Havelange presented me with *World Soccer's* World Team of the Year award. We were on a high but never got a chance to prove that status on the pitch.

The best team in the World. Collecting the World Team of the Year Award from FIFA President, Joao Havelange. (Author's Collection)

—⊖—

UNABLE TO TEST EVERTON at the ultimate level, I trained my focus on domestic competition. Eighteen breathtakingly successful months had left a healthy bank balance. I had a transfer pot that would enable me to improve the best team in the world. I didn't want us to be one-season wonders. I wanted to build on our success and make us even better. There was no room for complacency.

The player I most wanted was Leicester City's forward Gary Lineker, who had finished joint leading goalscorer in the First Division the previous season.

Gary was unlike anyone I had at Everton at the time. He possessed a blistering turn of pace, which was my main reason for wanting him. Neither Sharpy, Andy Gray nor Adrian Heath were particularly quick, relying instead on their guile and bravery. Gary, by contrast, was like lightning. I don't think there were any First Division defenders at the time that could live with his pace. In the penalty area he was fantastic. He had that sublime knack of being in the right place at exactly the right time. He had his weaknesses: he couldn't head the ball, he wasn't much use outside the area and was a bad trainer. He used to have a warm bath and do stretching in the bath before he went out to play; but he was as sharp as a razor from the first whistle. I bought him for £800,000 and he did very well.

I had also signed the England under-21 international Paul Wilkinson midway through the previous season, so it meant I had a surplus of forwards at a time when there was still only one substitute allowed. Getting the right balance was always so important to me as a manager. Having competition for places is a good thing, but what you don't want is someone kicking around the reserves resentful because there are no opportunities at all. I would have to sell somebody. That player, I resolved, was Andy Gray.

We'd had the best two years we could ever get out of Andy. He'd been absolutely fantastic for us, but he was nearly 30 and I didn't want him to spend the rest of his days with us as a substitute and not play one week and then have ten minutes the next. I didn't want him to be a reserve or a fringe player; he deserved better than that.

With Gary Lineker, who won every individual award going, but whose goals didn't bring Everton a trophy. (Author's Collection)

While I was setting up the deal to buy Gary, I set in motion with the Aston Villa manager Graham Turner Andy's transfer back to Birmingham. It was a Sunday morning when I found out it was going ahead. Andy had just moved into a new house in Formby and I thought, 'I'm not going to phone him to tell him about the deal with Aston Villa, I'm going around to the house.'

When I got there, there was a fellow installing a cooker in the kitchen. I didn't know how to tell Andy because of what he'd done for us. He'd been unbelievable for us for the past 20 months. He had written himself into the Everton history books. In the end I simply said to Andy, 'Tell him to stop working.'

'Oh no,' he replied.

So we sat down and I told him what had been set up. I firmly believe that if it hadn't been Villa, he wouldn't have gone. But because it was his old club and the reputation he had there, he agreed to move. Had it been any other club he would have held on, without a doubt.

Andy was very good about it. There was no anger or frustration; if anything there was an appreciation about what I'd done in terms of setting up the deal with Villa. I don't think at first it was a particularly popular deal with Evertonians. They deluged the local press and me with letters protesting at Andy's sale. But as a manager you are paid to make difficult decisions and this was one of them.

If any Evertonian had misapprehensions about Gary's signing he quickly went about proving his doubters wrong. His form for us that season was quite simply stunning. In total he would score 40 goals in all competitions as well as finishing top goalscorer at the 1986 World Cup in Mexico. Within the space of 11 months he went from being a First Division player at a mid-ranking club to a global superstar.

Gary changed the style of our play. We became more direct. His pace was such a good outlet that sometimes it was just too easy. We would ping a long ball forward knowing that he could outrun just about any defender. I don't think we became one-dimensional or even overly reliant on his goals – Sharpy scored 23 in all competitions – but the focus was much more centred on our strikers, whereas the previous season the goals were shared around. Back then Trevor Steven had scored 16 in all competitions, Derek Mountfield 15, Sheeds had got 17. This time there wasn't the same spread of goals from those not in forward positions.

I think the First Division was a bit more competitive that season. Along with Liverpool, Manchester United and West Ham challenged at the top. They were all in the mix for long parts of the season. We were disrupted by injuries too: Peter Reid and Derek Mountfield were absent for long stretches and, at times, Kevin Sheedy struggled. We were helped by the strength of our squad, but at times I was having to play youngsters in key positions or rely on the versatility of the likes of Pat Van den Hauwe, who could deputise at centre back.

One player who made the step-up that season was Ian Marshall, whose progress I had tracked since he was a kid. I used to go in early on Saturday mornings and watch the kids play with the Youth Development Officer, Ray Minchell. They were all typical Everton players: five foot three, five foot four, quick, skilful players with good control. But we had nothing at the back, no size up front. So I had a word with Ray and just said to him, 'When are you going to get some size in this team?'

The next time I went along there was this big gangly centre forward who was falling all over the place. So I asked Ray, 'Who's brought him?'

'Well, you wanted some size, didn't you?' he replied.

That awkward kid was Ian Marshall. We put him at centre back and he did well. He had an ungainly walk or run, but he got there; and it was one big surprise to me that he made it. It just shows you, you need special ability to find young players. It's all right a manager scouting professionals, but if you go to schools and you're looking for a good player, it takes a special talent to spot them. I could have been totally wrong on Ian, thinking he didn't have a chance in hell of becoming a footballer. But he did and he had a good career.

On 22 February 1986 we travelled to Anfield. It took us 73 minutes and a touch of luck for our first goal, when Kevin Ratcliffe hit a long-range shot which slipped under the body of Grobbelaar. Minutes later Lineker beat the Liverpool offside trap to chip Grobbelaar and seal the points. It was Liverpool's first defeat at Anfield in 11 months and only their third at home to Everton in 16 years. After the other two in 1970 and the previous year we went on to win the League Championship. With twelve games left, the win put us three points clear of Manchester United in second place and eight ahead of Liverpool.

I don't think things went particularly wrong after that day. Our form remained very good. When we were beaten by Luton Town on their Astro-Turf pitch on 22 March it was the first time we had lost a game in more than three months. I firmly believe that that game cost us the league title. We were leading 1-0 with just eight minutes to go, but Steve Foster and Mike Newell scored late goals. It was just a slip, but a costly one at a time when Liverpool's was form was incredible.

The destiny of the League Championship was still in our hands, but four days later I had more bad news. I received a phone call at home to tell me that Neville Southall had been badly injured playing for Wales against the Republic of Ireland in Dublin. There were fears of a broken leg, but the injury was perhaps even harder to treat: a severe dislocation and ankle ligament damage that was to keep him out of contention for the remainder of the season and for the start of the next campaign too.

However, I had the England Under-21 goalkeeper, Bobby Mimms, who I'd signed from Rotherham United the previous summer. Despite his inexperience Bobby did very well as Neville's deputy and kept clean sheets in six of his first seven games. But losing the best goalkeeper in the world, even if it might not have affected our performance, represented an incalculable blow to my team.

Over the previous 27 months our league form had been extraordinary. In our 100 previous matches we had won 64, drawn 18 and lost 18, scoring nearly 200 goals. Gary Lineker had just won the PFA and Football Writers' Player of the Year awards and had bagged 35 goals in an Everton shirt already. If we won our last four league games we would retain the League Championship. Everything was in our hands.

On 26 April Nottingham Forest came to Goodison and recorded a goalless draw, after which Peter Reid hobbled away on crutches. It was unfortunate, but not a disaster. The title was still ours to lose. The following Wednesday we travelled to Oxford United, where our renaissance was sparked two years earlier. If we won, and followed it up with victories in their remaining fixtures at home to Southampton and West Ham, we would be champions by at least a point.

It was a thoroughly depressing evening. Peter Reid had failed a morning fitness test and Kevin Richardson took his place. Gary Lineker, who could simply not stop scoring all season except for that night, missed three or four decent chances. We lacked a killer instinct. As we pressed for a win Oxford hit us on the break and struck a late winner. At the same time, Liverpool were playing Leicester at Filbert Street where goals from Ian Rush and Ronnie Whelan gave them a 2-0 victory. (To add insult to injury, Leicester had been the only team to beat us home and away.) It meant the League Championship was now in Liverpool's hands. All they needed was to win their final game at Chelsea the following Saturday, which they duly did. Of the final 36 points available, they won 34. In most ordinary years our tally of 86 points – two short of Liverpool – would have brought us the title.

WE STILL HAD ONE LAST STAB AT GLORY a week later. For the third season running we had reached the FA Cup final. Our run had been enjoyable and dramatic and full of the never-say-die attitude that had brought us such great success. In the quarter-finals we pulled back a two-goal deficit at Luton Town to draw 2-2 and then win the replay at Goodison. In the semi-final against Sheffield Wednesday at Villa Park our injury-depleted team held firm to win 2-1 after extra time in an epic end-to-end game. In the closing stages, Bobby Mimms came of age by saving Peter Shirtliff's stunning drive, which ensured our victory and another appearance at Wembley – or Goodison South as some fans had taken to calling it. It would be our sixth appearance there in 26 months. In the previous 62 years the stadium had stood we had played there just four times.

The final was against Liverpool, the first all-Merseyside FA Cup final. It was a chance to overcome our disappointment or have our nightmare reaffirmed.

Our best play came early on and I believe the final result would have been very different had we been awarded a penalty when Steve Nicol wrestled with Graeme Sharp in the Liverpool area on 18 minutes. The irony that the man who turned down our appeals was Alan Robinson of Hampshire – the same referee who had somehow missed Hansen's handball in the 1984 League Cup final – was lost on no one. Ten minutes later my disappointment eased when Peter Reid struck a superb through ball that Lineker raced on to. He took the ball around Bruce Grobbelaar and put us in front. Things were so bad for Liverpool that their players were arguing among themselves. At the time I could only envisage one winner and that was us.

It was against the run of play that Jan Molby – Liverpool's best player – latched on to Gary Stevens' poor crossfield ball shortly before the hour mark. The Dane played in Rush – who else? – and he sidestepped Mimms and pulled Liverpool level. Liverpool had never lost a game Rush had scored in before; suddenly my optimism looked misplaced.

I substituted Gary Stevens, bringing on Adrian Heath, but Liverpool were now on the front foot. Craig Johnston put Liverpool in front on 63 minutes and then six minutes from the end Ian Rush applied the *coup de grâce*. My Everton teams faced Ian for a time span of some 17 years and he was always a nightmare for us, but never more so than on that day. Liverpool had won the double, but in the end we had lost it by just two games. Such are the margins between defeat and football immortality.

The worst aspect of our cup final defeat was having to travel home with our conquerors the next morning, and then traverse the city on an open-top bus. It was an initiative agreed before the game to show the unity of the city, but not everybody agreed. Much to my annoyance, Peter Reid refused to take part and went absent without leave. Watching at such close proximity our greatest rivals celebrate two trophies we had been so close to winning was devastatingly cruel. Maybe being so close to their uncontained joy heightened my resolve to make sure Everton would regain their title.

THE CRUELTY OF DEFEAT had been heightened by the fact that just days before the FA Cup final, Barcelona lost to Steaua Bucharest in the European

*With my assistant
Mick Heaton in 1982.
(Welloffside)*

*Pictured with Philip Carter in 1982. As chairman he
was a great ally to me when times were hard. (Colorsport)*

*Some supporters even
distributed leaflets calling
for my dismissal as manager
in the autumn of 1983.
(Courtesy of Jez Wyke)*

The brilliant John Bailey celebrating with supporters on the Highbury pitch after our 1984 FA Cup semi final win over Southampton. (Welloffside)

Presented to the Duke of Kent before the 1984 FA Cup final. (Author's Collection)

With Watford owner Elton John prior to the final. (Author's Collection)

Celebrating with Colin Harvey on the Wembley pitch in 1984. (Welloffside)

The first trophy is always the sweetest. My 1984 FA Cup winners. (Getty)

Instructing my players prior to extra time in the 1985 FA Cup semi final. What they didn't know was that amidst the fatigue and elation I'd forgotten there was extra time to be played! (Colorsport)

A blood splattered Peter Reid in the now legendary European Cup Winners Cup semi final v Bayern Munich. I was fortunate indeed to have players who knew exactly what needed to be done. (Getty)

Celebrating the 1985 League Championship win with Graeme Sharp on the Goodison pitch. (Colorsport)

Philip Carter's patience with me was fully vindicated when I became the only Everton manager to lift a European trophy. Here we are in the airport on the way home. (Author's Collection)

Champions again, after securing the 1987 League Championship at Norwich. (Welloffside)

With the League Championship trophy after our 1987 title success. (Author's Collection)

Arriving at Bilbao in 1987, where I'd enjoy 28 wonderful months. (Author's Collection)

Back in an English football hotseat, this time at Maine Road. (Author's Collection)

With Peter Reid, one of several players I brought from Everton; something that was not always met enthusiastically. (Colorsport)

The second coming. My return to Goodison in November 1990. (Offside)

The 4-4 FA Cup draw with Liverpool in February 1991 was easily the most memorable encounter of my second spell as Everton manager. (Welloffside / Mirrorpix)

*After unhappy times in Greece and Nottingham, I found
the winning feeling again with Sheffield United. Here I am with my
assistant, housemate and friend, Viv Busby.* (Colorsport)

*Last minute defeat at Wembley again in the 1997 Play Off Final
was tough to take.* (Colorsport)

I had a premonition that Gareth Farrelly was due a goal the night before the crucial game v Coventry City that decided Everton's fate. (Colorsport)

There was not much to celebrate, but plenty to be glad about in surviving relegation. (Colorsport)

*With Sir Alex Ferguson (above) and receiving the
Everton Manager of the Millennium Award from Bill Kenwright
and Sir Philip Carter.* (Author's Collection)

Cup final. It was a competition we had been robbed of the chance of entering, and watching two ordinary sides battle out a war of attrition brought home to me how much we had lost because of the Heysel disaster. I would have backed us to beat either of the two teams.

I'd had my own brush with Barcelona a month or so before that match. They were not a club who stood on formality in any way. Red tape didn't seem to bother them. One day I was at Bellefield when I took a call from a Barcelona official telling me that Terry Venables was likely to leave as manager that summer and on Terry's recommendation they had identified me as the man to take over. I didn't know Terry at all and had had virtually no dealings with him in the past. It's not the sort of phone call you receive every day. I was staggered by the informality of it.

Although I loved Everton and was very happy, I was intrigued and flattered by the opportunity to manage one of the biggest clubs in the world. The desire to compete in European competition also burned within me. There was unfinished business, both from my time as a player and a manager. If the offer was confirmed there was much to think about, both for myself, my family and Everton.

I told Philip Carter about the approach and with his blessing travelled to London to meet Barcelona representatives at the Connaught Hotel. The delegation included José Luis Nunez, the club president, and Joan Gaspart, its chief executive, in London. Over lunch we verbally agreed a deal for me to succeed Terry in Spain and I was offered a provisional contract. The Everton board were resigned to losing me and even went as far as offering the job as my successor to Colin Harvey. Colin was obviously my first choice as assistant manager at the Nou Camp and he said that he would have gone if he had not been offered the chance to succeed me at Goodison. Colin was the right and logical choice to be Everton manager and, if I'm honest, I never believed that the board would even contemplate another candidate.

And yet none of this happened. A few weeks later Terry Venables signed a contract extension and the deal fell through.

Despite my disappointment at missing out on the Nou Camp, the idea of managing outside England had been firmly implanted in my head. It created a longing which burned deep inside of me and one which I knew I had to get out of my system.

$\ominus$

ALTHOUGH A MOVE TO CATALONIA did not happen for me, for Gary Lineker the chance came. Barcelona had inquired about his availability towards the end of the ultimately disappointing 1985/86 season and a deal was agreed. He went with my blessing, because I don't think that you can stand in a player's way when a club like that comes calling. Although he had scored so many goals I didn't think his departure would cause irreparable damage to our team. Indeed, to the contrary, I felt it might heighten the teamwork that had brought us such outstanding success a year earlier. As it happened, that was the case.

We agreed a deal before the World Cup, not knowing Gary would return as a national hero. Had we been able to foresee that we might have been able to inflate the £2million asking fee by a million or two. Equally, had he endured a nightmare tournament I don't doubt that Barcelona might have dropped out of the deal.

I often get asked if the sale of Gary to Barcelona was linked to my possible arrival there as manager. I can unequivocally state that that is not the case. The deals and the timeframes involved were completely different. In any case, I would never – under any circumstances – work against the interests of a football club I was managing to further my own as a manager elsewhere later on. That just wasn't the way I worked.

Going into the 1986/87 season I was quite happy with my squad and initially told the board I didn't need any of the £2million that was now sitting in our bank account. Coming within two points of the league title and 33 minutes of winning the FA Cup did not suddenly make us a bad side.

After some of the injury problems we had encountered, however, I soon decided we needed some experience and versatility. The previous season I'd been to see Manchester City play at Watford. It was a horrible mud-bound pitch and not a very good game. But almost gliding around it was the City captain, Paul Power. He was in his early thirties, but he was as fit as anything and was the best player on the field. I called John Bond, the City manager, after the game and inquired about him. 'He's the one player everybody asks about,' he said. 'I could sell him ten times a season.' Paul was due a testimonial at Maine Road, but I managed to persuade him to come to Everton. I think a few fans may have been a little underwhelmed, but Paul soon proved them wrong.

On the eve of the new season it became clear that the injury problems Derek Mountfield had suffered over the previous year were going to remain a concern and that I couldn't rely on his fitness. The man I wanted was Dave Watson from Norwich. Like Alan Harper and Kevin Sheedy he'd been at Liverpool as a young professional, but hadn't made the breakthrough. He went to Norwich and worked his way up to be captain, and played for England too. The Norwich manager Ken Brown didn't want to sell, saying it was 'like cutting off my right arm'.

Money, however, often talks in those situations, and we had a lot of it. It took a club record fee to sign him – £900,000 – but I think over the next 13 years Dave repaid every penny of that. Only two players – Neville and Brian Labone – have appeared more times in an Everton shirt than Dave. When you sign a player I don't think you instinctively look at their leadership qualities; it's not something you see until you're in the dressing room or on the training ground with them. Some players, they give their maximum and they're not able to give any extra. Others seem to have this natural – almost subliminal – gift of guiding other players around them. Dave was one of those players, and not just on the pitch, either; he was an example to everybody at the club in terms of how you go about your training.

The deal was done on the very eve of the new season. I wanted him to play on the Saturday, so we met midway between Merseyside and Norwich – at Villa Park – on the Thursday, to get there in time to register him before the 5pm deadline. The negotiations were fine; we signed the contract, put the registration forms through and then realised we were late. He was going to miss the season opener against Nottingham Forest, so I thought on my feet.

I looked up and there was a clock on the Villa Park wall. So we turned it back by an hour and got Dave to stand there and pose signing the form with the clock above his head to prove he'd signed on time to make his debut on the Saturday! It worked too: the Football League accepted it and Dave made his debut.

We started the 1986/87 season more slowly than previous years, but were always there or thereabouts. We suffered from injuries to key players, like Neville, Pat Van den Hauwe, Gary Stevens, Paul Bracewell, Sheedy and Reidy, but we showed that football could be more than just a team game, but a squad game too. Paul Power was magnificent, playing at left back and all over the midfield; so was Alan Harper, who fulfilled similar duties in Gary Stevens' regular berth and in midfield.

I added to my squad at key moments too. I'd spotted Ian Snodin playing against us as sweeper for Doncaster Rovers in the FA Cup a couple of seasons earlier, and his career had progressed following a move to Leeds United. I was impressed by his pace and tenacity and in January I spent £825,000 on him. To the delight of Evertonians he chose Everton over Liverpool. I think Kenny wanted him to play wide-right in the midfield, and I wanted him to play in the centre. I think that swayed him because financially he was going to get what he was after from both clubs. He was a good athlete, a good reader of the game and two-footed. He added some fresh impetus at an important stage of the season.

The other very important signing I made close to the transfer deadline was Wayne Clarke from Birmingham City. He scored some hugely important goals for us, but I felt he never got the recognition that he deserved. I don't think he was ever fully appreciated by the fans. He had this lazy look about him; it was as if the fans could look at him and say, 'Well, he loses it and doesn't chase back to win it back again'. I suppose there was a lot of jogging in his game rather than a sprint and a rest, but technically he was absolutely fantastic and did well for us.

It probably took us until December to kick into our stride. We turned over a very good Norwich City side 4-0 at the start of that month, scoring some lovely goals. The best was the fourth goal, in which Heath exchanged passes with Sheedy who indolently scooped the ball back into the path of Inchy, and he hit it while still running on the volley past Bryan Gunn in the Norwich City goal. 'When we have everybody available,' I said afterwards, 'I will have an embarrassment of riches. It is nice to be embarrassed.'

I often think the psychological aspects of management are underplayed. In January 1987 we went to play Queens Park Rangers on their dreaded AstroTurf pitch at Loftus Road. Jim Smith, who was in charge of Rangers at the time, was a master of little ruses. Rangers' pitch was particularly bad; it was basically carpet on top of concrete, an awful surface, which gave the home side a considerable advantage. Just before we were about to go out the QPR trainer came into the dressing room with a big jar of Vaseline and said, 'You'd better put this on your lads, because if you go down it's going to scrape all your skin off, and it'll burn.' And I thought, 'You clever sod. That's no courtesy; that's to dissuade our lads from tackling.' We won that match 1-0, a rare victory on plastic, and it increased the conviction that this might be our year again.

Later that month we went to Bradford City to play an FA Cup fourth round tie. The pitch was icy and a couple of hours before kickoff we went out to inspect it. There was the referee and linesmen, the Bradford manager Terry Dolan, and myself checking it. Dolan was saying, 'It's fit to play,' but I was vehemently opposed. The referee in the end decided to play it. So when you talk about mind games I'm thinking, 'What do I say in the dressing room – it's not fit to play?' So I went in the dressing room and told the players, 'I've said it's fit to play, but Bradford wanted to cancel it. Come on then, get out there and do it!' And they did; we won 1-0.

Just as the title had been lost over a few days in April the previous year, so it was won the next year. We went to Arsenal on 28 March and after keeping them at bay for attack after attack, Wayne Clarke scored a sublime lob over John Lukic's head. The same afternoon Liverpool lost at home to Wimbledon and the advantage passed to us. The following Saturday we returned to London and this time it was Alan Harper who scored a fantastic goal, this time to beat Chelsea and send us top. We were on a roll now, beating West Ham 4-0, Aston Villa 1-0 and Newcastle 3-0 with a Wayne Clarke hat-trick. Liverpool beat us 3-1 at Anfield, but I think that our supporters knew the title was coming back to Goodison by the way they chanted 'Champions!' defiantly in defeat.

The title was sealed at Carrow Road on 4 May 1987, where we won thanks to Pat Van den Hauwe's early goal.

Winning the league title for a second time as manager was almost completely different from 1985. I wouldn't say it was more rewarding, because the first time is always the best, but it represented a very different challenge. It wasn't an easy process as had been the case a couple of years previously. There were more obstacles on the way and the season was a far greater examination of my abilities as a manager. Winning had been easier before and my teams had largely picked themselves. Injuries to key figures now meant I was forced to adapt. It was much harder and as a manager I was tested more. We used a lot of pieces and components to earn our success. Some of those players weren't necessarily big names and it didn't work out for them long-term at Goodison, but they did a good job for a crucial period of time. Full credit to them for rising to the task.

CHAPTER TWELVE
BILBAO

MY DECISION TO LEAVE EVERTON in June 1987 and manage Athletic Bilbao was the culmination of a process that had started – in my mind at least – when I first received that approach from Barcelona a year earlier. Being approached by the Spanish giants whetted my appetite and served as a reminder of what I was missing out on in European competition. I suppose the roots of that footballing wanderlust lay with the Heysel ban. I'm quite confident that had it never happened Everton would have asserted their domestic dominance on the European stage and I would never have had itchy feet.

The fact that a Liverpool executive helped in the initial stages of setting up the Bilbao deal will come as a grim irony to many Evertonians. It was the actions of some supporters of his club, after all, that had resulted in the Heysel ban. I didn't see it at the time as an attempt to unsettle Everton, but in summarily dismissing the approach for Kenny Dalglish and putting me in the frame it was, of course, just that. That said, I was leaving Everton in the strongest position possible and Colin Harvey was unanimously considered the right choice as manager. The assumption was that he would continue the success he had already been such an important part of, just as Bob Paisley and Joe Fagan had after Bill Shankly at Anfield.

Many people were surprised at my choice of club. Athletic Bilbao were not a Barcelona or a Real Madrid, but they were a formidable club with a great history and proud tradition, very much like Everton. It's a club that is linked with England; with Sunderland precisely, because it's a ship-building place, and the club wore red stripes on the shirts in reverence to their English cousins.

The club is one of the great upholders of Basque nationality and tradition, employing a Basque-only recruitment policy for its playing staff. Even today, 20 years after Yorkshire County Cricket Club stopped restricting itself to players born from within the county, that proud policy continues, slightly at odds with the modern world.

The Estadio San Mamés, also known as The Cathedral, is a wonderful stadium, with the crowd close to the pitch. It is the oldest purpose-built stadium in Spain and can fit 40,000 people. Sammy Lee

The Estadio San Mamés was a wonderful stadium, with fantastic, passionate supporters.
(Author's Collection)

once told me that when he played there with Liverpool he thought it was the best football stadium he'd ever played in. It had atmosphere and history and passion; like the club that played within it. When Marcelo Bielsa took a wonderfully talented Bilbao team to the 2012 Europa League final, supporters back in England finally got a proper glimpse of what a proud and wonderful club it really is.

As well as asking me why I joined Bilbao, the question people often ask me today is: *did Everton do enough to keep you?* The answer to that is yes. I was never made to feel unwanted at Everton. The supporters and the players valued me, as did my chairman, Philip Carter. My wish to leave Goodison was about football and never about money. There was never any notion that I'd play one club off against the other to up my wages because that wasn't me, but it wasn't until the last minute – and I mean the last minute – that Everton offered me comparable terms to Bilbao, by which time it was too late anyway.

'I'm sorry,' I told the board. 'It's too late. The deal is now done.'

Would I have changed my mind had that offer come earlier? Maybe. Certainly my decision to leave would have been even more difficult than it was.

Only a few years before my arrival Bilbao had won back-to-back La Liga titles, but now they were struggling. They had only survived relegation after winning a play-off at the end of the season, a night of high drama and passion that I'd been lucky enough to witness at first hand.

I wasn't expected to win the league, as Barcelona and Real Madrid were expected to sweep up everything. Cup success would be a bonus. I was expected to go and prove that Basque football could compete, and also to qualify for Europe. I thought it was a great challenge. It excited me.

They were truly lovely people connected with the club and they made me feel very welcome. The only problem was that we couldn't find schooling for the kids. Perhaps if we'd been in one of Spain's big cities there would have been an international school, but that wasn't possible. My children were also at a certain age where it was difficult to move them. After lots of talks with the club and my wife, we resolved that the family would stay in England and I would work in Spain. School holidays and close season we'd spend together, as well as every weekend possible. Of course, it was a big decision to make; financially it was good; but there were lots of sacrifices too. That was the negative part of moving there, but for me the football side of it was more important.

My whole life in Spain revolved around football. I even lived at the training ground. They had dormitories and rooms for some of the players, including a room for the manager, which had a single bed and an en suite bathroom. It was small and unprepossessing, but it struck my fancy. A family ran the complex, an ex-player with his wife and two sons. I asked, 'Can I stay here?' So I paid a certain amount of money for my lodgings and they looked after me. It was basic enough, a single bed, bathroom, TV and desk, like a three-star hotel, but every morning I was simply going downstairs and getting changed and going out on the training ground. It was fabulous. They were a great family and it was a great experience.

I tried to impose my own standards and routines on the club, sometimes with more success than on other occasions. There were times when I was rightly overruled. For example, every day around 100 or so locals would congregate at the training ground to watch me put the players through their paces. It wasn't something I was particularly pleased about at first.

'I don't want anybody on the training ground to watch my sessions,' I told Fernando Ochoa.

'Impossible!' said Fernando.

'No,' I said. 'I don't want anyone in the training ground watching my sessions.'

'Impossible!' came the reply.

I soon found out how it was impossible. They were mostly old men coming down every day with their berets on to watch the training. That was their day out. They'd come and watch the training and have a look at the players and watch the sessions, then go down into the bar at the complex, have a little beer or glass of wine and play cards. That was their life. I soon loved having them there. The more of them that came the better the atmosphere was on the training ground. From being vehemently opposed to it, I actually swung around to the view that it's a mentality that could work in England if it was conducted properly.

One of the things I was unable to do was prevent supporters from watching training sessions. I was overruled, and rightly so. I think it's something that could be tried in England. (Author's Collection)

The players loved having a massage. They had a massage before training, after training, at every opportunity. I used to be out there on the pitch waiting for them, looking at the watch for a 10am start. The supporters would be saying, 'Mister! Mister!' pointing to their watches. 'Mister! They're going to be late, you know.'

The players would come out at their leisure all rubbed down, five, ten minutes late. It was a problem. I thought to myself, 'How do we get out of this?' So one day I just looked at the watch. It was spot on ten o'clock and they were just strolling up, so I decided to take action. Press-ups. The first player there did just one, the second two, and so it went on. All day long the old men were clapping me. 'Well done, Mister!' After that the players were sprinting there to be first. No one was late the next day!

Sometimes I faced more puzzling problems. The training ground is below a mountain and is a beautiful set-up. As well as the pitches and dormitories, they had classrooms so that the young players were taking lessons then going training, then taking lessons, then going training again. Kids were bussed in from all over the Basque region because we couldn't afford to lose a quality player at a young age. I did a session one day and the players were dead to the world.

I said to one of the coaches, 'What's wrong with the players?'

'Oh, Mister,' he said, 'it is the wind from the south; they get headaches from the wind from the south; headaches.'

I didn't have a headache.

I said to one of the players, 'Wind from the south?'

'Oh yeah,' he said, and started pointing at his head. 'Headache.'

'Tell me next time the wind's coming from the south before the training.'

So I went out with a ball in my hand, got them all in a centre circle and said, 'Wind from the south, eh?'

'Yeah, yeah.'

'See those mountains up there?' I said. 'Would you like to run up those mountains, or would you like to play with this ball?'

'Oh, ball!'

I've no idea what 'wind from the south' was meant to be other than some sort of local superstition. It was a load of rubbish; it was just something that gave them headaches, so they said.

The other trick I borrowed from Catterick came soon after, when I gave them a night out in Madrid. I took their keys and they came in late, of course. They had to come to my room one by one to reclaim their keys. The president was not happy at all.

'We must fine them a lot of money,' he said. 'It doesn't help the young players if they're seeing that.'

'Leave it with me,' I said.

So I booked a restaurant: there was tapas, champagne for the staff, wine and whatever they wanted for the lads.

'It's down to you two,' I said to the two ringleaders. 'You're paying.'

The third one, who I knew had bribed one of the porters to get back into his room, was going for more champagne and more tapas. He was very generous. At the end of the night I presented the three of them with the bill.

'You three, you're paying this,' I said.

The whole place just erupted because they knew that he was guilty and he thought he was getting away with it.

There was an element of bonding there as well. I've always believed in that; the need to bond together is so important. You needed to have the players with you rather than looking up at you or down at you, or even not liking you.

I did the same pre-season routine as I did back home. Lots of ball work, minimise the running, make it fun. We did some skill exercises, which was split into little groups, and the captains of the teams had to select the worst player in the group. But the captains all selected themselves the first day. I was incredulous, but it turned out that they didn't want to upset their team-mates, so they picked themselves.

I used to get six captains together and do a little skill exercise; whoever failed it wore a yellow jersey for the next day, until the break, and then someone else was going to have it. It was meant to be a bit of fun, but the next day it was a full-page story in the sports papers: 'Worst player of the day'. The irony was completely lost on them. The players didn't dare select anybody the following day!

I also taught them head tennis, a staple of Bellefield routines. We had a little draw among the players and coaching staff and I reached the final. It was all set up, everybody was watching, but the player wouldn't play me. It turned out he had negative headlines in mind: 'Manager beats player in head tennis final'.

I made some good friends with the Basque staff and other people associated with the club. Javier Clemente, who had led Bilbao to the La Liga title and was then in charge of Espanyol, was sometimes around. Txetxu Rojo, who succeeded me as manager, was a coach. I struck up a tremendous friendship with Angel Iribar, the goalkeeping coach. He was the only one that really stood by his principles, and I didn't agree with them. I always believed that a goalkeeper with strong hands pushing the ball back into a dangerous area is worse than soft hands pushing for a corner. I could not get that through to him. It still happens these days, especially with the foreign goalkeepers. They have strong hands and the ball is going into a dangerous area when they do it. It's almost as if they don't want to concede a corner.

I never found the Basque-only transfer policy limiting or frustrating. I knew what I had to work with and enjoyed working with what I had. You could bring in players from elsewhere in Spain or southwest France, so long as they were Basque. The French World Cup winner, Bixente Lizarazu, was one such player who joined the club in the 1990s, from Bordeaux. I'd gone over the border in the 1980s when he was a teenager to scout him and tried to sign him. It is limited, but it's not limiting because the organisation and set-up at the club is absolutely incredible, and they try and use everything they have to make the policy work.

I think they were all genuinely nice people connected with the club. We used to have board meetings in city centre restaurants. It would be me, the coach, the president and Fernando, the general manager. Fernando spoke English; not brilliantly, but it was enough to help me understand their plans for the club. They used to frequent different places because they were voted into their positions, so they couldn't be seen to forever be going into the same restaurant. In any case, they liked to be seen in and around the city.

I remember one restaurant we went to and the wine came out in a pewter jug.

'Taste the wine, Howard,' said Fernando. So I tasted the wine. It was beautiful. 'You like house wine?' he asked, and he winked at me. It was the most expensive wine in the place, of course, but they couldn't be seen to be drinking the good stuff because the supporters would be looking and saying, 'Hey, that's our money they're spending.' So instead they brought it out in a jug.

During the 1987/88 season, my debut campaign, we finished in fourth place, far behind champions Real Madrid, but two places above Barcelona. We encountered disappointment in the King's Cup, in which we were knocked out by Castilla, the second team of Real Madrid, but it had otherwise been a good campaign. The club was happy, the fans were happy, and so was I. After the final game I was asked to go up into the boardroom, and there was a painting hanging on the wall depicting a bridge.

'Do you recognise that?' the club president asked me.

I looked at it closely.

'Yes,' I said. 'That's the Tyne Bridge in Newcastle.'

'Mr Kendall, where do you want it?'

'For me?'

Towards the end of the season they had sent a famous painter from Bilbao over to Newcastle to paint something that I would recognise from where I was born. It was an absolutely fantastic gesture, the thought that had gone into it. It reaffirmed my belief that I was a part of a very special club indeed.

EVEN THOUGH I WAS OUT OF VIEW to many back home in England, I was still a manager in demand. Barcelona showed further interest in my succeeding Terry Venables. When I look back on it, we were playing Barcelona, but when I had the meeting with Joan Gaspart, who was now president, he was fishing around asking me my opinion on players and didn't go much further than that. I wasn't quite sure what to make of it at the time, but looking back I think he'd used me.

Barcelona's interest may have been tentative, but Newcastle United were rather more forthright. A delegation came over from Newcastle to try and take me back to England as Willie McFaul's successor. I met a director, went out for a meal in the bar, and we had a good chat. I said, 'Your timing is wrong. I'm happy here. I'm settled.' It was a very difficult situation because the Bilbao people found out about him coming over and trying to tempt me back, and confronted me. 'What's your decision?' they asked. I said, 'I'm here; I'm staying.' But your home-town club, your own supporters, your own people asking you to go back and be the manager. It was very tempting, but I didn't think it was right because the timing was wrong.

Our UEFA Cup challenge began well in 1988/89, with a 2-1 aggregate win over AEK Athens. But in the next round we had the misfortune of being drawn against Juventus. At the Stadio Delle Alpi they just overran us 5-1, and in the second leg at The Cathedral they took a 1-0 half-time lead through Michael Laudrup. It looked like it might be a humiliation for us, and at half-time I tried to instil some pride and defiance in my players. Shortly after the interval we scored two goals in a minute and ten minutes later our centre back Genar Andrinúa made it 3-1 on the night, 6-4 on aggregate. Had we pulled it back to 6-5 I believe we would have gone on to complete one of the most dramatic comebacks in the history of European competition, but it was not to be. Roberto Galia scored a second crucial away goal, and we bowed out 3-2 winners on the night with at least some pride restored.

We ended the 1988/89 season seventh, a single point off Europe. It was desperately disappointing and pressure was building because the club's presidential elections were occurring. The club can become fiercely political as presidential candidates vie for power, making all sorts of promises. This, of course, can breed instability for a manager, and while I tried to stay immune from it, you have to live with certain consequences. In an effort to make an impression the new board sanctioned the purchase of a defender-cum-striker called Loren from Real Sociedad. They paid £1.5million, which was a lot of money for Bilbao, and I didn't think he was worth it. In a pre-season game in the Netherlands I brought him on as a centre back – which was where he'd played earlier in his career – and was slaughtered by the newspapers the next day, who accused me of spending big money on a player of dubious quality.

The club had a special hold over me and I was very happy there. But as the 1989/90 season kicked off there was a growing sense that all was not quite right. It was nothing specific that I could put my finger on and I didn't feel that my job was on the line, but there was a feeling that something was wrong. I'm not sure why, but something had changed. Newspapers were overly critical, leading me to believe there were people unhappy with the job I was doing. I had a run-in with one of Spain's most distinguished sports journalists, who apparently disliked the idea of an Englishman infiltrating Bilbao's Basque-centric creed. The interview descended into a dreadful row, which upset members of the board.

Results were inconsistent and a few weeks later my side faced a daunting schedule of matches. Over the course of a week we faced Seville at home, Barcelona away in the cup and Real Madrid away. It was a horrendous schedule with results to match. We lost to Seville, lost to Barcelona and then got hammered 4-0 in Madrid.

After the Madrid defeat it was a bit of a media free-for-all. I was surrounded by a huddle of reporters firing questions at me. People were shouting too loud and speaking too quickly and my language skills weren't up to that. It concluded with a Bilbao radio journalist asking a question, which I thought I had answered. I obviously misheard because he started repeating the question at an even more rapid pace. Believing I'd answered him, I stood up to leave, said, 'Goodnight' and walked out. It was a bit of a faux pas; you just don't do that sort of thing in Spain – least of all in front of the nation's football media.

Afterwards I went into town for dinner with some friends who had flown over to see the game. Over dinner we resolved that after two and a half years it was time for me to be heading back to England; that the time was right to return.

Not that the decision would necessarily be mine. Afterwards a TV crew was waiting for me at the hotel.

'Do you think you'll be in charge for the next game?'

'You need to put that question to my president,' I said.

'We did,' said the reporter. 'He said he didn't know.'

I knew then that my time was up, whether I chose or not.

I went back to Bilbao the following day and met Fernando, the man who had brought me there.

'We've got a board meeting this afternoon,' he said.

'I know what's going to happen,' I said. 'I'm volunteering.'

We came to an arrangement and everything was perfectly amicable. The club got together and put on a farewell party for me at a restaurant that I liked. All the directors came, friends came and they had a singer who sang some Roy Orbison, who they knew was my favourite. It was an absolutely superb send-off. When I was meeting the board for the last time, one of the directors shed tears when it was time to say farewell.

I have no regrets about my time in Spain at all and have only fond memories. It was difficult in some respects, having to leave my young family and adapt to a new culture and language; not being able to wheel and deal in the transfer market as I was used to in England was limiting too. But as a cultural and footballing experience it was wonderful. It sated my desire for European football, filling a gap in my career that existed after the cruel European ban on English teams. But now I was ready for fresh challenges.

CHAPTER THIRTEEN
MANCHESTER

SHORTLY AFTER REJECTING THE NEWCASTLE UNITED JOB, I met representatives of another big English club. I never entered negotiations with any club in my homeland with a man still in the managerial position, but if there was a vacancy I was always prepared to listen. Leeds United had been one of the great footballing forces during my playing days, but had fared badly in the 1980s, much of which had been spent in the Second Division. One of my old sparring partners, Billy Bremner, had just fallen victim to the managerial axe after failing to win promotion, and Leeds were looking for a new boss.

I agreed to meet Bill Fotherby, the Leeds managing director. Bill is a persuasive man and sold the merits of restoring a fallen giant very well. It was an intriguing prospect; intriguing enough for me to listen to the terms laid out before me. What should have represented an offer was more like a set of demands from the Elland Road board: guarantee promotion from the Second Division at the end of my first full season in charge; work closely with the media to maintain the club's good public relations record.

Managers can guarantee many things, but something like promotion – as I knew too well from my Blackburn days – is not one of them. It was never made clear what would happen to my contract if I failed to end the club's exile from the First Division. The second stipulation seemingly overlooked my quarter-century in football, through which I had always maintained excellent media relations. I declined the offer and Leeds went for another Howard –Wilkinson – who did a superb job at Elland Road and brought them not just promotion but the League Championship too.

Although I was mostly happy with life in Bilbao, I did miss home, missed living with my family, and I think subconsciously you tend to think about your next move in these situations. Realistically my scope for managerial work was limited. The children were in school and I didn't want to move them, which limited me to the Northwest. Although this was one of the great hotbeds of football in Europe, it was more limiting than it might have seemed at first glance. Everton were off my radar because Colin was there and you would never even countenance a friend failing at his job. Liverpool could be excluded for obvious reasons. Blackburn, Blackpool, Bolton, Preston, Stoke and Wigan would, with respect, have represented considerable backward steps at the time. That left the two Manchester clubs.

It seems inconceivable now, but Alex Ferguson had been having a rough time at Old Trafford. In September 1989 newly promoted City beat United 5-1 and supporter pressure was mounting. Famously a supporter displayed a banner at Old Trafford imploring him to resign: '3 YEARS OF EXCUSES AND IT'S STILL CRAP TA RA FERGIE'. Alex held on and went on to claim the FA Cup that season. The rest is history.

From the moment of my return to England the newspapers were full of speculation about my next move. I would have been naive to think that they wouldn't, but it wasn't something that always sat comfortably with me. Speculation about Alex Ferguson's impending departure and my succeeding him made me feel very awkward, for Alex is someone I respect greatly and it was totally unfair. Journalists would call asking me to comment on Alex's situation, despite my insistence that I wouldn't talk about any managerial job unless it was vacant.

It wasn't long, however, before a vacancy arose. The perpetual instability at Manchester City had, by November 1989, claimed another victim. Mel Machin had taken City to promotion and overseen that famous 5-1 win over United, but it wasn't enough for the club's chairman, Peter Swales, who was never shy in making changes. On 27 November Swales sacked him and a day later I received a call from a third party asking if I was interested in taking over at Maine Road.

I met Swales at his home to discuss the vacancy. When it came to asking about my contractual conditions we hit an impasse. I wanted two clauses in my contract, the same as had existed in my previous deals. Firstly that if another club was to meet a set figure of compensation it would secure my release; likewise, in the event of my dismissal I would be guaranteed a set sum of compensation.

The second was concerning the England manager's job. Bobby Robson's tenure as England boss was almost certainly going to end after the World Cup in Italy and there would soon be a vacancy. I'm not sure exactly who the FA had in mind or whether I would have even wanted the job, with all its pressures and intrusion, but I at least wanted to allow for the possibility if it arose. When I was in Bilbao I had fielded a couple of calls from someone acting on behalf of the FA inquiring about my contractual situation, so I was aware that I would at least be in the running for the position.

Swales, who ironically sat on the FA's International Committee and had a say in the selection of the national manager, was unimpressed by this.

Obviously he was concerned about me taking the City job and then walking out a few months later. He said that City should be entitled to receive compensation if this was to happen. I disagreed, pointing out that my previous clubs had found such a clause acceptable. We couldn't seem to reconcile this difference. I left his house believing that I would never manage Manchester City.

A couple of days later, my old team-mate Joe Royle emerged as the frontrunner for the City job. Joe had done a fine job at Oldham Athletic and was considered one of the brightest young managers in English football. He seemed set to take the job – until he discovered he was not first choice. After he spoke to Swales, Joe called me at home to ask if I had been approached. I could have been economical with the truth at this stage and paved the way for his appointment, but Joe was someone I went back with for years and was a good friend. I gave him the honest answer and Joe said he was pulling out.

A day or so later I was at Manchester Airport, awaiting a flight to Spain so I could tie up some loose ends in Bilbao, when City approached me a second time. Swales had sent a representative down to meet me and tell me that the contractual clauses I had asked for had been accepted. I shook hands with him and told him to tell his chairman that Manchester City had a new manager.

My tenure at Maine Road started on 6 December 1989. I had been out of work for little more than a month and was delighted to be back in football so quickly, managing one of the best-supported clubs in England. We were 20th in the league, but we were no more than a couple of wins off safety. The situation wasn't irreversible.

The first thing I learned was that it was like no other club I'd worked at before. There was no transparency between the boardroom and the manager's office. I was introduced to the club's silent financial backers when I took over. One of them told me, 'We're paying you a load of money [it was actually the same money I was offered to stay at Everton two years earlier]. You'd better keep us up.'

'I can't guarantee that,' I said, 'but I wouldn't be here if you didn't think I was the right man to keep you up.'

It was the type of attitude that I had to face a lot of the time. I didn't like it at all. At Everton you had board meetings once a month. I had one in 11 months at Maine Road and beforehand Peter Swales went through my notes, advising, 'Don't tell them that, don't tell them that.' I think I was only in there for about five minutes. But although Peter had a reputation for Machiavellianism, scheming and interference, on the whole I never really encountered any of it. The dysfunctionality that seemed to characterise City's reputation in the 1980s and 1990s never really seemed to impact on my managerial reign.

The only time Peter seemed to interfere was when it became clear that Bobby Robson wouldn't be remaining as England manager after the World Cup. Peter was one of the key people in the selection process for the job, and although I was on a shortlist with Joe Royle and Graham Taylor I was never under serious consideration by the FA, despite being the only manager on the list to have won something.

'You didn't want the job, did you, Howard?' he said to me slyly; thus dismissing in a sentence all those hard-fought negotiations. I'm sure I might have been a more credible candidate in his eyes if I had been managing just about any other club.

Bernard Halford was the club secretary and, as with Jim Greenwood at Everton, we ran the club together. I love Bernard to bits, but he was very careful with money. He ran a very tight ship – so tight in fact that getting money out of him could be like getting blood out of a stone. This showed itself when we signed Niall Quinn from Arsenal. I took a bit of a chance on Niall, but he was absolutely fantastic. I didn't realise how good he was going to be, but Bernard's dealings upset him at first.

When he moved up, I got Niall into the hotel in which I stayed when I didn't go back to Merseyside. I knew the manager and could get a room for £15 a night at a time when the United players were staying in the centre of

Manchester for £100 a night. I had a call in my office one morning and it was Bernard, who was gravely concerned.

'Quinn's got extras on his bill,' he said. 'Two jugs of orange juice he hasn't paid for.'

'But Bernard,' I explained, 'we got him at a fifteen-pound-a-night hotel.'

That issue passed, but soon afterwards I had a meeting with Niall's advisor.

'There's something wrong in the contract,' he said.

'What's that?'

'He hasn't got his signing-on fee.'

Typically a signing-on fee is structured so that you get half upfront, which would help you with your moving costs and give you a bit of money to settle in, and you'd get the second half after 12 months. But Bernard being Bernard had structured it so that Niall wouldn't get anything at all for a year. Assuming everything was in order he'd just signed the deal, but now he was in Manchester without any money. The sum wouldn't have been inconsiderable; probably the best part of £10,000.

I went to see Bernard straight away.

'We've just paid £800,000 for a player and you're trying to save ten grand,' I said. 'We're starting off with him being unhappy here. You can't do it.'

So they changed it. Bernard put his hands up and said, 'I tried to get away with it; it didn't work this time.' But that was just Bernard and the way that City was run.

It was a funny club in other ways too. I inherited a large backroom staff, which included two former City managers, Tony Book and Jimmy Frizzell. This was a bit of a strange situation and invariably you're a little bit cagey about having two of your predecessors around. Tony, for example, had done every job going at City: he'd been manager a couple of times, he'd been assistant manager, he'd been first-team coach. My immediate thought was, is he trustworthy? Is he one of mine? But I soon realised that he was absolutely tremendous, a good ally, and I appreciated the work he did with me.

Jimmy was a little bit different. He was on the staff, but he was doing next to nothing to be honest. He was fine, but he unexpectedly emerged at the centre of one of my biggest problems.

The big disappointment of my time at City was the fractious relationship I had with a local journalist, Peter Gardner from the *Manchester Evening News*. Everything I was doing, signings, the way my team was playing, he was criticising. There were leaks too, about transfer targets, team selections and all the business of the football club. I even got a phone call from Alex Ferguson one day and he asked, 'What have you done to Peter Gardner? He says he'll have you out within twelve months.'

I thought about what I'd done to upset him and after a while I realised what it was. I'd stopped him travelling on the team bus. For years he went everywhere with the City team, sat at the front with a cigar in his mouth. When I came in I stopped this.

'I don't want anybody on the team bus,' I explained to him. 'It's nothing to do with you, Peter; that's simply my way of doing things, I want the lads to relax, not to be saying something that you're going to follow up and put in the newspaper.'

This apparently upset Peter, and I felt his wrath in the pages of the *Manchester Evening News* each week. But where were his stories coming from?

All the coaching staff used to have a little get-together on a Friday. Work was done and we'd have a little chat about the week, a couple of drinks in the office to finish the week off and look forward to the next day. Jimmy, who is as honest as the day is long, just turned round to me one Friday afternoon and said, 'I'm the leak and I'm sorry.'

I was completely perplexed.

'What are you on about?'

'Peter phones me every morning to find out what's going on and puts it in the paper,' he confessed. 'So, I'm the leak and I'm sorry.'

I didn't know what to say. The situation had obviously been playing on his mind. I could probably have sacked him on the spot, but I didn't; I realised he was now in my camp, that I could depend upon. So I just laughed and said, 'No problem.'

What a character, though; what a bonus that is for a manager, that someone owns up to being a leak !

Peter Gardner played on my mind quite a bit at the time. I probably shouldn't have let him bother me, but he did; probably because I'd always had such a good relationship with the press until then. A few years later when I was at Notts County he had moved on from writing about City to writing about Oldham or Rochdale and we came face to face again. He met me in the press room after the match and handed me a cigar and said 'sorry'. It was a big gesture by him and one that I appreciated. But when I was at City I felt he was totally wrong because of the way he fuelled the fans against me.

My 11 months at City were defined by some fairly busy activity in the transfer market. As well as Niall Quinn I brought in some familiar faces: Adrian Heath, Wayne Clarke, Alan Harper, Peter Reid and Neil Pointon. I signed Tony Coton from Watford, who would go on to be one of English football's stand-out keepers in the early 1990s.

The signing I faced most competition for was probably West Ham's Mark Ward. He was a feisty midfielder and coming under my charge brought his career full circle. Eight years earlier when he was a teenager at Everton I had released him. It was actually Gordon Lee's decision to release Wardy, even though it happened under my watch. Shortly after I took over we took him to play in a testimonial game at Rochdale or somewhere, and I remember asking Colin Harvey after the game, 'Are we sure about letting him go?'

'Gordon nearly did it last year; he's done it again.'

I thought, 'Fair enough, I'm not going to step in.' So Mark left the club and went non-league. Then Joe Royle took him to Oldham; then it was on to West Ham. I went to Blackburn to watch a game to look at someone else and I had a serious look at Wardy. He was terrific; I thought, 'You'll do.' I took him from Upton Park to Maine Road and later took him back to Everton again. He was an example I always gave to young players who I had to tell that I wasn't going to offer them a contract. 'That's not to say that you can't make a living in football,' I'd say. 'Look at Wardy and the way he went from Everton to non-league, and look what happened.' It wasn't going to happen to everybody but it showed what was possible.

The deal to bring in Wardy was one of the more complicated ones of my career. It was a crazy day at Maine Road, a Sunday not long after Christmas, and I had agreed a deal with Lou Macari, who was West Ham manager, to bring in Mark. I also needed money to buy a goalkeeper, so I agreed to sell to West Ham Ian Bishop (who I'd previously sold to Carlisle when he was a kid at Everton and was now selling again, much to the anger of City fans to whom he was a favourite) and Trevor Morley the centre forward as well. City were struggling and I needed a warrior, not a luxury player like Ian, and a goalkeeper too. £200,000 was also coming City's way to help fund the Tony Coton deal. So on the Sunday I had Mark Ward coming up to Maine Road; Ian Bishop was there with his agent, Trevor Morley with his agent, managers, secretaries and all sorts of other people. It was chaos. We were in and out of meeting rooms all day long.

All of a sudden Wardy announced, 'We've got a hitch; we've got a problem.'

'What's the problem?'

'My wife's got a horse. Is it covered by relocation expenses as well?'

'Trevor Morley's wife's got a horse as well; why don't you swap horses?'

'No, my wife loves the horse,' said Wardy.

You don't think about things like that in a complex transfer deal. The horse was scuppering everything, but we got through it anyway.

The best player that I had at Maine Road was not a signing, but one I was lucky enough to inherit. Paul Lake was a graceful, athletic midfielder and defender. He seemed to have everything; he was an elegant presence that bestrode the Maine Road pitch. He could pass, he could run, he could tackle, he could head; he could do everything. Other managers used to call up about him all the time. I used to ask for £10m when clubs asked about him, but that was in the days when clubs couldn't afford that sort of money.

Perhaps Paul's only problem early in his career was his versatility and never having a position to call his own. It was very early in pre-season when I asked Tony Book, 'What's Paul Lake's position? What's his best position?'

'Well, he's played wide right, he's played wide left, he's played centre midfield, he's played full back,' answered Tony.

So I thought, 'Big tall lad, good athlete, good feet, good spring; I'm going to settle him in the centre back position.' It was a big surprise at first, but he was outstanding, absolutely outstanding. I made him captain and gave him a five-year contract, but I'd also found a position for him. I thought he was awesome. He would have been an England international for years, comparable to the likes of Rio Ferdinand at this present time. But it wasn't to be. We were playing Aston Villa early in the 1990/91 season and he just went down on the edge of the area. From where I stood on the sidelines it seemed innocuous. The trainer went on, brought him off and that was essentially the end of his career. He'd ruptured his anterior cruciate ligament.

Yet Paul couldn't quite leave it. He'd been such an outstanding talent. He battled for five years to save his career and went to America and all over the place to try and get it corrected. Later, he wrote a superb autobiography, *I'm Not Really Here*, in which he was critical of the way that City treated him, saying that the medical staff cut corners. Given what had happened when Niall Quinn joined the club that didn't surprise me at all. Possibly they didn't think it was that serious at the time, and didn't feel that they wanted to flash any money about sending him to America. It was only in the later stages that they realised they might lose him, when it was probably too late, that they took it as seriously as they needed to. It was tragic, because Paul was a special player; one of the very best I ever managed.

———⊖———

FROM BEING STUCK AT THE BOTTOM OF THE TABLE at the time of my arrival, City ended the 1989/90 season 14th, comfortably clear of relegation and level on points with Manchester United. We started the following campaign well, and lost just one of our opening 11 league fixtures. We were playing good, progressive football and my new signings had started to click. Of course, I knew many of them from my Goodison days and the only thing that was missing, some joked, was the royal blue shirts for my new club.

Not all City fans were happy with being dubbed 'Everton reserves' by some of English football's more caustic observers. When Adrian Heath made his debut as a substitute, his arrival in place of Ian Brightwell was greeted by chants of 'What the fuck is going on?' Many didn't forgive me for selling Ian Bishop, but what they didn't recognise was that I was buying players for the job in hand. City had been in trouble when I took over and my signings brought them well clear.

But I had reason to think that our progress might have inspired pride. When we played Everton on 1 September Adrian Heath's goal gave us a 1-0 win over my old club.

The win over Everton left them bottom. It was their third straight defeat since the start of the season, and it would take them until almost October to record a league win. After three years in charge, Colin's managerial reign was unravelling.

When I left Goodison I allowed Colin to follow his own path. He didn't need me lurking in the background or phoning him up every five minutes. The only two bits of advice I'd given him upon leaving Everton were to keep the Chinese restaurant routine going and maintain the end of season trip to Majorca.

At the end of October, following a League Cup defeat to Sheffield

United, the Everton board sacked Colin. I was incredibly disappointed for him when I found out. The club had been part of his life for almost 30 years and I knew that all he wanted was to win something for a group of supporters he considered himself one of. He was also my friend, colleague and for many years my right-hand man. I was devastated for him. He was so intense and dedicated to the job, I was really sorry he hadn't won anything. I knew how much he felt for the club.

My sense of shock at his sacking and my preoccupation with managing City meant that in its immediate wake I never gave much consideration as to who the Everton board might appoint as Colin's successor. The newspapers were full of speculation linking Joe Royle to the job, and given the club's tradition of appointing former players to the role, he seemed a natural candidate. It certainly never crossed my mind that I would be asked back.

Forty-eight hours after Colin's dismissal I was contacted by a go-between asking if I was interested in returning to Goodison. I was frankly staggered by the question. I simply couldn't believe it. I never sought out the manager's job. I never even considered it. My first reaction was, 'Oh no!'

It later transpired that what had prompted Everton's interest was a journalist friend implanting the idea in the mind of a director. This friend had broken the news to me that Colin had 'taken a taxi' – the phrase given to the sacking of Everton managers following Johnny Carey's infamous dismissal in the back of a cab in 1961 – while I was at a luncheon in Manchester, and had decided for himself that I'd be receptive to a move back home. Nothing that I'd said in that short conversation had ever betrayed that idea.

But now, after this involvement, I was faced with a huge dilemma that would be played out in newspapers and on TV stations a few days later. On the one hand there was no logic to my return. They say you should never go back. Everton were struggling at the wrong end of the First Division and reportedly riven by internal divisions and a split dressing room. Neville Southall had very publicly made his displeasure known on the opening day of the season when he stomped out of the dressing room at half-time and sat beside his goalposts. A clear-the-air night out at a Chinese restaurant had then ended in a brawl between Kevin Sheedy and Martin Keown that made it into the newspapers. City, on the other hand, were on the up. We had a good mix of experienced professionals and exciting young players, like Paul Lake and David White, and were playing good football. There was every reason to hope for the future.

And yet. Everton were *my* club. I wasn't a Scouser, I hadn't started out with them. I'd played for four other clubs and managed three besides Everton. But we had a bond. The supporters had taken me to their hearts and I'd given them everything I could, first as a player then as a manager. We had enjoyed some great afternoons and nights together. It's difficult to explain, but perhaps Alan Ball did so best when he said, 'Once Everton touches you nothing is ever the same.' I didn't ever have that link with the City fans, some of whom had been openly hostile to me. There was a pull and a push back towards Merseyside. The question was never 'why?' it was 'why not?' Did I want to go home for a third time? Yes. Did I want to restore Everton to glory? Definitely. Did I have the freedom to do so? Absolutely.

I met Philip Carter at his home and the negotiations were probably as straightforward as they have ever been for any top-flight manager. I handed him my City contract and said, 'Just cross out Manchester City and put Everton's name in its place. I don't want any more money or anything to change.' That was it.

I then met Peter Swales at Maine Road and told him what I was going to do. But he knew, because I had a get-out clause in my contract, there was nothing he could do. He couldn't stop me and he couldn't sue me. Everton would pay a fee and I would be released from my obligations to City. It was exactly the same when I left Everton to go to Bilbao.

Later Bernard Halford told me what happened next. I rank it among the finest compliments that I ever received, like when Bill Shankly tried to resign after not signing me as a player.

Peter Swales phoned the City director, Freddie Pye.

'I want you down at the ground now, Freddie,' he said.

'I'm busy.'

'No, I want you down at the ground now.'

'Why, what's happened?' asked Freddie. 'Has the stand burned down?'

'No,' replied the chairman. 'It's more serious than that. Howard's leaving.'

CHAPTER FOURTEEN
EVERTON

I'M NOT SURE WHO WAS MORE SHOCKED BY MY RETURN to Goodison Park. Me, or English football in general. There was a cloak of secrecy to the moves to rehire me that seem completely inconceivable in today's world of rolling news, social media and internet. When I stepped from behind a screen in one of Goodison Park's lounges on 6 November 1990, there was a touch of theatre to proceedings, almost like a new Pontiff being unveiled before St Peter's Square. Certainly there was a hush of incredulity from the assembled press as a battery of camera flashes lit the room.

'When you talk about Manchester City you talk about a love affair,' I told them. 'But when you talk about Everton you are talking about a marriage.'

On my right, as he had been for so many years, was Colin Harvey. I had absolutely no doubt about inviting him back as my assistant manager. Although there was no hesitation in his accepting my offer, I'm sure he must have been greeted by a confusion of emotions, having just days earlier been shown the door. Certainly I thought it was a brave decision to return, but it was a mark of how highly everyone at Everton Football Club thought of him that he was welcomed back unquestioningly.

I don't think much ever fazed Peter Swales, but he made clear his disappointment at losing me. 'In my seventeen years in football I've had a few surprises, but this was the most shattering. I feel let down,' he said. My decision to leave Maine Road wasn't a popular one with the City fans. When I came out of my office for the last time and went down to my car, I found that its tyres had been slashed.

I recommended Peter Reid as my successor and it met such a chorus of approval from the City supporters that he became irresistible. I think the fact that he was the fans' choice never sat easily with Swales. It was like the Chelsea situation with Roberto Di Matteo, where the chairman possibly didn't want him but he was successful and forced Abramovich into doing it. I don't think Peter Reid was Swales' choice, which is why he got rid of him at the first chance. But what disappointed me was that as soon as I left, after a period when there was no money for transfers, Reidy was given several million to spend on Wimbledon's Keith Curle and Terry Phelan. That sort of money was never available to me!

One of the disappointing things I encountered on my return to Goodison was the vitriolic reaction of the City fans. A lot of it was fed by the Manchester media, who ran headlines like 'Kendall wins the Pools' and 'Judas'. It was a lot of nonsense, really. I was neither on more money nor better terms.

The newspaper headlines ran counter to the reality of my brief contract talks with Philip Carter, which fuelled a lot of anger and a lot of misconceptions. To the blue half of Manchester I was now 'Judas Kendall', which was sad because it simply wasn't like that all. The situation persisted for years. A couple of seasons later I took Everton back to Maine Road on the last day of the season. We absolutely slaughtered them and won 5-2. They were redoing the dugouts at the time and Dave Watson wasn't playing. We were sat in chairs on the edge of the pitch and didn't have the protection of the dugout. The City fans were having a right go at us and were even throwing eggs. Dave Watson got one on the back.

We went in at half-time and one of the players said to Dave, 'What's that on your back?'

'It's an egg.'

'How did you get that?'

'Well, I looked around and I saw this egg going straight for the gaffer and I dived in front to stop it hitting him …'

I can laugh about it now, but at the time it wasn't very nice.

It was good to be back at Goodison, good to be back home. But I was in no doubt that a lot of hard work still needed to be done. My first task was to reappoint Colin as my assistant manager. He loved the club and was as obsessed and committed as a coach could ever be. I was deeply disappointed that things hadn't worked out for him as manager, but that was then; now I was looking to the future. It must have been a brave decision for him to accept my offer, but he did and I was glad to have him as part of my staff.

So much of our success in the mid-1980s had been built on a good team spirit. When you have that, and a situation in which players are inherently comfortable in each other's company, they drive each other on. Because they're close, they can criticise each other – slaughter each other in some cases – and in doing so, improve.

I arrived back in November 1990 to an unhappy dressing room. It was cliquish, and I just felt there were two different groups going out to play together, going out to train together, but changing in the same dressing room. The split was between the 'old guard' whom I had managed previously, and the newer crop of players Colin had brought in. One or two players straddled the divide, but there was a definite division. It was my job to try and do something about that.

You could point the finger at both sides in that situation. There were the ones who had done it, had won trophies and caps and written their names into Goodison lore, and they would turn around and say, 'We've got no chance of doing it again with what we've got at this club now.' Then I would look at the other ones who were saying, 'What chance have we got, because Howard is going to come back and he's going to select the Ratcliffes and the Sheedys and people like that; we've got no chance of getting in. They've done it for him before so he's going to be loyal to them.'

It's a dangerous situation if you have groups, cliques or whatever you want to call them splitting a dressing room. In fact you've got no chance; you've got to do something about it. And unfortunately you've got to make tough decisions; you've got to turn round and say, 'Sorry, it's time for you to go.'

I suppose, looking back at it, I was pretty ruthless. I worked with some ruthless people, like Catterick, but it was something I had got from within myself. I always tried to treat players in the way that I myself wanted to be treated; and that was to be completely straight with them. I never believed there was room for sentiment in football. It was something I had learned as a player. When I wasn't wanted by Billy Bingham or Willie Bell I understood that I needed to find another place to play football. Did the players I moved on share that view? Probably not. But my job was to improve Everton Football Club, not worry about their feelings. Your duty as manager is to make tough decisions. That's what you're paid your money for.

In the 12 months following my return to Goodison I sold Graeme Sharp to Oldham and ended the Everton careers of Kevin Sheedy and Kevin Ratcliffe. These three players were as synonymous with Everton's mid-1980s golden era as Colin, Bally and I had been with the club's late-1960s heyday. It wasn't easy and it wasn't nice to have to do. I still felt they had something to offer football, just not at the level I aspired for Everton.

By the end of the 1991/92 season only Neville Southall and Alan Harper, who I'd signed for a third time, this time back from Manchester City, were there from the 1985 team, along with Dave Watson who lifted the title with them two years later.

Looking back at this spell in charge, I think it would have been easier for me if my absence from Goodison Park had been longer than three years. You look at Jose Mourinho returning to Chelsea after a gap of six years and hardly any of his former players are still there; I think because of that his second spell will be easier than mine was.

Off the field so much had changed at Goodison in barely more than three years. The disharmony in the Everton dressing room was matched by discord in the boardroom. Everything had been so much easier in the old days, when it was a simple axis running the club: me, Jim Greenwood and Philip Carter.

On a night out with Jim Greenwood, Philip Carter and friends.
Their declining influence at the club would undermine my second
spell as manager. (Author's Collection)

In the first board meeting that I attended in my second spell, they were talking about finances, which never came up in the past. Previously the directors always had a separate financial meeting before the official board meeting. But finances were discussed this time and the club's debt was brought up. Philip Carter joked, 'Nothing changes, Howard, does it?' I always remember that statement: *nothing changes, does it.* But it had changed.

Although he remained on the board Philip stepped down as chairman in 1991 and was replaced by Dr David Marsh. David was a lovely man, a gentleman; but really he was just a figurehead. I don't think he had anything to do with decision-making. Because of this, there existed something of a power vacuum in the boardroom. With hindsight you could tell it would end in disappointment for me.

I felt for Philip Carter at that time because he still sat on the board but all of a sudden he'd gone from the top chair down the table. A lot of the power rested with Desmond Pitcher, who ran United Utilities – the conglomerate that supplied a lot of the power and water in the Northwest at the time. I never took to him. He invited me for dinner and introduced his wife to me as 'my future ex-wife'. My wife immediately took to his wife after that, but it wasn't a gesture that amused me. I found the board meetings excruciating. I recall one when, just before my manager's report, Pitcher, without saying a word, popped the papers in his briefcase, picked it up and walked out. He never said, 'Sorry, gentlemen, I've got another appointment and need to leave.' There was not a bloody word. I thought, 'You ignorant man, you're undermining not just me, but all the other directors in this boardroom.' This was a big difference between my second period as manager and the first one. We didn't have a disunited boardroom or figurehead running the club in the mid-80s. Now it was not a nice situation.

Jim Greenwood was, however, still around and he remained absolutely fantastic. Despite the problems going on above us, we ran the club together; we had trust in each other and everything went between us. But there had been a simplicity about things in the past that we couldn't replicate. For example, when I signed Trevor Steven, Jim simply said, 'You'd better phone Philip Carter.'

I did and said, 'Philip, I want to sign Trevor Steven; it's £300,000.'

'Yeah, do it.'

And that was that. It was great. Jim and I were brilliant together; we got things done. There was no messing around at all. But it was complicated now. At first I generally knew where I was with finances. There was a level of transparency and I knew what I had to get on with. But this was to change.

⊖

EVERTON WERE IN A POOR POSITION when I returned, but it was far from irreversible. It took a few weeks to turn around, but we were soon earning the points that would hoist us to mid-table and respectability. We ended the season ninth, which was no disgrace, but I knew that Evertonians expected more. Certainly I did.

The game everyone remembers from the 1990/91 season was the FA Cup fifth round tie with Liverpool. The game went to two replays, but we should have won the first match, a goalless draw played in front of the TV cameras at Anfield. Gary Ablett brought down Pat Nevin in the Liverpool penalty area and the whole stadium – indeed the whole country – could see that it was a definite penalty. Everybody except for the man who mattered, the referee Neil Midgley.

It meant a replay three days later at Goodison. It was as well that Midgley missed Ablett's foul because if he hadn't he would likely have deprived us of one of the most extraordinary and exciting nights in Goodison's history. For 120 minutes the momentum ebbed and flowed between the two teams in a night of high drama. Liverpool led through Peter Beardsley's first-half goal and at times threatened to overrun us. Then Sharpy pulled it level just after the break with a header, but we couldn't hold on. Beardsley regained the lead for Liverpool, but Sharpy seized on a defensive error to equalise. On 77 minutes Ian Rush headed home Jan Molby's cross and it looked like the game was heading Liverpool's way.

I watched this unfold from the dugout, where alongside me I had my last substitute, Tony Cottee. I'd used Tony infrequently since returning three months previously, but I told him to warm up and with four minutes to go brought him on for Pat Nevin. With just seconds remaining, and just one previous touch to his name, it paid off. Stuart McCall flicked the ball on and Cottee ran in to tuck it past Bruce Grobbelaar. Three-three. Extra time.

There were further twists to come. Southall saved brilliantly from Rush and Venison, before John Barnes put Liverpool ahead with a curling 30-yard shot into the top corner. Many sides would have crumbled, but Cottee was in inspired form. Six minutes from time he equalised again to set up another replay a week later, again at Goodison. We took that match 1-0, thanks to Dave Watson's first-half goal and some dogged second-half defending. But the 4-4 draw had already reaped its biggest consequence.

Less than 36 hours after it was all over, my counterpart Kenny Dalglish shocked football by announcing his resignation as Liverpool manager. Although Liverpool have fared better than Everton since then and have continued to win cup competitions, league success has remained elusive for both teams. It was really the end of an era of winning for Liverpool that you could trace back to 20 years earlier and that dramatic FA Cup semi-final defeat of the Everton team I was playing in.

After we'd won the second replay I had a word with Neil Midgley about Gary Ablett's foul on Paddy Nevin in the first match.

'You've caused Kenny Dalglish to retire, I'm having a heart attack in the dugout,' I said. 'If you'd have given the penalty in the first game possibly Kenny would still have been manager of Liverpool and I would be okay.'

'Yes,' he said, 'it was a bad decision. But look at it this way, I've earned your club an extra £500,000 in gate receipts because of it!'

A colossal disappointment was the quarter-final tie with West Ham United at Upton Park 12 days after knocking out Liverpool. It was on a Monday night, under the floodlights, and Upton Park is a difficult place to go in those circumstances. The atmosphere was incredible. We were slaughtered by their left winger, Stuart Slater, who was absolutely brilliant on the night. Had we won we would have progressed to a semi-final with Nottingham Forest that I felt we could have won, but it was effectively the end of our season.

There was, however, a visit to Wembley, in the final of the much-maligned Zenith Data Systems Trophy against Crystal Palace. It was a no-holds-barred sort of game, which left several of my players battered. Mike Newell and Martin Keown had to be taken off after receiving a kicking. Palace would finish third in the top flight that year, so they were no push-overs. We held our own until extra time, but ended up losing 4-1. Little could I have imagined then that it was the last time I would lead Everton out at Wembley.

DESPITE THE CHALLENGES THAT I FACED, I inherited a decent crop of players. Neville Southall was still the best goalkeeper in the country. Dave Watson was the sort of defender that any manager in football would put on their teamsheet without thinking, knowing he would do a good job. There were others, however, who while good footballers didn't seem to fit into the mould of what I considered an Everton-type player. And the situation was made more difficult because of the rifts that existed in the dressing room.

I knew I had to change things around. I wanted players who would excite Evertonians and help revive their great club. I wanted flair and verve and energy; players to excite the fans. I thought Dean Saunders would have been one of those figures. He reminded me of Adrian Heath because of his work rate and when I looked at who was available at the time, he was the best around.

At the time his club, Derby County, were in difficulty with their finances and were asking for offers for Mark Wright and Dean. It sounds crazy by today's standards, but their system was that you had to go down to the Baseball Ground and present your offer in an envelope and the club would consider it. So after we'd done that, Jim Greenwood and I elected to meet Dean in the Post House near Stoke to discuss the move. But he didn't turn up. I think because Dean's father had played at Liverpool it was a big draw, and looking back I think the move was all cut and dried by then. A few days later he joined Liverpool in a British record transfer deal. It was a wasted journey, going to Derby County.

Saunders' move to Anfield meant that Liverpool needed to move players on. I was alerted to the availability of Peter Beardsley and felt that he was the right sort of player for Everton. Graeme Souness, who had succeeded Dalglish, said to me, 'He won't sign for Everton; he hasn't got the bottle to move across the park.' But Peter proved him wrong. It's very difficult to make that switch, but I think he had enough experience to deal with it. It wasn't the case of his being born and bred in the city. Professionally it's a lot easier if you've not come from the area.

Ian Rush was another player I tried to sign. Gordon Lee had been after him a year before I first arrived as manager. He apparently had a choice between Graeme Sharp and Rush, but what a partnership Ian and Graeme might have made! He was going to the races at Ascot and we met at the Bell House in Beaconsfield. There were six Evertonians around him in the lobby of this hotel, all trying to persuade him to come over the park, and I thought I had him. He was, after all, a boyhood Evertonian. But he said no in the end. It was understandable, I suppose, but Rushie was one player Evertonians would have been thrilled to see signed. At least it would have ended some of their derby-day nightmares.

Another player I tried to buy was the Romanian international Gheorghe Hagi. I had a call from a contact in Spain alerting me to his availablity. So, myself and Jim Greenwood flew to Spain and met the Real Madrid president, Ramón Mendoza. There wasn't an issue with the fee, but at the time English football could not have supported the wages he asked for. There was just no chance, they were far in excess of what we could afford. He was an Everton type of player though; someone who the fans would have taken to immediately, and I think that was important at the time because things weren't going as planned. Fans were a little bit restless, and I think his arrival would have given everybody a lift.

When you look at foreign players I think you're always better trying to get them on loan and seeing whether they settle in. But sometimes a loan deal can be a little bit false. I experienced that with the Polish international Robert Warzycha, who joined the club in spring 1991. He came over on a loan basis from Gornik Zabrze and what a player he seemed at first. I remember one game at Villa Park when he scored twice and he was just exceptional. Then all of a sudden the problems started – the family had to come over and settle. I think now you would have someone finding them a property and opening bank accounts, and finding schools for the kids, but there was none of that then; it was just Jim Greenwood and I. And his performance just dropped. As soon as he signed that contract his performances went down and down; and yet to this day I don't think any manager would have not signed him after seeing what he could do during his loan spell.

Throughout my first two periods as manager, there was always a need to balance the books. The board would push what profit there was towards my transfer funds, but generally I needed to sell to buy. That's just the way that football was back then. There weren't huge TV and commercial revenues; instead you wheeled and dealed. As well as moving on some of the older players, I sold a few of Colin's signings to free up transfer funds. Mike Milligan, Neil McDonald and Stuart McCall were all sold during the summer of 1991 or soon after. There was, of course, no transfer window back then, which reduced some of the pressure on me.

The Premier League era transformed the game, but even in the early 1990s there were still lots of unconventional business dealings. One lower-league player I tried to buy from an up-and-coming manager, who is still involved in football today, showed this. It wasn't a big deal – less than £100,000, and we haggled over a £20,000 price difference before he struck upon an unusual compromise.

'I tell you what,' he said. 'My horse is running on Saturday; tell your chairman to put the sixty grand on my horse. If it wins, we'll halve it, and if it doesn't win, we'll give the lad a free transfer.'

At first I didn't know if he was joking. But I'd known this manager for a long time and soon realised he was serious.

'We can't do that,' I said. 'This is Everton Football Club. That's not how we do business here.'

We left the transfer at £60,000; no bookies, no bets, just a straight cash deal. I went to meet the player and his family on the Saturday, have lunch and tie up the transfer. I'd completely forgotten about the 'indecent proposal' until I was in the car on the way back and the racing results were read out. The horse won at 9-1. Sixty grand at 9-1; can you imagine?

Another player I sold was Mike Newell, who I didn't think fitted the Everton mould. I know that's being a little bit cruel, but Mike was a different type; he was a workhorse, and I just wanted a different sort of player up front. In autumn 1991 Blackburn came in and offered a very good fee for him, which I accepted because I'd been alerted to Maurice Johnston's availability at Rangers.

With Mo I thought I was getting a good deal; a proven goalscorer and Scottish international. I remember going up to watch Rangers and Mark Hateley and Johnston were up front; and they'd forced a player of Ally McCoist's calibre to the substitutes' bench. I'd seen Mo when he was starting out at Partick Thistle years earlier, but I couldn't make my mind up and he signed for Graham Taylor at Watford instead. I looked at his history of goals and games played and I thought, 'Well, I'm getting quality here.' Although he scored in a couple of derby games, at £1.5million it's got to go down as one of my most expensive flops. His on-the-field performances were very, very disappointing given the money I paid for him.

On the other hand, and contrary to a few perceptions, Tony Cottee was never a player I had any real issues with. He was an outstanding goalscorer, but his goals seemed to come in short spells; two goals, three goals, and then nothing, then two goals again, and then three or four. He was a real goal poacher, but his style was frustrating for me and frustrating for some of his own team-mates. Sharpy had been used to Andy Gray charging all over the place and making an impact; even Adrian Heath charging or helping, going down the channels. Then suddenly he was expected to be doing all the hard work while Tony was waiting in the penalty area. I think Graeme possibly wasn't as geared up as he would have been when playing with some of Tony's predecessors. In fact you didn't have to talk to him about it, you'd see it.

Tony asked for a transfer a couple of times, but no one came in for him or if they did it was at a time when I never had the right replacement. As he showed in the 4-4 game, he had that knack of scoring goals at certain crucial times. There were, however, times when he would be left out of the team and would be disappointed by that, which was understandable. The only times we came into conflict were when Tony let out his frustrations to the press. I remember one interview in which he said, 'How am I expected to score goals if players around me are not giving me the opportunities?' I sat reading that in my office and my immediate thought was, 'He's having a go at his fellow players.' So I got them together downstairs and just said to Tony, 'You've got two choices; you apologise to these lads here, or you train with the kids.'

'I didn't mean it,' said Tony. 'I was misquoted.'

'Hey, I'm sorry, lad, you said it.'

'I don't want to train with the kids,' he said.

'You've got to train with the kids, or apologise to your team-mates and take them out for a Chinese.'

I sent him off to play with the A team at Morecambe, but he quickly backed down. I think he was shocked after realising one of his opponents was his window cleaner!

I never liked taking money off the players, fining them and them not knowing where it was going. If it came back to them via a Chinese meal it was easier for me to deal with. I used to keep a list of who was late, or who was out of order, or sent off, and we'd reel off who had contributed.

We did, nevertheless, have some more serious issues with discipline as well. One player agreed to buy a house and came to an agreement with the vendor that he was going to pay him 30 grand in cash to save on stamp duty and put the rest through the books. The sale went through, the player moved into the house – but then he wouldn't pay the rest of the money. At every board meeting letters from this poor chap to the board begging for help to get his money back were read out.

I think generally the players were becoming more powerful. During the 1960s and 1970s we used to get fined for anything: being overweight, being late, breaking curfew. We weren't earning that much, so it affected us more. The impact of discipline was more important in those days than it is now. If you fine players these days, it doesn't mean anything to them. I don't know how you hit players these days; I don't know how you hurt them. These sort of problems were beginning to come to the fore in the early 1990s.

The incident that everyone remembers was when Peter Beagrie drove through a hotel lobby window on a moped in the summer of 1991. People made light of the situation, likening it to Evel Knievel, but it was pretty horrendous. We were very near Bilbao, and we played in a tournament a little further down the coast. I was meeting up with friends and all of a sudden the police came in. I'd given the players a night off; it was the first one that they'd had.

'Kendall, problem. *Beeezy.* Hospital.'

My first thought was, 'Oh no, not Peter Beardsley.'

'No. Beagrie.'

'Thank goodness for that!'

So I went to the hospital with Jim Greenwood and Beagrie was screaming the place down because he'd had a drink and his arms were cut to shreds. I held him down when he had the operation to put stitches inside and outside the wound. It was pretty bad; there was blood everywhere and he was in a lot of pain.

I found out later that the lads were playing a daft bloody game and he'd 'borrowed' a motorbike and gone through this arcade and run straight through a window and slit his arm. I had a word with Jim and we decided to pay the man off whose motorbike was damaged, pay off the hotel for the window, and get Beagrie bandaged up and out of there as if nothing had happened.

The first few parts of the plan went surprisingly well, but when we got back into Manchester airport all the press are waiting. It must have been the hotel receptionist; he'd seen what had happened and tipped them off so we didn't get away with it.

One player we had particular problems with was Billy Kenny. He broke into the first team in the 1992/93 season and was outstanding. He had great potential and gave a man-of-the-match performance in the derby. Unfortunately it was a difficult time for the club and for Billy. There were excuses coming in for absences, which we checked up on and found out that they hadn't been true. It emerged later that he was involved in not just serious drinking, but also recreational drug use. We couldn't have that going on at the club, and we came to an agreement on his contract. Joe Royle took a chance on him and took him to Oldham, and he was let down as well. It was a terrific shame because the lad certainly had great potential; he was a very good young midfield player and had a great future ahead of him.

DESPITE AN OPENING-DAY DEFEAT at Nottingham Forest, we started the 1991/92 season with great promise, beating the champions Arsenal 3-1 at Goodison in our first home match. A few days later we ran Manchester United ragged at Old Trafford and yet somehow only came away with a goalless draw. We played some good football, but only had one win from the first eight games to show for it. The season ended with Everton in 12th position and without even a decent cup run to our name. It was that sort of season; indeed it was that sort of inconsistency that defined my second spell as manager.

I was trying desperately hard to find the winning balance by making the transfer deals that would make Everton competitive again. There wasn't much in it. What we needed was an Andy Gray, a real blood-and-guts centre forward who would galvanise a group of largely decent players.

At the same time we tried to pick up promising young players who would serve us well in the future, and also promote good young players. One of those was Stuart Barlow. Colin had signed him from the local amateur leagues when he was working as a butcher. He had pace to burn and could have been a local hero. There were so many times he was through on goal because of his speed, and nothing came of it. He got the nickname 'Jigsaw', because he went to pieces in the box. It was a little unfair on him but it's what people were seeing. He was a smashing lad and a dream to work with, and missing all those chances didn't put him off getting there. He'd keep going, he'd outpace defenders, and he would get one-on-one with the goalkeeper. And miss. I remember a derby game at Anfield and he was put through a couple of times. He could have written his name into the history books, but the chances went. Liverpool had a similar player in Ronny Rosenthal, but the difference was when he came on you had the old sinking feeling in the dugout; indeed he punished us that particular day.

It was also becoming harder and harder to bring in up-and-coming talent. The days of picking up a Sheedy or a Mountfield for loose change were coming to an end. I remember one situation where Ray Hall, the youth development officer, told me, 'We need to go and get Joe Cole from West Ham.' He was an exciting young player and he was available at that time. But he was only about 12 and they wanted £1m for him. I said, 'Forget it.' The lad was a gifted player but there was no way you could bring in a new player who was years away from the first team for £1m.

Signing local lads was also proving harder. Even today Goodison supporters bemoan a lost generation of Evertonians who played for Liverpool: Steve McManaman, Robbie Fowler, Michael Owen and Jamie Carragher. It wasn't through want of trying though. Ray Hall and our local scouts were well aware of all these players. Michael, in particular, was a player Ray was very keen to sign. I'd briefly played in the late 1960s with his dad, Terry, a young Welsh lad who played on the wing. It wasn't actually a connection I knew about until the end of Michael's career. Robbie Fowler was another young player we were just desperate to sign. Maybe the incentives offered by Liverpool were better than Everton's at the time. I'm not saying that Liverpool didn't, but we certainly played everything by the book. I think sometimes, however, you've got to look at the real reasons why they didn't sign for the club that they supported.

There wasn't a great deal of money to spend, so I had to be careful with what I had. In the summer of 1992 I bought Paul Rideout, Barry Horne and Preki. I'd always remembered Paul playing as a schoolboy international at Wembley in the early 1980s. He was considered the outstanding talent at the time, but his career never really took off the way it should have done. He was a bit slow but technically very adept. He had started to play as centre half at Rangers, and I thought he still had more to offer as an attacking threat. He didn't do too badly for me, but when you look at what he did afterwards for Everton you realise his importance.

Preki was an indoor-league player in America, and received the country's award for the 'Most Valuable Player' two years in a row. He was recommended to me by an agent and I got permission to bring him over to play him in a friendly. In terms of technical ability he was absolutely brilliant and I thought he was worth the chance. He was alright, but I think he found it difficult switching from indoor to outdoor football. He was a little like Hagi, who was obviously a much better player, in that he was a clever left-sided player with quick feet.

I also wanted somebody in the midfield who was dogged; a bit of a Peter Reid-type player, someone with some guile. I called Peter Shreeves, who'd been his coach with Wales, to sound him out about Barry.

'He's a good lad, a good player, he'll put his foot in; he is intelligent and a leader,' said Peter. 'He's got one problem though.'

'What's that?' I asked.

'His passing!'

What he meant by that was that Barry was infectious in the middle of the park in terms of closing people down and winning tackles, but in possession he wasn't so good. I used to have to say to him, 'Just give it to the nearest blue shirt,' because he became edgy once the ball was at his feet. I think in the current Everton team, Tony Hibbert is a little bit like that at times. He does some good work and then there's a little bit of a jittery spell and you can see the thought cross his mind, 'Where am I going to put it?' I just told Barry, if you give it to the nearest blue, you've done your job. Of course, he had a very good career at Everton and scored a vital goal as well.

These probably, in fairness, weren't the players to capture the imagination of the Evertonians though. They weren't the likes of Hagi or Rush or Saunders that they – and I – aspired to bring to Goodison Park. But the transfer market was a difficult place to navigate at that time. There weren't many exceptional players available and promising ones were harder to come by. Instead I was left to sign good players who could do a job and bide my time for very good ones to come along.

We started the 1992/93 season in emphatic fashion, beating Manchester United 3-0 at Old Trafford and Blackburn Rovers – then one of the big names in the new Premier League – 3-2 in a thriller at Ewood Park, but we couldn't sustain it. I don't know why. There was no obvious reason as to why we fell away. It was just something that happened. If I'd had the answer then my second spell would have been more of a success.

I looked again at the transfer market. It was a centre forward we so desperately needed; someone with a bit of guile, who could make things happen in the box. There wasn't much money, however, and I had to sell before I bought. Crowds were disappointing too, often below the 20,000 mark, and we failed to make inroads in cup competitions, so the likelihood of a windfall was slim. So I had to look at my most saleable assets.

Martin Keown was someone who had risen to play for the England team while I was manager. But I was never quite convinced by him: I looked at the games that he played and the number of times he was responsible for goals we'd conceded and he was involved in a lot of them. He was a superb athlete, but I don't think his football brain was the best. Although he was a very good player, I think Neville got him out of a lot of bad situations.

Martin wasn't always easy to deal with. I don't think the lads in the dressing room thought he was one of them either, but that didn't matter to me. I'll always remember one day when I'd done all the set pieces in training on the Friday; we were all set for the weekend when Martin Keown said, 'I think I pulled a hamstring and I won't be able to play tomorrow.'

So I went to the treatment room and said to the physio, 'You're going to have another one in here in a couple of minutes; he's got a problem down there.' Then, pointing up to my forehead, I added, 'But I think his biggest problem is up there.'

Martin was standing right behind me. You can imagine the face that was on him; it was a frightening experience just turning around and seeing him!

Bill Kenwright, who was a director at the time, and David Dein, the vice-chairman at Arsenal, were very close friends; they started to do a little bit of talking about a deal, and I think that Martin knew about it. In the end I elected to sell him for £2million in early 1993. Possibly that was one of the bigger mistakes I made, but I felt it was a good deal at the time. However, it turned out to be an even better deal for Arsenal.

We ended the 1992/93 campaign on a high note, beating Manchester City 5-2 at Maine Road, but it wasn't good enough. Everton finished their first season in the newly formed Premier League 13th.

That summer I was preoccupied with trying to buy a centre forward. I sold Peter Beardsley to Newcastle to bring in some more cash. Peter had been fantastic for us in his first season when he scored 20 goals (only one Everton player – Yakubu – has managed such a feat since), but after that things started to dry up. I felt he was getting into the wrong positions too often, trying to take too much responsibility, I suppose. I'd see him outside the penalty area, or going to take a corner or a free kick, when really he should have been in the danger zone making it count.

One of the players I tried to make a move for then was Duncan Ferguson, who was at Dundee United. I called their manager Jim McLean about him.

'He's going to Rangers,' said Jim.

'But he's been down at Leeds United,' I said, knowing that he'd spoken with Howard Wilkinson. 'He went for talks at Leeds.'

'Yes, but he's going to Rangers.'

'Can I talk to him? If Leeds United talked to him can I talk to him?'

'No, he's going to Rangers.'

And that was that. Everton was becoming such a hard sell I wasn't even getting in the door with the top players. I looked at Niall Quinn, Mark Hateley, Mark Bright and Brian Deane, but clubs either weren't prepared to sell or asked for silly money.

One player I was definitely interested in was Dion Dublin. The centre forward had been fantastic for John Beck's Cambridge United as they made it to the brink of the Premier League, a notion that seems inconceivable two decades later. I'd tried to buy him a year earlier when their promotion bid failed, but at the last moment – having failed to sign Alan Shearer – Alex Ferguson had bought him for Manchester United. Early in his Old Trafford career Dion had suffered a nasty leg break and Ferguson brought in Eric Cantona while he was absent. After his recovery he was a peripheral figure, largely an impact substitute, but he was on my radar.

My solitary signing that summer was Graham Stuart. He's got the nickname 'Diamond', and he deserves it; he's a cracking lad and was a good player. He impressed me when he was at Chelsea and he's one of the few that moved up north and excelled there. He was a great pro and could play in a couple of positions I needed strengthening, and his versatility was the reason why he turned out so well for Everton. Like Barry Horne, he would make decisive interventions for the club.

We started the 1993/94 season much like our previous campaigns. We were very good at times, and at others very poor. We won the first three games of the season and went top, then lost the next three. We won another three on the bounce, including the derby, but could not sustain that form. Crowds were down, but I maintain that we weren't far from having a team that, while it might not have been challenging for the title, would have been competitive in the top half of the Premier League.

I was also confident of finally getting my centre forward. At the end of November we played Manchester United in a midweek League Cup fourth round tie at Goodison. They beat us comfortably 2-0, but afterwards I resurrected the idea of a deal for Dion Dublin with Alex Ferguson. To my delight he was quite receptive and we sat down and agreed a transfer.

In the past I'd have simply phoned Philip Carter and Jim Greenwood and the transfer would have been waved through. Now, however, things were different. I called David Marsh the next day, the Thursday, to tell him about the transfer. He neither said yes or no and that was that until the next morning when I received a call at Bellefield. I was preparing for a league match against Southampton. It was Marsh.

'We don't like the deal,' he said. 'The deal's off.'

'I've agreed everything with Alex,' I protested.

'We don't like the deal,' he repeated. 'The deal is off.'

'As far as I'm concerned then I'm no longer the manager of Everton Football Club,' I answered. 'See you.'

I think, looking back, what had happened was that Dion played against us at Old Trafford after his injury, and he had a little bit of a limp. Someone had made a passing comment about him being a bad signing and I said, 'It looks like it.' Then a few months later I was in for him. Maybe the board thought I was desperate. I certainly wasn't. Even to this day I firmly believe he would have been another Andy Gray for me. We needed that bravery in the area, and I think Dion would have provided that. I think he proved it too, having an excellent career with Coventry and Aston Villa and earning England caps.

The disappointing thing was that I was no longer in charge. If the signing failed I'd maybe get the sack, but at least I would have had a say in my own fate. But the money was there and available.

I turned up at Goodison the next day for the Southampton match and walked out across the pitch with Marsh.

'I meant what I said yesterday,' I said.

'Yes,' he replied, and then turned to me. 'You will be professional today, won't you, Howard?'

I was surprised he would ever doubt my professionalism.

'As always,' I answered.

And that was that. After the game, which we won, he asked me: 'Are you serious about this?'

'Yes,' I replied. And then I went to meet the media and announced my resignation as manager of Everton Football Club.

CHAPTER FIFTEEN
GREECE

WHEN I LEFT EVERTON my immediate priority was to get back into work. Football had been my entire professional life and my career extended more than 30 years, unbroken except for the month between leaving Bilbao and starting at Manchester City. I was still a relatively young man, the right side of 50, and felt that I had a lot to offer. I was still hungry.

I was introduced to Xanthi by an agent, to whom we'll merely refer to as 'Jimmy the Greek'. He had approached me shortly after I left Everton to see if I was interested in a move to Greece. If you're out of work, you'll listen to anything that comes your way, and what Jimmy proposed sounded plausible. A Greek top-flight club, bankrolled by a wealthy car executive, that wanted to meet me in Athens. So I said I'd go and meet them, and after doing so agreed to take up the position.

Really, I should have done my homework on the club a bit better, but I wasn't the only one. The *Liverpool Echo* ran the headline: 'Kendall Goes to Island in the Sun', thinking that I'd accepted an offer to join a club on Zante, the Ionian holiday island. I had to call the paper's sports desk to tell them to change the headline: Xanthi was no paradise, it was situated far away from anywhere in the northeast of the country near the Turkish border.

Xanthi was a small club, with a 9,500-capacity stadium. It had been promoted to the Greek top flight in 1989 and has stayed there since then. There was very little in the city to do for an English football manager who didn't speak the language. I believe it has tried to market itself as a tourism destination now, but that wasn't the case 20 years ago. It was a stopping-off point, a staging post.

The club put me in a hotel on the main road and I thought, 'What am I doing here?' There was a derelict garage across the road and the hotel backed on to a petrol station. But I thought, 'I'll get on with it, I'll give it a go.' The players were good to work with. We had to do pre-season training early in the morning and late in the afternoon because of the heat.

A lot of my memories are of living in the hotel. You could hear everything from the room next door to you, and that was unsettling. After training I didn't have anywhere to go. One night after dinner I decided to go and sit on the balcony, have a cigar and contemplate why I was there. So I lit the cigar up and puffed it out, didn't inhale it at all, just puffed it out. All of a sudden this Greek came over in a panic, shouting, 'Oh no! No! No! Kendall!' I'd forgotten about the petrol station underneath and the lorries were filling up there. If I'd put the ash out the cigar would have sent the place sky-high.

The conditions were primitive, backward even. The players rode on motorbikes and things like that. I was lent a Skoda 105 car – the sort of old-fashioned East European car that my children made jokes about at school (this being the days before the company was taken over by Volkswagen) – as the club was owned by the Czech car company. The club president, who was one of its executives in Athens, later offered me a top-of-the-range Skoda if I stayed, but it wasn't much of an incentive.

There was a habitual lack of trust in Greece. We'd have a director sitting in the changing room before games, and I'd be telling the interpreter to get him away. It was because of the mistrust and the corruption that was endemic throughout the Greek game. He was there to make sure players weren't being paid off to lose. My opposition to his being there was purely because I didn't feel board members should be anywhere near a dressing room, but it caused problems with the board because they were so suspicious of everything. I suppose they assumed that without a director's presence there was scope for some sort of manipulation.

It wouldn't have surprised me that match-fixing was prevalent during my time in Greece. I'd had my own bad experience there as a player more than 20 years earlier and nothing I encountered during my time as manager changed that view. There was a whiff of corruption, but it's difficult to point the finger, hard to ascertain what was really going on. My guess is that the paranoia that was prevalent confirmed my worst suspicions.

Results were acceptable during my first spell in Greece and I don't think I let anyone down. I liked my players and enjoyed working with them. However, I found it hard to adapt to life in Xanthi. It was a long way from home. It was remote. It wasn't an especially happy time for me. I gave it my best shot, but it wasn't working out and so I tendered my resignation.

I returned to England but didn't have to wait long for a job. Back in Liverpool Derek Pavis, the Notts County chairman, called me to see if I'd be interested in taking over at Meadow Lane. County were rooted to the bottom of the Division One (then the second tier below the Premier League), but I was always restless and keen to get back into the game. So in January 1995 I was appointed County manager.

Shortly after taking over Peter Reid, who had spent time there as a player after being sacked as Manchester City boss, told me, 'I wish you'd phoned me before you took the job on; I would have told you all about it.'

Very quickly I learned what 'all about it' meant, which was why I wasn't there too long.

The chairman was an overpowering figure. Pavis had made a fortune in the plumbing and heating business and had bought the club, having previously been involved with Nottingham Forest. It was his club really. He ran it as his fiefdom, modestly naming a stand after himself (by contrast, Tommy Lawton, the club's greatest player, had to make do with a bar). He supported me in a way – he let me bring Stevie Nicol down from Liverpool as player-coach – but he also micromanaged to a ridiculous level.

I decided to have a day off in Liverpool and let Stevie take training one day. I got a call from Pavis, asking, 'What's going on here?' Because County didn't have a training ground we used to hire training facilities. Anyway, this day Steve had decided to take them onto the Meadow Lane pitch. All of a sudden it poured down with rain so it cut the pitch up like I don't know what. 'He's cut my pitch up. What's going on down there?'

'I don't know,' I said. 'I'm in Liverpool; Steve's in charge.'

The pitch, of course, wasn't his concern. It was mine and the grounds-man's, but here I was getting it both barrels. He thought that everything to do with Notts County Football Club was him. I was in with a journalist doing the morning report once and he came charging into my little office.

'Sorry, sir, I want a word with my manager,' he said to the journalist, then said to me: 'Come 'ere.'

'Yes?'

'Come 'ere, I want to show you something,' he shouted. 'They're taking the piss out of you and they're taking the piss out of me. Come here, I'll show you.'

Two players, Paul Devlin and Michael Johnson, had travelled from Birmingham as they did every day for training. There was some sort of seminar going on in one of the rooms upstairs so the car park was full. The players had arrived fairly late and parked in the chairman's spot. Pavis, who had been forced to park somewhere else, was incandescent.

'They're taking the piss out of you and they're taking the piss out of me,' he repeated.

'All they did was park the car there. I'll tell them to move it.'

'Fine them two weeks' wages,' he ordered.

I hated fining players at the best of times, but over something as trivial as that I wasn't happy at all. I tried to make light of it but the chairman was having none of it. 'I'm telling you, fine them two weeks' wages,' he shouted.

I pulled over the two players later and told them, 'You parked in the chairman's spot; you're fined two weeks' wages.'

They were shocked rather than angry; that was a massive amount to the two of them. In the end I dragged them in the next day and told them I'd let them off with the same rate the council charged for clamping, around £30. Boy, did I have them playing for me the next week; they were so grateful to me. It was a brilliant way of getting players to play for you, having an out-of-touch chairman. It got you that little bit extra.

There was one game and the opposition was down to nine men; they'd had two players sent off. I'd brought in John Burridge on loan, and he made a right bloody mistake near the end of the game. We were playing against nine men, and it was a corner against us. I'd got everybody back, similar positions to what it would be if we were playing against 11. They scored.

Afterwards Pavis was waiting for me.

'Cloughie wouldn't have done that, would he?'

'What?'

'He would have left two up the field and kept three of them back so there was hardly anyone in the box. Cloughie wouldn't have done that.'

'Well, I do that,' I replied. 'It was a mistake from the goalkeeper that cost us the game.'

'No, but Cloughie wouldn't have done that.'

I was a very good manager with a proven track record, but I wasn't Brian Clough. No one was. He was unique.

I always felt very privileged to meet celebrities throughout my career. Here's Roy Evans and I with Norman Wisdom, and with Ken Dodd, whose charity functions I always try to attend. (Author's Collection)

Things didn't go so well in the league, but it's difficult to take over anywhere mid-season and I inherited a club that had won just four league games in the first five months of the season. I did, however, take County to Wembley after beating Stoke City in a two-legged semi-final in the Anglo-Italian Cup. This was a short-lived competition for the second-tier clubs of England and Italy. Perhaps it was a derided competition, but it's one that we won. Ten years after leading Everton to European success against Rapid Vienna in the Cup Winners' Cup, I oversaw County's win in the final of the Anglo-Italian Cup – a 2-1 win over an Ascoli team that included the German international forward Oliver Bierhoff.

I was at Meadow Lane for just 79 days. The end came when we played Barnsley at home. We took an early lead through Paul Devlin but couldn't maintain it and ended up losing 3-1. Afterwards myself and my assistant Russell Slade were summoned to the boardroom and fired. Derek Pavis wasn't even there; someone told me he was on holiday and had phoned in the instructions.

It wasn't, frankly, the best of experiences. Later Pavis tried to trash me in the press, making all sorts of ridiculous allegations about my conduct. I'm not saying I was perfect, but there were lots of untruths spoken and it demonstrated to me what a nasty piece of work I'd had to deal with.

I was neither sorry nor disappointed to leave Notts County. I was better off out of there. Pavis wanted a miracle worker to get County out of the mire, and I didn't have what he demanded. I don't think anybody would have done.

⊖

I WASN'T PUT OFF BY THE NOTTS COUNTY EXPERIENCE. I still wanted to manage, I thought I had something to offer. I wasn't yet 50 and knew there were still years left in me. My next stop was Bramall Lane, where I was appointed manager in December 1995. After seven years, Dave Bassett had been sacked as manager with the club in danger of slipping down to the third tier.

I found Sheffield United in a bad place. I needed someone to liven the dressing room up because it was dead; we lost somewhere down south without a whimper and I knew something had to change. So on the train on the way back up to Liverpool I was thinking about names and my old friend

John Bailey came to mind. Bails had finished playing a few years earlier and was exactly the sort of person we needed to liven the place up. The next day I phoned him and told him to be at Lime Street station first thing Monday morning. He was going to be my new coach.

He asked what the terms were, but he wasn't really listening until I mentioned a free trip to Majorca at the end of the season if we stayed up. 'That'll do me!' he said.

So we went down to Sheffield; I took Viv Busby with me and the three of us had rented accommodation in the city. We were housemates and we got the results. We avoided relegation by a mile, finishing ninth, and Bails was fantastic in the dressing room, absolutely brilliant.

The United fans were great too, really passionate and loyal, but they weren't easily impressed. Shortly after my appointment we'd met Arsenal in third round of the FA Cup, drawn with them at Highbury and then beaten them in the replay in Sheffield. It was a tremendous achievement against a very good team and we were drawn against Aston Villa in the fourth round. The following day myself, Viv Busby and Bails arrived at Bramall Lane after training. There were queues stretching around the stadium. When we got out of the car we expected them to be in the throes of cup fever, but they stood there silently. There was no 'Well done, lads' or 'We're going to win this next week' or anything that fans anywhere else might have said. Nothing. They didn't even say, 'Good morning!'

At the end of the season I looked to revitalise the team. Safety was fine, but a club the size of Sheffield United needed to be aspiring to the Premier League. The man I wanted to bring to Bramall Lane was someone who had haunted me for years and who I'd tried to sign a couple of times before: Ian Rush.

After 16 years, interrupted only by a brief spell in Italy, Rushie was finally leaving Liverpool. He was in his mid-thirties, but I knew he could do a job in the second tier, and that he'd be a great asset for a club like Sheffield United. He was available on a free transfer and I got him to Sheffield to talk about a contract. He arrived at Bramall Lane; there were press and photographers and TV outside, and I thought, 'Yeah, I've finally got him.' That the chairman backed me signified how much Sheffield United wanted to be successful.

But then I got a phone call from him the next day to say, 'I'm signing for Leeds.' I was agog; I thought everything was done. I spoke to him on the phone and said, 'You could be a hero in Sheffield; why are you going to Leeds?' They were in the Premier League. I said, 'You'll be sitting on the subs' bench in the Premier League; why don't you come down here and be a hero?' But it was a 'No' again. Kenny Dalglish had advised him to stay at the top as long as he could. So he went to Leeds, and was playing wide right and was on the subs' bench. He made a big decision, which I don't think was the right one. I think the right one was to come and play for me. The move was a disappointment for everyone. Rushie scored just three goals for Leeds that season; he could have had 20 had he dropped down a division.

After avoiding relegation at Bramall Lane, I had one full season in Sheffield and we did really well. It was a fabulous club and I liked being there. We played good football and I enjoyed being a manager again. We had a good mixture of fine, experienced players – like Nigel Spackman, David White, Paul Parker and Andy Walker – and younger players such as Don Hutchison, Chris Short and Carl Tiler, who were very good at that level.

Towards the end of the season we were blighted by injuries, which may well have cost us an automatic promotion slot. Bolton were runaway league leaders, but we finished just seven points behind Barnsley, after our form in the final quarter of the season slipped away a little. It was still enough for us to claim fifth spot and a place in the playoffs.

In the semi-final against Ipswich Town we showed tremendous fortitude and spirit, despite sometimes facing adversity. In the first leg in Sheffield we led for a long stretch thanks to Jan Age Fjörtoft's goal, only to concede late on. It was a shattering blow with the second leg at Portman Road still to come and lesser teams may have folded, but my players picked themselves up and I was impressed by their persistence.

We travelled down to Suffolk and, despite being under pressure for a lot of the first half, took an early lead through our Belarussian striker Pyotr Kachura. Ipswich fought back, equalising and then going ahead with just 16 minutes remaining. But almost immediately I pushed my players forward and Andy Walker scored a crucial, crucial equaliser. The game went into extra time, but we dug in despite heavy pressure and secured a victory on away goals.

It meant another Wembley appearance, my tenth as manager, for the playoff final against Crystal Palace. I think sometimes that a team can view a semi-final win and a looming appearance at the home of English football as victory in itself, and I suspect that that is what happened with the Blades that day. We didn't play especially well, particularly in the first half. I was forced to take off Don Hutchison at half-time after he had broken his collarbone and had already lost to injury our first-choice goalkeeper, Alan Kelly, in the run-up to the tie. But still we held on and there were moments when we might well have snatched it.

The breakthrough didn't come, and in the dying seconds – as the game neared extra time – we were defeated in the cruellest manner. Palace forced a corner, which Carl Tiler cleared easily. The ball dropped to the Palace captain, David Hopkin, and he curled a right-footed shot into the corner of our net. I'd experienced a last-minute defeat as a player in the FA Cup final, but this was just gut-wrenching. I was so disappointed for my players and the Sheffield United fans.

I had wanted, desperately, to win promotion with them, to test myself in the top flight once more. Little did I know that that opportunity was going to present itself sooner than I could have imagined.

CHAPTER SIXTEEN
HELL

WHEN I HAD LEFT EVERTON IN DECEMBER 1993 the club
was 11th in the table. Although the squad needed strengthening in some
key areas, I felt that I hadn't left it in a bad position. At the end of that
season relegation was only averted by my successor Mike Walker on the
final day following a dramatic victory over Wimbledon. Despite having a
lot of money to spend, the start to the 1994/95 campaign was the worst in
Everton's history. Walker was sacked in November and relegation was again
only narrowly averted under Joe Royle's management. Joe won the FA Cup
then took Everton to sixth place in his only full season, but then fell out with
the chairman, Peter Johnson. Relegation in 1996/97 was avoided by just

two points. Everton had struggled at times during both my first and second spells, but relegation battles were never a factor.

Throughout all this time I followed the club from afar. I was working a lot of this time, and even when I wasn't I still kept away. They were still my club, but they didn't need me in the background. I listened to the fateful Wimbledon match on the radio and didn't attend the 1995 FA Cup final.

Peter Johnson made all sorts of grand promises to the Everton supporters about a successor to Joe. But the hunt took nearly three months. All manner of names were suggested, but, after lots of speculation and a rejection by Bobby Robson, by June only two names were being seriously considered for the job: Andy Gray's and mine.

I was in Majorca on holiday when I got a tip-off that I was under consideration. I knew that Andy was also in the frame, and the Sheffield United chairman understandably wanted to know what the situation was. I wasn't making a decision on the matter; I was waiting to see what would happen and who they wanted – me or Andy Gray.

There was talk of a two-man 'dream team', but that possibility was never mooted to me. It's not one that I would have considered, nor is it one that Andy would have contemplated either. He wanted to be his own man and rightly so.

I was in contact with Sheffield United and they wanted to know for definite whether I was staying or not. Because I wouldn't give them an answer the speculation grew. Then I got a phone-call tip-off that they were having a board meeting at Everton and that Andy had got the job. So I said, 'Fine, no problem.' I telephoned Sheffield United to tell them, 'I've thought it over, I'm on holiday; I'm definitely staying.' The club got me to speak to some local journalists to tell them of my decision, which was, of course, splashed all over the Sheffield press.

That should have been the end of the matter, but the next morning I got a phone call to say, 'Andy's turned down the job, it's yours. You can expect a call from Peter Johnson in thirty minutes.' My first instinct was to say, 'Oh Jesus,' not because I knew I was going back to Everton but that I'd be letting Sheffield United down.

I've never been so sorry about anything. It wasn't the right way to act, but in a way it wasn't my fault either. Andy had decided to stay in TV, and it was possibly the right decision at the time for him. He didn't have to win games every week, he was well paid by Sky and very good at his job. Being a manager the pressure is totally different. It was very, very disappointing what I had to do to Sheffield United. But I had no qualms about returning to Goodison, even if Andy had seemingly been Johnson's first choice. They say you should never go back, but this was the fourth time I was entering the club: once as a player and now three times as a manager. When Everton ask, as I know so well, it's very difficult to say no.

The fact that I was third or fourth choice didn't really ever bother me. People say I was only asked back because I was the most successful ever Everton manager. What that tends to overlook is that I was still a very good manager. There were the unhappy spells in Greece and with Notts County, but look at what I'd done in my time in Sheffield. I was proud, too, of my time at Blackburn. I was proud of my time at Manchester City and avoiding relegation with them. I was proud of getting Athletic Bilbao into Europe at the first time of asking. Much as I took pride in my record at Everton, there was more to me as a manager than those glorious six years I'd spent there in the mid-1980s. Yet people don't talk about any of that.

As previously, I was told by the board to instigate a backroom clear-out. It was never easy. In 1990 I'd had to get rid of Mick Lyons, who I'd played with and managed. This time one of the coaches was John Hurst, who had been such an important part of Harry Catterick's great team in the late 1960s. It was never an easy or nice part of arriving at a club.

I think harder still were the decisions about senior players I was faced with over the course of the season. Neville Southall and Dave Watson were the only remnants of the mid-80s glory days, but they were coming to the end of their careers. I tried to move Dave on. He had taken over as caretaker manager the previous season and done well. I was trying to do my best for Dave. I knew he enjoyed the managerial side but I was back now. I thought it was best for him, because he was nearing the end of his career, and Manchester City – who had dropped down a division – came in for him. I think maybe he thought I was simply shifting him out, but I wasn't; I was trying to help him. I said, 'Go and talk to them. You may end up as manager there. Go and talk to them.' But I don't think he was really listening. I think I lost Dave Watson on that morning. It was disappointing but I was only trying my best for him. I thought, 'You haven't got long left, the legs don't last forever.' But I was wrong to do that and I got a good season out of Dave.

Neville was even harder because he had been my first signing 16 years earlier and had been present throughout my Everton managerial career. By some distance he had played more games than anyone else in Everton history and was – to use an oft-misused phrase – a legend. There was nothing misplaced about describing the Welshman as such. But by 1997 I felt that Neville had started to lose some of the agility that had once made him such a great player. I didn't really want him to be extending the length of his career and having people point the finger at him, because he was too good for that. I remember bringing him up to my room on the morning of a game against Leeds, and I was absolutely choked having to tell him I was leaving him out. It was one of the hardest things I ever had to do. It felt as if it was a family loss because I'd been with him so long. I also knew just how much it meant to him, but he took it well.

All the time that I was at Everton I never once pointed the finger at Neville for conceding a goal. I think, given how long he was there, that's the highest compliment you can pay him. He was a great, great player and crucial to me and Everton for many years.

My inheritance as a manager was a mixed one. There were some big-name players –Gary Speed, Duncan Ferguson, Slaven Bilic, Nick Barmby – but throughout the squad there was an overall lack of quality. There were a couple of players like Neville and Dave at the end of their careers and another crop, like Michael Ball and Richard Dunne, about to come through, but there was not much in between.

Duncan, of course, was the centre forward I had wanted to sign four years earlier. He was the type of player who would have made all the difference in my second spell. He was big, strong, brave, powerful; technically very good. He had all the attributes to be an outstanding footballer. But he also had his problems. His manager at Dundee United, Jim McLean, once told me that he'd fined Duncan more than he earned. I thought that was a classic. On inheriting him I got word from Joe Royle to say that he could be difficult but also that his spell in prison for an on-field assault on a fellow player had deeply affected him. He had a distrust of authority. But I got to know him and thankfully he liked me and the way I worked him.

*Duncan Ferguson was someone I got the best out of
and we remain firm friends. Here I am with Duncan,
Alan Stubbs and the snooker player, John Parrott.*
(Author's Collection)

As a manager you treat the players as you would want to have been treated when you were a player. That was my main principle that I went back to all the time. Obviously, you're going to meet different characters so you have to adjust a little bit, but I don't think you need to apply that much difference if you've already wheedled the oddballs out. I felt I got the best out of him because I liked him, and I think he liked me, but it was very difficult to convince him to do something that he didn't want to. Duncan under my charge, nevertheless, had his most successful season in English football.

Slaven Bilic, on the other hand, was a different proposition. He was a strange player. He wasn't a Joe Royle signing and he wasn't one of mine; he was in the drawer when I arrived. He was Croatia's captain and highly educated, trained as a lawyer. He had come to English football late; Harry Redknapp had brought him to West Ham and he'd done well there. He was touted as a long-term successor to Dave Watson. I found him very difficult: committing himself in the penalty area too often and giving penalties away. He was one of those centre backs that you can't trust. I liked to see defenders that you can trust implicitly. Sticking a leg out in the area isn't trustworthy play. He was on a very good contract at Everton at the time, but I didn't take to him. As a player I thought he took too many chances at the back.

There was a story that went around about somebody bumping into his wife and asking her, 'When is your husband going to play again for Everton?'

'My husband?' she allegedly replied. 'My husband is a barrister; he's a part-time footballer!' He was on £1m a year at the time! That said, I knew he was a part-time footballer because he seemed to get sent off every bloody week.

With Nick Barmby the problem I had was that I didn't know what his best position was. He used to tell me that he had his best time as a player at Tottenham playing 'widish on the left-hand side'. I'd say, 'Yes … but you were playing alongside Gary Lineker, Teddy Sheringham and Jurgen Klinsmann – no wonder you had your best time there!' I just couldn't work out his best position. He was a little like Joe Cole: an outstanding young player, technically very good. But I still ponder to this day, was he a striker, was he a wide player, was he a centre midfield player, was he a floater? He was a good player, but where did you play him?

I had no such problems with Gary Speed, although he too was versatile enough to play in a number of positions. Gary was absolutely superb in the air. He had this great knack of coming in around the back of defenders and getting his head to the ball. His technique was good; he had a bit of composure and style. He was a good player and a good lad. I made him captain of Everton. Dave Watson had been captain and I thought, 'Dave's going to give me everything, whether he's leading the team out or not.' I may have been wrong in doing it as Dave was very proud to be Everton captain, but I thought, 'How much extra can I get out of Gary Speed if he leads them out?' He was a boyhood Evertonian and had watched us through the glory years, so I was sure what it meant to him. When I gave the job to Duncan I got a hat-trick out of him. My view was that I was still going to get the extra 10 per cent from Dave Watson, but if I was getting 70 per cent from Gary Speed I'd get 80 to 90 per cent with him wearing the captain's armband.

Besides this group of senior professionals I had some talented youngsters, like Tony Grant, Michael Ball and Richard Dunne.

Granty was someone that I really liked. He was in the reserves during my second period in charge and even then he was better than some of the senior players in terms of the skill side of the game. He was a brilliant passer, but he had no pace.

A few years younger than him was Richard Dunne, who had broken through under Joe. There were glowing reports from the youth side about this big, powerful Irish lad. But he came back after the summer and had put on a tremendous amount of weight. I told Ray Hall to go down to his digs and give his landlady a diet sheet listing the foods that he could and couldn't eat. It's always difficult, a young lad coming over from Ireland, put into digs; you'd get lonely, wouldn't you? It was understandable in a way, but we weighed him about two weeks later and he'd put a few more pounds on. So I sent Ray back down again to the digs to get some answers from the landlady.

'Why has he put a few extra pounds on?' he asked. 'We gave you a diet sheet a couple of weeks ago.'

'Well, yeah, I stuck to that,' she said. 'But after he's finished mine he goes out for a McDonald's!'

You can't monitor them all day and night, can you? I don't think there was any doubt of Richard's ability though. I knew that the older he got, the better he would get, because those habits go. He'd get married, have a family and have other diversions. I felt he wouldn't start showing his worth until his mid-twenties. And he certainly did that: he captained Manchester City, earned a lot of caps, and played for Aston Villa too.

Michael Ball was someone who had outstanding ability. He was a proper Evertonian, a local lad who grew up following the team and had been selected for the FA national school at Lilleshall. He was a very good prospect, but I was unsure what his best position was. He had lots of talent, but was it left back or was it left centre-back? Because of his reading of the game and good distribution, you'd say it was possibly left centre-back, but he didn't really have the height. But he settled into wherever I played him and did very well. He was someone who should have played for Everton and England for many years, and it was disappointing – although he still had some very good clubs – that his career was to finish prematurely because of injuries.

With the likes of Earl Barrett, Graham Stuart, Andy Hinchliffe and Craig Short, this represented the nuts and bolts of my Everton squad going into the 1997/98 season. There wasn't a great deal of money to spend and I would sell Hinchcliffe and Stuart in order to bring in fresh faces as the campaign progressed.

When I looked to make deals over the summer of 1997, I was seeking a Kevin Sheedy or Alan Harper type of signing, but these were becoming harder to make because clubs held on to their players for longer. I bought the full back Tony Thomas from Tranmere Rovers, but the step up to the Premier League was probably a bit much for him.

One signing that would pay off in the most dramatic circumstances was the midfielder Gareth Farrelly. I was in the process of buying Gareth for Sheffield United when I went back to Everton. I'd seen him pretty regularly but he was playing reserve-team football at Aston Villa. He was outstanding at that level and I thought he was worth a chance for United. I then went to Everton and again thought I'd give him a chance. He was a good goalscorer, but at reserve-team level; and he hadn't had many opportunities at Villa. We took a chance with him.

From West Ham I part-exchanged David Unsworth for their midfielder Danny Williamson. I'd seen Danny playing for West Ham and I thought he was super on that showing. He absolutely dominated the midfield that day and when he became available I had no hesitation in sending David the other way. What a terrible mistake that turned out to be. Danny was probably one of the most disappointing transfer deals of my career. I'd seen him a number of times and he was outstanding at West Ham, and I thought I'd probably got the better end of the deal. He played just 17 games for Everton, but just didn't impress. He suffered from a few injuries and his career would end a couple of years later. But I don't know what went wrong with him; I haven't got a clue.

From Grimsby I bought John Oster. He was an exciting, incredibly skilful winger. Watching him at Blundell Park reminded me of scouting Trevor Steven 15 years earlier. I couldn't believe that a player with so much natural ability hadn't been snapped up. Trevor excited me, and John Oster excited me. He had so much talent, it's a shame that he didn't make the most of it.

THE PREVIOUS SEASON had been tumultuous indeed for Everton. At one stage they were talked of as title outsiders, but as their league form collapsed and they lost their best player in Andrei Kanchelskis and manager, so it impacted on the pitch. I don't think the lengthy search for a successor to Joe really helped either. Players like stability and certainty. Three months without a manager would not breed either of those things. I think the upheaval and poor form affected confidence a little bit and this carried over into the opening of the 1997/98 season. We didn't start particularly well, but that was partly the consequence of still getting to know each other and the personnel changes I was making and still needed to make. Many things needed to change at Goodison if I was going to make Everton competitive again.

The process of change was hard and there were some bad moments. We were dumped out of the League Cup, losing 4-1 at Coventry City. Afterwards I became embroiled in an argument with Craig Short as the Everton players trooped off the field without applauding the travelling fans. It had been a dreadful performance and I was disgusted. You could see our fans in the corner were as well. But I did the wrong thing after the game and sent them back out to applaud the supporters. It was something silly like Phil Brown did in front of the TV cameras when he was Hull manager and sat them down on the pitch at half-time. I wanted to show the players how much I cared and they didn't. It was an attempt to get the players into line, but Shorty said 'No' and went straight in the dressing room. I could understand it because they weren't all to blame and I was punishing the lot of them.

I probably deserved the reaction at the time. It was the wrong thing to do. I should have got them in the next day and run the bollocks off them, but I never believed in that either because that was what was done when I was a player. What good is it running someone the day after to punish them when they haven't performed?

Unfortunately the row was caught on TV and by all the newspapers. It didn't do the name of Everton any good, but sometimes these things can have a galvanising effect. Three days later we were playing Liverpool in the Goodison derby. I restored Neville Southall to the line-up and took a chance on Danny Cadamarteri, our dreadlocked teenage striker. As bad as we were at Highfield Road we were good at Goodison. We took the lead on the stroke of half-time thanks to a Neil Ruddock own goal and never looked like giving it up. Fifteen minutes from full time Danny robbed the Liverpool defender Bjorn Tore Kvarme, ran 40 yards and let fly with a rasping shot that sealed a 2-0 victory. It was a brilliant goal and probably the highlight of our season.

Danny was a really good young player. He had pace, he was direct. After his derby goal the chairman wanted to award him a new contract straight away. I liked him, but I preferred Francis Jeffers because I thought he was more head-up, technically superior, and had a better eye for a goal. Peter

Johnson was determined that Cadamarteri had to sign; we didn't want to lose an outstanding young player, and basically he gave him what he wanted. I'll always remember coming in the morning after he'd signed the new deal: he had a four-by-four with the ghetto blaster blaring away in the car park. I'm not sure whether he was parking in my spot, but he was somewhere he shouldn't have been.

I think some players really think in those circumstances, 'I've made it, I've got a new contract, I've signed as a professional, that's it.' But of course he had a long way to go and never fully realised his potential.

Big money was starting to come into football and Danny would have been one of the first players to have benefited from it throughout the duration of his career. It was affecting the game in all sorts of ways. Players were harder to sign, there were more agents; but in the dressing room things were changing too. Discipline was increasingly a struggle. Fines, as I've mentioned already, had less of an impact than in the past. There was an away trip we had to Southampton and Slaven Bilic got sent off. I'd told him at half-time to take it easy, they'd had a player sent off, and he shouldn't do anything rash in the penalty area. What did he do in the second half? He just went in, right from the back, penalty, red card, we lose the game. So I slaughtered him. I said, 'You're going to be suspended now; I'm going to fine you.'

I took all the players to the Chinese restaurant. Bilic was there, and I had a list of the other fines. And he said, 'I've got to go now; one of the kids has got to go to the dentist; I'll leave my card.' So he left his cash card in the Chinese and said, 'Give it back to me tomorrow.' Well, the Moet et Chandon came out, the lot came out. That's how much they loved him. I'm not talking about me having Moet; I'm talking about everybody having Moet. It must have cost him a small fortune, but with the amount he was earning he would hardly have noticed. That's how hard it was.

There were, however, some good times. I'll always recall appearing at a pro-celebrity golf tournament on the Wirral and the organisers were looking to save a few quid, so they asked if I would mind sharing a room with another one of the celebrities. I told them it wouldn't be a problem, and to my surprise I was put in with the Liverpool manager, Roy Evans. We were settled in for the night and had Match of the Day on the television when we decided to share a nightcap, so we called room service and ordered two scotch and dries. Imagine the bellboy's surprise when he entered the room to find the managers of Liverpool and Everton sleeping together!

Roy Evans and I gave a hotel bellboy
the fright of his life while room at a charity event
during the 1997/98 season. (Author's Collection)

On the pitch our form nosedived sharply after the derby win. We went eight games without a win, including a run of five straight defeats. Supporters were protesting against the chairman and there was a sit-in demonstration by some fans after a home defeat to Tottenham which left us bottom.

Peter had a reputation as being an awkward chairman; meddlesome in some respects, completely hands-off in others. To me he was a stranger. I couldn't tell you what he was like because I didn't know him. I had virtually no contact with him at all. What contact I had was through the secretary Michael Dunford (Jim Greenwood having retired) or his henchman Clifford Finch.

It certainly wasn't the same cosy atmosphere that had predominated in the 1980s. At times it could be quite testing. I was, however, helped greatly that year by Bill Kenwright, who sat on the Everton board. He was a great ally to me, just as he remains a great ally to Everton Football Club to this day.

The Tottenham game was the inauspicious conclusion of Neville Southall's 750-match Everton career. With a view to being Neville's long-term replacement Joe Royle had bought the England Under-21 international Paul Gerrard from Oldham a couple of years earlier. Paul had a decent career and was more than useful, but sometimes you can't help but compare players to those that have preceded them. I'd given Paul a try-out, but dropped him after the Coventry game and wasn't entirely convinced.

The first time I saw Neville all those years earlier I liked him. It's not very often you can see goalkeepers perform and make your decision on one game. But it was a similar situation with the Norwegian goalkeeper Thomas Myhre. I got word on Thomas, who was at a Norwegian club, from an agent and we flew him over to have a closer look at him. I got permission for him to play a reserve game at Blackburn reserves, and went along. It was one of those lucky evenings: they had a strong side and he had a lot of work to do, and he performed really, really well. Again, like I did with Neville, I said 'Yes' to a goalkeeper after seeing him just once.

So we signed him. A couple of days afterwards I went down into the bathroom before I went out training and I saw him standing over the sink putting contact lenses in. I immediately went back upstairs and said to the club doctor, 'Did you give Myhre an eye test in his medical?'

'No, why?'

I said, 'Well, surely that's the first test that you make on a goalkeeper? He's wearing contact lenses!'

Short-sightedness aside, our new goalkeeper was very good and I had no hesitation playing him straight away – even if it meant bringing an end to the career of our Welsh colossus.

Goals remained a problem and we struggled to score from open play.

To help alleviate this, in January I signed the France international centre forward Mickael Madar. I did my homework on him through my contacts in Bilbao. They told me there was no doubt about his ability, but there were a few questions about his character. So I went over to Valencia to see him for myself and he was sub, which was just my luck. But he got on for about the last 10 or 15 minutes and I saw enough there in him along with the information that I had been given to take a chance with him. He was alright; in fact he was more than that – he scored some fine and very important goals.

Other transfer deals were more controversial. The one I get asked about today is the sale of Gary Speed to Newcastle United, then managed by Kenny Dalglish. All sorts of conspiracy theories have been bandied around about Gary's sale, most of which are nonsense. There was no real bust-up. It was a messy transfer, complicated by the fact that he was the club captain and a lifelong Everton supporter. I didn't want to lose him. He was one of my best players, my captain; someone I had made captain. It wasn't clear whether I would ever see the money his sale generated.

Through January 1998 there was all kind of speculation that Newcastle United wanted to sign him. The situation came to a head at the end of the month when Speed refused to travel with the team to West Ham after supposedly learning from a journalist that he would be dropped and stripped of the captaincy. It was disappointing because to my mind I think the most serious offence that a player can do is not turn up for a game. But just like when I was a player and I didn't want to play for a manager who didn't want me, so as a manager I didn't want a player who didn't want to play for me. The only option left was to sell Gary quickly and for as much money as possible.

It has since been suggested to me that someone associated with Newcastle – maybe an agent – was advising Gary that the way to get a move was to do what he did. I'm not saying for one minute that the instruction came from Kenny, but I think it came from someone connected with the deal. I also think that to put a player under that sort of pressure was wrong. He knows he's not going to be well liked by the club he's left after that. Not just on his return, but he probably won't be remembered for what a good player he was and the good performances he put in for the club. Gary had been a great signing for Everton and I was the last person who wanted him to leave. It's just a shame that the nature of his departure spoiled some of the good memories Evertonians should have had about him.

If Gary was one person I didn't want to sell, the deadline-day acquisition of John Spencer from Queens Park Rangers was a signing that the chairman didn't want to go through. He wanted out of the deal; he didn't like it for some reason. (At the end of the season he was publicly critical of John.) He wanted me to contact Rangers with some sort of excuse to scupper the deal. And I said, 'You're going to blacken that lad, you'll tarnish that lad's career if you do that.' I didn't do it. I thought it was naughty; an unprofessional way of doing business. Of course, he was undermining my position too; the situation bore echoes of what went wrong with the Dion Dublin deal. But I won the battle over Spencer: it was the difference between me being a manager and not.

Because we were increasingly in trouble I was really after players who could make an impact. I was also trying to wheel and deal and bring in bodies. I swapped Graham Stuart with Sheffield United for Carl Tiler and Mitch Ward. Carl had gone for a record fee for a centre half to Nottingham Forest a few years earlier. He was a decent defender but Cloughie probably found out that at the highest level he fell a bit short. You like to hope that he's going to do a job for you, but he was a disappointing signing and I probably should not have let Graham leave.

I went back to Sheffield United later in the season and signed Don Hutchison. There was some scepticism from Evertonians because of his time at Liverpool, but he'd grown up a bit since then and matured into a very good player. He was strong, he could pass, he was good in the air and technically very good; he could also play in midfield or up front. I remember watching him from the directors' box with Alex Young, and Alex saying to me, 'Aye, he's a player.' He turned out to be a very good player for Everton indeed.

Wins were hard to come by after Christmas. We drew a lot of matches, but there were some bad defeats as well. We lost 4-1 at home to Aston Villa and 3-1 to Sheffield Wednesday. In our penultimate game of the season Arsenal beat us 4-0 at Highbury, in the process lifting the Premier League title. That put us in the relegation places for the first time since Christmas. We were really in a lot of trouble. We went into the final game of the season against Coventry needing to get a result better than Bolton, who were away at Chelsea. If Bolton won, Everton were relegated.

Sunday 10 May 1998 was the day of reckoning. Mike Walker had been in the same position four years earlier. Like him, I understood the enormity of our situation, but I think it would have been far, far worse for me than it would have been for him had we gone down given my association with the club. For me it would have been a killer. I was the most successful manager in the club's history and had a great record as a player. To be relegated was just unthinkable.

A lot of planning went into that match, but it was elements of chance that saw us through. I held the pre-match press conference a day early to afford us the opportunity of a day without distractions, and made a few jibes about hoping that Chelsea wouldn't be 'playing with their flip-flops on' that I hoped would get to their players and inspire them to raise their game. I spent a lot of time with my backroom staff preparing for the game. The nightmare that I had every night was that I'd be remembered not as Everton's most successful manager, but the one that had taken them down.

The night before the match I had an epiphany. Gareth Farrelly couldn't find the back of the net all season. His form had been patchy and he was in and out of the side. I'd had a little meeting with my staff the night before – we stayed away from home the night before the game – and agreed on the team. Then I changed my mind during the night. I woke up and thought, 'He's due one,' and went back to sleep. I don't know for what reason, but I went down next morning to the staff and said, 'I'm playing Farrelly.'

There was a tense and volatile atmosphere inside Goodison. We needed the crowd to get behind us and to do that we needed an early goal. Cometh the hour, cometh the man. Six minutes in Gareth Farrelly let fly with a shot from 25 yards that flew into the roof of the Coventry net. Goodison erupted, but we failed to settle. Coventry had the better of much of the game and the best chances. Tempers were becoming frayed on and off the pitch. Then, with 15 minutes left, a sudden roar, unconnected with events on the pitch, erupted. Chelsea had scored through their player-manager Gianluca Vialli. The Gwladys Street sang his name.

With five minutes remaining, Cadamarteri was played through by Barmby's flick header. He was tackled, probably fairly, by the Coventry centre half but the referee gave a penalty. It was the sort of break that you pray for in these situations. Nick Barmby took the ball, placed it, but shot poorly, and Marcus Hedman saved.

Four minutes later Goodison was silenced. David Burrows went down the left and sent in a cross for – of all people – Dion Dublin, whose header slipped out of Thomas Myhre's grasp and into the Everton goal.

The crowd howled for the final whistle and amid the screaming of whistles came another roar to signify that Jody Morris had scored a second goal for Chelsea. Moments later came the final whistle at Goodison and the players ran for the dressing room as the crowd stormed onto the pitch, singing and dancing in relief. I looked up to the stands and picked out Bill Kenwright, who gave me the thumbs-up.

The unrestrained joy of Goodison soon turned to anger. Before the Main Stand stood 10,000 angry fans calling for Peter Johnson's head. My team huddled in the dressing room celebrating our safety. There was, of course, nothing really to celebrate.

THAT WAS MY FINAL ACT AS EVERTON MANAGER. My penultimate one had occurred at Goodison three nights earlier, when the youth team lifted the FA Youth Cup. Leon Osman, Tony Hibbert, Francis Jeffers, Richard Dunne and Danny Cadamarteri all played a part in the two-legged win. Between them they would make more than 800 appearances for Everton and three of them would earn international recognition. The credit was all Colin's really, for he was youth-team manager at the time, but it happened under my watch. I suppose you could say it was the final act of a partnership that had lasted off and on for more than 30 years.

I remember asking Colin at the time who he had coming up through the ranks. Colin doesn't mess about; he's very direct. If someone stands a chance of making it that won't be enough; it's got to be special for Colin to pay attention. He looked for something outstanding, extra special.

'Only one,' said Colin. 'He's twelve years old. His name's Rooney.'

FOUR WEEKS AFTER THE COVENTRY GAME, the board met and backed Peter Johnson in a decision he had made to sack me. The first I knew about it was when a journalist phoned me on holiday in Spain to ask me for my reaction to the rumours. News had been leaked to the press and Johnson was meant to meet or phone me to tell me it was all over but that never happened. It wasn't very nice being left to answer speculation about my own future.

I was still in Spain when I received instructions to fly out to meet Johnson at a hotel near Lake Como. So I made the long journey across Europe to go and see him. I got there expecting the worst, but what followed was just the strangest meeting.

There was a plate of sandwiches awaiting me, and he offered me one. I declined. We chatted in general terms for 20 or so minutes, and I sat there waiting for him to sack me. But he didn't. It was as if he was unable to face up to doing so. I returned to England in this kind of limbo. I had to wait several weeks for the telephone call that told me I would no longer be manager of Everton Football Club. A total of six and a half weeks had passed between the Coventry City game and the day of my dismissal, 24 June 1998.

I don't ever regret going back to manage Everton for a third time. What I didn't like was the manner in which I left. If Johnson and Clifford Finch didn't think I was the right man to manage the club then I felt the least they could have done was come out and say it to me. They didn't have to put me through that time. When people are coming up to you – your own players – asking what is going on, and you're not able to tell them, then it's a terrible thing. They're undermining you and your position as manager by not coming out and telling you their intentions.

It got worse than that during the summer of 1998. I felt undermined not just as a manager, but as a person too. I was hurt, no doubt about that. It didn't sour my love of football or Everton – nothing could ever do that – but I do think it dimmed my relationship with managing.

DESPITE MY HURT AT BEING SACKED BY EVERTON I still wanted to be involved in football. I still felt that I had something to offer, that I was a good manager. My desire to get back in the game, however, saw me make a bad decision. I should have been chastened by my earlier experiences in Greece, but I wasn't. I made a mistake. I took a call from Jimmy the Greek and on his word got a new job.

This time the club was Ethnikos Piraeus in Athens. It was a terrible mistake. The 'Hell' to which this chapter refers was not at Goodison Park – I was saved from that by Gareth Farrelly – but at Ethnikos. They were probably like a Greek version of Luton Town, in that they were a small club with top-flight pedigree, but their existence was slightly tenuous. Although they were in the top division while I was there they were about to embark on a slide through the league that would take them to the fifth tier of Greek football.

All the paranoia and suspicion that had undermined my spell with Xanthi was present again. I had a goalkeeper who hid in the toilet at half-time and wouldn't come back out. He was from a local village and we were playing their team. He'd let a couple in in the first half and the home crowd were really getting on his back, claiming that he'd been paid to do it. And he just wouldn't go out for the second half. I had to go in the toilet and get him out.

Jimmy the Greek was as bent as a nine-bob note. The club president didn't understand English and Jimmy was telling me that he wanted four English players. I was on the phone trying to bring English players over. John Richards, the Wolves managing director, agreed to let me have the Irish forward Dominic Foley; he scored a hat-trick in his first game, so I was happy with that. I went to Burnley and got a couple of players from there. But they were arriving at the airport and I hadn't a clue who they were.

It was Jimmy the Greek who organised all the business side: the English club had continued to pay the players' contracts, and were billing the Athens club for reimbursement. But they weren't paying the English club and they, in turn, after a while weren't paying the players. Jimmy was getting the money and just giving them a little bit of spending money here and there. There was a local derby game and a bit of a hostile crowd – Greek crowds can get very nasty – and they started throwing coins at the players. The English lads were picking them up because they hadn't been paid. Fortunately I was getting paid. It wasn't regular, but they fulfilled their obligations in the end.

It was a crazy club, and I had to get out. During my last game the general manager ran onto the field and hit the referee. I had a friend visiting from England, watching in the stand. I looked around from the dugout at my mate and shook my head, and he helped me pack that night. I made an excuse that I had family problems and I had to leave. It wasn't the right thing to say but I just had to think of an excuse to get out of the madhouse. That was the end of my managerial career.

There are plenty of statues in Greece, but I think Jimmy the Greek deserves one of his own.

I LEARNED A LESSON from that sorry experience in Greece. On my return to England I was approached by other clubs, but I was always very careful when considering what they put on the table. Hull City offered to make me 'the best-paid manager in the Third Division'. I asked for more details and the chairman said, 'We'll give you a mobile phone and a two-bedroom bungalow.' I told him I didn't need two bedrooms, there'd only be me. 'The other one's for me in the afternoons!' he replied. I didn't take him up on that.

Football had changed rapidly during the 1990s and not always for the better. The money in the game meant it was increasingly difficult even for big clubs like Everton to do much more than put a cup run together. The chances of building a team again like the class of 1985 was virtually nonexistent. Because you know there is no way you can be as successful again, it dampens your enthusiasm for the game. If someone had offered me the time and the money, it might have been different. But I didn't see any club telling me, 'You've got five years and plenty of money.'

What I missed the most were mornings on the training grounds. I was never one to stand on the side of a pitch in an overcoat looking on. I liked to get involved, to play with the lads, even when I was in my fifties. There was nothing better than joining in a brisk training session on a cold winter's morning. I found being without that part the hardest.

I was settled and happy on Merseyside, which had become my home.

I started to do work in the local media, writing a weekly column for the *Liverpool Echo*, which I enjoyed. There was always interest on the after-dinner circuit and I have spoken many times about great days as both a player and a manager. The pleasure comes not in reflecting on past glories, but in coming into close proximity to those that I hopefully brought some happiness too once in a while.

People ask me how I'd like to be remembered. I've had a good life and a fine career, both as a player and a manager. It would have been nice to have saved the best until last, like Bob Paisley and Alex Ferguson were able to do at their clubs, but that wasn't to be. Yet I've had far more highs than I have lows and possess some wonderful memories from my life in football. My wish is simple. I'd like to be remembered as someone who as a player and manager brought enjoyment to supporters. That's all.

AFTERWORD

To Lil and families, hope you enjoyed reading, love Howard.

INDEX